LANGUAGE AND COLONIAL POWER

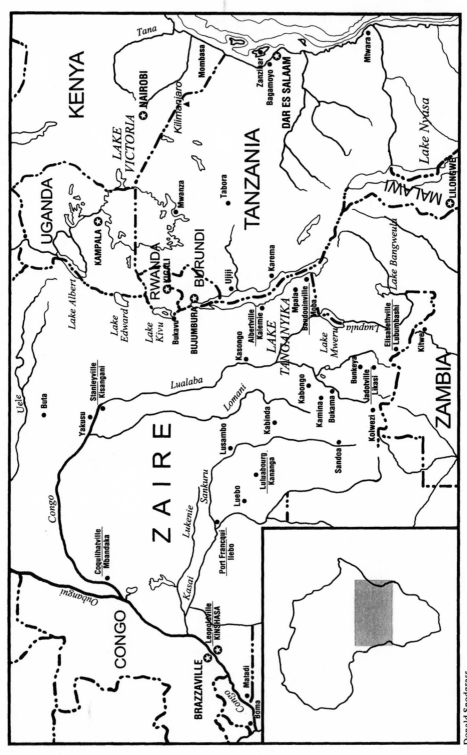

Donald Snodgrass

LANGUAGE AND COLONIAL POWER

The Appropriation of Swahili in the
Former Belgian Congo 1880–1938

JOHANNES FABIAN

Professor of Cultural Anthropology, University of Amsterdam

Foreword by Edward Said

UNIVERSITY OF CALIFORNIA PRESS
Berkeley • Los Angeles • Oxford

University of California Press
Berkeley and Los Angeles, California
University of California Press, Ltd.
Oxford, England

© Cambridge University Press 1986

Library of Congress Cataloging-in-Publication Data

Fabian, Johannes.
  Language and colonial power : the appropriation of Swahili in the
former Belgian Congo, 1880–1938 / Johannes Fabian.
    p.   cm.
  Reprint. Originally published: Cambridge ; New York :
Cambridge University Press, 1986. Originally published in series:
African studies series ; 48.
  Includes bibliographical references and index.
  ISBN 0-520-07625-7
  1. Swahili language—Social aspects—Zaire—Shaba. 2. Shaba
(Zaire)—Languages—Social aspects.   I. Title.
PL8704.Z9Z283   1991
496'.392'0967518—dc20   91-15091
                                                                 CIP

Printed in the United States of America

9   8   7   6   5   4   3   2   1

The paper used in this publication meets the minimum requirements of
American National Standard for Information Sciences—Permanence
of Paper for Printed Library Materials, ANSI Z39.48–1984.   ⊚

Contents

v

Contents

Foreword

Johannes Fabian's *Language and Colonial Power* is a work of very high scholarship and of a particularly valuable cultural critique. In a way that no other analyst of imperial practice has done, Fabian shows that European scholars, missionaries, soldiers, travellers, and administrators in Central Africa during the late nineteenth and early twentieth century used Swahili as a mode of extending their domination over African territories and people. The language was first studied and characterized, then streamlined for use among laboring people, then regulated as such fields as education and finance were also regulated. The novelty of Fabian's approach is not only that he shows how ideology informs discourse, but also how the inflections deriving from history itself from differing situations, and individuals affect the historian's perceptions of this subject. A central feature of this book is that "the appropriation of Swahili" is seen to be a constantly changing contest, occurring at the level of micropolitics as well as at the level of international politics. This study is a fascinating, even gripping work that places the civilizing ambitions of Franco-Belgian colonialism in a much more precise, disturbingly demystifying light. Any student of what has been called Africanist discourse, or of imperialism will find *Language and Colonial Power* an invaluable and path-breaking work.

Edward W. Said
Old Dominion Foundation
Professor in the Humanities
Columbia University

Acknowledgements

Recognition and gratitude are due to many persons and institutions. I can name only some of them. William J. Samarin pioneered inquiries into the social history of language and colonization in Central Africa (see, e.g., 1982a and b). Personally and through his studies on the origins of Sango and Lingala, two 'vehicular' languages whose history in many ways parallels that of Congo Swahili, he has been a source of inspiration and encouragement.

Most of the documentary material I found in the library and archives of the former Ministry of Colonies at Brussels, in the library of the Benedictine Abbey of St Andries near Bruges, in the historical archives at the Royal Museum of Central Africa at Tervuren and at the departments of African languages and linguistics at Leiden and Cologne. The director and the staff of these institutions have been helpful with expert advice. Fr R. Lamey, archivist of the White Fathers in Rome, generously provided bibliographic and other information.

Completion of the book was made possible by leave from the University of Amsterdam spent at the Institute for Advanced Study, Berlin. I thank the library and secretariat for help in completing the bibliography and typescript, and my colleagues for having been sympathetic and encouraging listeners to these exotic tales.

Berlin
April 1984

A note on names and orthography

Writing on African history requires choices regarding nomenclature and orthography. Selecting and imposing names and ways of writing them, in fact, belonged to the exercise of colonial power over language. When the Belgian Congo became an independent country, African politicians and scholars began to restore traditional names and, in many cases, to introduce innovations appropriate to symbolize the end of colonial rule. This is legitimate even if it disturbs geographers and bibliographers. However, to employ current names would make it necessary constantly to refer to earlier usage (which, needless to say, did not remain unchanged from 1880). So as to keep confusion within bearable limits, I have adopted place and other names, as well as their transcription, as they occur in the sources and during the period treated in this study. No political offence is intended, therefore, when I write Congo instead of Zaire, Elisabethville for Lubumbashi, Katanga for Shaba, Tanganyika for Tanzania, and so forth. Ethnic terms and names for languages are most of the time rendered without prefixes unless such a modification is distinctive (as in Tshiluba and Kiluba, varieties of Luba in the Kasai and in Katanga respectively). Language quotations from printed and manuscript sources are always as in the original. Their inconsistencies and linguistic deficiencies often contain precious information.

Introduction

I compiled a register of two, three hundred basic words in the Russian language; these I had translated into as many languages and jargons as I could find. There are already more than two hundred of them. Every day I took one of those words and wrote it in all the languages I could get together ... Only because I would eventually have regretted it had I burned this mass of paper ... did I ask Professor [Peter Simon] Pallas to come and see me. After a thorough confession of my sin, we agreed to have these translations printed and thus make them useful to those who might have the desire to occupy themselves with the fruits of someone else's boredom ... Those who are so inclined may or may not find some illumination in this effort. This will depend on their mental disposition and does not concern me at all.

This is how Catherine the Great, Empress of Russia, described the beginning of an ambitious linguistic undertaking: a monumental collection of vocabularies, and one of the first to include several African languages.[1] The result was *Linguarum Totius Orbis Vocabularia Comparativa, etc.* by Peter Simon Pallas (2 vols., Moscow 1787 and 1789).

István Fodor restored this text to its historical significance for African linguistics. His study of the project's origins, sources, and contemporary context makes fascinating reading. The idea for the project seems to have come from the Empress. It is possible that she conceived of it as a pastime, to while away long hours in her 'well heated' room in the Hermitage (Fodor 1975: 19), but there was method in her boredom. After all, she was the absolute ruler of a vast colonial empire, and what began as a playful distraction soon turned into a model of linguistic information-gathering, anticipating polyglot wordlists and dictionaries that were put to colonial service in Africa in the second half of the nineteenth century. In its later phases, Catherine's project did not remain an armchair affair. Lists were sent out to the governors of the Empire to be forwarded to official interpreters and translators. 'Consequently,' Fodor notes, 'translations were regarded as official business and the wordlists became documents of state, witnessed to with stamps and signatures' (1975: 9). Nor was the search limited to Russia. Through its ambassadors in Madrid, London and The Hague, the lists reached Spanish, English and Dutch colonies, and even China. George

1

Washington took a personal interest and asked the governors of the United States to participate in the collection of material (Fodor 1975: 10).

Pallas' vocabularies, in other words, were a serious contribution to 'statistics' as it was then understood: as filling administrative 'space' or rubrics with information of interest to the State. They were mirrors of ethnic and cultural diversity; they could become instruments of government inasmuch as they imposed a semblance of order on a bewildering multitude of languages and helped to create a frame for language policies. Pallas himself and his learned predecessors and contemporaries undoubtedly had detached scholarly interests in comparative language studies; but, like the *philosophes* of the Enlightenment (whom Catherine knew and consulted), they pursued their scientific interests with constant attention to the use to which their findings could be put by their absolutist sponsors.

I had given little thought to such deep connections between language, linguistics, and politics when in 1978 a sabbatical leave should have given me the leisure to 'write up' the results of field research in Zaire. Between 1972 and 1974 I had worked in Shaba and collected material on the role of Swahili in the context of industrial and other kinds of work. But the monograph would not take shape. My difficulties began with a vague feeling of discontent caused by the historical shallowness of my knowledge of Shaba Swahili. At the same time I lost whatever faith I still had in two assumptions that underlie much anthropological work on language. One asserts that language is somehow a representation of the world and that it is used, above all, referentially as a system of signs labeling objects in the 'real world'; the other one holds that the object of our inquiries into language, be they linguistic in a strict sense or in a wider, sociolinguistic, sense, must have the description of (a system of) rules as their object. Both problems I tried to address in ways I was capable of, but the result was articles and a theoretical treatise, not the expected monograph.[2] I let myself be side-tracked, as I saw it then, by collecting more or less circumstantial evidence for the history of Shaba Swahili. This began – perhaps because it is in the nature of studying language from a safe distance (see Catherine's *divertissements*) – as a pastime and a passion for obscure and odd vocabularies. A. Verbeken's *Petit Cours de Kiswahili pratique* had been my first introduction to the language of Shaba in 1966. Search in archives and libraries (mostly in Belgium) soon unearthed numerous predecessors whose amateurish descriptions had been eclipsed by scholarly works. At first I thought that my findings would make a bibliographic essay with limited appeal to a small circle of Swahili experts. Then I became convinced that a story could be told that would be of much wider interest.

The result was a book about colonial power – another book about colonial power. The literature on the subject is vast; students of 'imperialism' have founded their own empires through specialization in several disciplines, anthropology and linguistics among them. How it all worked and works, in global terms of domination and exploitation, is by now pretty well understood. What remain obscure, as far as I am aware, are some of the preconditions for the exercise of colonial power. Inquiries into power tend to become tautological – this has been observed by students of language-spread, among others (Lieberson 1982: 41–2) – unless objects, targets (in short, the content of power) can be established in such a way that they remain outside a narrow circle of reasoning (example: Power is the ability to control X; control over X is evidence for power).

Among the preconditions for establishing regimes of colonial power was, must have been, communication with the colonized. This went beyond the (trivial) fact of verbal exchanges, because in the long run such exchanges depended on a shared communicative praxis providing the common ground on which unilateral claims could be imposed. Granted that use and control of verbal means of communication were not the only foundation for colonial rule; but they were needed to maintain regimes, military, religious – ideological and economic. In the former Belgian Congo, our area of interest, brutal, physical force as well as indirect economic constraints never ceased to be exercised, and they have been the subject of historical studies; much less is known about more subtle uses of power through controls on communication. That concept, overworked as it may be, can be fruitful if it is understood historically and politically. The aim, at least of this study, is then not to seek in Africa instances for some general theory or typology of communication (that was done long ago by L. W. Doob 1961), but to tell the story of an emerging praxis of colonial controls as they were imposed in specific ways on a specific means of communication – a variety of Swahili spoken in the southeastern part of the Belgian Congo.

Shaba Swahili, sometimes labeled Lubumbashi Swahili after the largest city of the region, is the product of processes which are by no means completed. In the course of three or four generations, counted from the end of Belgian rule in 1960 and taking us back to about 1870, Swahili – or, to be precise, several varieties of Swahili – grew from a small basis of perhaps only a few hundred speakers to acquire several million, virtually the entire urban and a great portion of the rural population of southeastern Zaire. Phonological, syntactic and lexical developments occurred as Swahili turned from a *lingua franca* into the principal, and sometimes the only, African medium of verbal communication.

Because that process is not concluded it remains problematic to use the designation Shaba Swahili (replacing earlier labels such as Katanga Swahili, Congo Swahili and, most misleading of all, Kingwana). I know of no study, not excluding Polomé's pioneering work and the descriptions and documentation we now have from Rossé and Schicho,[3] which would demonstrate that Swahili spoken in this area can be regarded as a single, distinct dialect or variant. Even if one were to accept the relatively short lists of phonological characteristics that can be established (mostly, however, on the doubtful premise that they mark 'deviations' from East Coast Swahili) and add to this morphosyntactic and lexical data, one would still have to accommodate under

3

the single label 'Shaba Swahili' regional and social variation whose existence is known but which has not been adequately surveyed.

Swahili-speakers in Shaba are conscious of that situation. While doing research I found much evidence for a tendency to evaluate Swahili in relative terms. I noticed, for instance, among people who spoke the language fluently and used it in most, if not all, communicative situations (including family life, leisure, sentimental matters, and so forth) a widespread reluctance to consider it on a par with autochthonous or European languages. Historical, political, and psychological factors would have to be considered to explain this attitude (including, of course, the simple fact that a given multilingual speaker – and there are no monolinguals to speak of in Shaba – experiences Swahili as a deficient medium for certain purposes and not for others).

There is less room for conjecture when we consider the semantic field covered by the term *Swahili*, often used with a qualifier. One can distinguish at least four types of usage: (1) First, as might be expected, the term serves to designate *a* language when it is to be distinguished from other labeled languages such as Tshiluba, Lingala, French, and so forth. (2) But I found evidence, regrettably not followed up at the time, for a notable deviation from the expected. *Kiswahili* may, for instance, be used as a synonym for *lugha* (or *kinywa*). Then it simply means 'language.' With this connotation it can be used in the plural. I have heard the expression *mu biswahili bwao*, 'in their Swahilis,' meaning 'in their languages, or in their manner of speaking'. (3) The meaning of *Swahili* is not exhausted by its functions as a proper name or generic term. In a somewhat more narrow and specific sense, it may designate a recognized variant of Swahili as it is spoken in Shaba. Thus *kiswahili ya monpère*, missionary Swahili (including Bible-translations and liturgical texts); *kiswahili ya Union Minière/Gécamines,* company-town Swahili (i.e. not only the often pidginized variety spoken at work, but also the specific dialect that developed in the 'compounds'); *kiswahili bora* (recently often *kiswahili ya Dar*), East Coast Swahili (the standard to which newscasts and newspapers are geared); *kiswahili ya Kalemie* (*ya Kongolo, ya Kisangani*, etc.), a regional variety recognized as alien to Shaba. The list is not complete. (4) Most intriguing (and, to me, theoretically most interesting) is a usage which appears to confound the medium and the message, as it were. Members of the Jamaa movement (see Fabian 1971) occasionally spoke of the founder's teachings as *kiswahili ya père Placide* (Placide Tempels, founder of the Jamaa). One may dismiss such instances by classifying them as metonymic extensions; I believe they give us much to think about with regard to language and culture and to the question whether the former should ever be regarded a mere vehicle of the latter.

In this study, inquiry will be directed to the past, and it will, for many reasons, have to reach into a past which is rather remote from present-day Shaba Swahili. The ethnographic examples I have just quoted are to underscore that my principal concern remains with a contemporary situation, namely the role of Swahili in the context of work, industrial, artisanal, and artistic. When it was first formulated, the aim of my project was to describe what might be called the workers' culture of Shaba, through analyses of communicative (sociolinguistic) and cognitive (ethnosemantic) aspects of language use. For reasons mentioned above, compounded by well-known problems with both – approaches to culture 'via language' and the notion of workers' culture itself – this project got bogged down. Complications also arose from what could be called the *historicity* of Shaba Swahili, its susceptibility to change on all levels. The point is this: language-centered anthropological approaches, even those that are inspired by the 'ethnography of speaking', need *not* assume that relations between linguistic and cognitive structures are fixed or in any sense straightforward and unproblematic. But they *must* ascribe a high degree of structural stability to the language(s) through which a culture is studied. In extreme cases anthropologists have treated linguistic data as the fixed, constant given, around which varieties of cultural expressions can conveniently be arranged in order to draw inferences about, say, ethnobiological knowledge or religious beliefs (examples of this include kinship terminologies and other types of folk-classification). Everything one learns about languages such as Shaba Swahili militates against linguistic determinism (or fatalism), be it of the structural–semiotic or of the older 'Whorfian' variety. Not only is Shaba Swahili a medium which *always* shares its territory with several other languages; it is itself characterized by so much internal variation and lexical permeability (in the form of 'borrowing' or 'relexicalization') that it simply makes no sense to regard it as a constant in language-and-culture studies. On the other hand, precisely because it cannot possibly be conceived of as a (relatively) stable depository of culture, Shaba Swahili gains weight as evidence for historical processes.

One can be wary of linguistic determinism, therefore, without having to give up the idea that language may be important in the study of sociocultural transformations. On the contrary, only when one realizes that the linguistic medium of communication is itself part of what is being produced as a 'culture' does one assign to language its proper role. This applies to all languages and is hardly a new insight (if we remember Humboldt); but nowhere is it more dramatically demonstrated than in the relatively brief history of colonial vehicular languages being transformed into 'creoles.'

Unfortunately, the historicity of Shaba Swahili which can be inferred from its present shape and state goes together with exceedingly poor historical documentation, at least at a first glance. What exists is widely dispersed in governmental, missionary, and private archives, in travel accounts and colonial biographies, in articles in learned journals and in now defunct popular magazines. Much remains to be unearthed, but it is safe to say that a straightforward history of Shaba Swahili – one that would present, for instance, successive forms of that language in chronological sequence – will never be written. For the period prior to World War II (a period crucial in the development of Shaba Swahili) I know of no recordings of *spoken* Shaba

Swahili. In the colonial newspapers of Katanga, Swahili with a local flavor (but never as it was actually spoken) appeared only in the thirties. Radio broadcasts and records of popular music, which must be the earliest actual recordings, go back to the forties. But even these, as poetic expressions or formal exchanges, cannot be taken simply as reflecting popular usage at that time.

Colonial administration, the missions, and the mining industry with its supporting services (railways, agriculture, manufacture, commerce and domestic service) are well documented, and we are beginning to see excellent analyses of labor policies, to which the development of Swahili in Shaba was closely tied.[4] Yet information about language in these documents and publications is remarkably scarce. We do know that Swahili has been by far the most important medium of communication with and among the African labor force at least since the first quarter of this century. What made Swahili so attractive in the eyes of colonial policy-makers? Why was it eventually adopted as a colonial *lingua franca?* And what happened to it in this role? These are some of the questions to which I hope to provide at least tentative answers.

Given the situation just described, it is understandable that the few authors who speculated about the history of Congo Swahili in general and about that of the Shaba variety in particular, took an extremely narrow view. The sketches that exist (e.g. Polomé 1967: 7–8; Schicho 1980: 3–10) approach the history of Shaba Swahili as a question of *origins*, that is, as a question of the time, place, and circumstances of the 'arrival' of Swahili in this part of Central Africa. Whiteley (1969: 72, preceded by Sacleux 1939: 387, under *kingwana*) credits Tipo-Tip, the famous Arab trader, with the introduction of the language into the Congo. Polomé located the center of diffusion for the southeast in a Swahili community established in Katanga at the Yeke capital of Msiri. He in fact states that Swahili was the *lingua franca* of the town (1972: 68). This was a reasonable guess, but it does not stand up in view of the evidence to be discussed in this study.

The Msiri hypothesis, as I shall call it, of the origin of Swahili in Katanga can be disposed of right away. Msiri was of Nyamwezi origin and spoke, of course, Swahili, having done his apprenticeship, as it were, as a porter in Swahili caravans. Operating from a home base in Usumbwa, east of Lake Tanganyika, his father had traded with local chiefs in the region later known as Katanga. The rather complicated series of events by which a network of trade relations was eventually transformed (through agreements and military force) into a political entity, an 'empire' known as Garenganze, need not concern us here. The fact is that, by 1860, Msiri and his Nyamwezi had conquered a vast region which they ruled from their capital Bunkeya (near the present town of that name). The population spoke Sanga, Lunda, Luba, Bemba and a few other languages. The conquerors called themselves Yeke, which was also the local name of their language. Commercially and politically the Yeke State competed with Swahili traders and rulers and set an effective limit to their southward expansion. But its territory also reached into the Luso-African sphere of influence, with its orientation to the Atlantic coast. Msiri sought to profit from commercial relations with both coasts.

Much of the information we have about conditions and daily life at Msiri's capital prior to the effective establishment of Belgian rule (which began, incidentally, with the execution of the chief in 1891) comes from a group of British evangelists who eventually organized themselves as the 'Garenganze Evangelical Mission' near Msiri's capital. Three of the more prominent pioneers in that group, F. S. Arnot, C. A. Swan and D. Crawford, eventually wrote accounts of their experiences which were widely read in Europe and America. Before these works were published they reported their impressions and experiences, while they were fresh, in letters and diaries to *Echoes of Service*, the monthly (later bi-weekly) journal of their home organization in England. A careful reading of these letters covering the time between Arnot's departure from Benguela on the West Coast (1885), his arrival in Garenganze (1886) and Msiri's death (1891) shows how much these missionaries were preoccupied with learning languages and, almost throughout this period, with deciding which language to choose. Coming from the West Coast, they first used Portuguese and Umbundu as vehicular languages, not only while they traveled, but also after they had settled near Bunkeya. For their evangelizing they depended for years on speakers of Umbundu and Portuguese. Until 1891 Swahili is not mentioned at all in their correspondence, not even when certain events such as the arrival of 'Arab' trade caravans would have been an occasion to do so. There is no indication whatsoever of a Swahili 'colony' existing at Bunkeya between 1886 and 1891.[5] The first to mention the language of these traders is D. Crawford; he speaks of Swahili, 'the language of Zanzibar, which, I believe, will be of no small use in the event of our working eastward'. This is stated, hypothetically and regarding the future, in a report describing, among other things, the events that surrounded Msiri's death.[6]

Swahili, in other words, is ruled out as a significant vehicular medium in Msiri's Katanga. What the missionaries describe is, instead, a situation of apparently stable multilingualism. Yeke, Sanga and Luba are all spoken and understood at the capital. The missionaries eventually concentrated on Luba in view of an eventual expansion toward the North. The letters contain many remarks on their approach to language(s). Only in some of the later remarks does one get the impression that a simplified form of Luba may have assumed the function of a vehicular language, but it cannot be ruled out that all three major languages were used in simplified forms. At any rate, D. Crawford is the first and only one to suggest that it was a 'natural result' of so many languages meeting in one place that they should 'form a sort of mongrel dialect, known, I might almost say, by everybody'. This sounds rather speculative and is not backed up by examples or other evidence, nor is the name of this dialect reported.[7]

To invoke Tipo-Tip and Msiri is correct insofar as it underscores

7

commercial and political links that contributed to creating an 'interaction sphere' in which Swahili could spread from the East Coast to the Upper Congo. But there are empirical and theoretical reasons to be dissatisfied with the notion of diffusion and the role assigned to 'big men' in these accounts. The problems I have in mind manifest themselves already in the ways one formulates the question. When we ask how a language 'spreads', how 'it got from there to here', or when it 'arrived' at a certain place, we are not only plotting events in space; we express our questions in spatial metaphors.[8] These metaphors should be recognized as such and critically examined. They 'spatialize' phenomena whose relation to space and time is by no means a simple one. More importantly, notions such as spread, expansion, and other synonyms of diffusion often encourage a 'natural', i.e. an a-historical and a-political, approach to linguistic change. A language never spreads like a liquid, nor even like a disease or a rumor. The danger of misrepresentation increases when these images are coupled with notions such as evolutionary stages (in the case under investigation this would be exemplified by the hypothesis that the process *always* starts with a pidgin form and then progresses either toward creolization or disappearance). Were one to follow ideas of this sort without criticism one would end up with a history of Shaba Swahili which was not only conjectural (for reasons alluded to above and to be discussed at length, we will never have anything but a somewhat conjectural history), but also imaginary. Studies of pidgins and creoles in other parts of Africa and elsewhere in the world have left simple evolutionary explanations in confusion. The case of Shaba Swahili will add further evidence to that effect.

Taken as symbols, Tipo-Tip, Msiri and later '*bwana* Union Minière' ('Master Union Minière') contain a kernel of truth in spite of all the theoretical and historical objections one may have against them. These personages or agencies signal the role of power in the social history of a language – power to impose and promote, and to control and restrict. To say that controls are being imposed presupposes something (or someone) that is being controlled, and the shape of power must not be taken for the shape of reality (as is frequently done by those who wield power). The delusions of politicians and of grammarians are comparable, and often the two are allies – as, I believe, can be demonstrated in the interplay between colonial policies and linguistic description. To say that the powerful suffer from delusions is not to detract anything from the effects of their decisions. There is in my mind no doubt that Shaba Swahili, like other African languages, has in its development been deeply influenced by colonial, administrative choices and by expert, linguistic decrees. Yet the constructs of power are frequently parasitic on the creative labors of the people, and they never fully explain what happens with and to a language.

Having rejected simple models of diffusion in general, and having in particular expressed doubt about the accepted view that Msiri's political influence explains the implantation of Swahili in Katanga/Shaba, I shall now formulate a number of assumptions which, I believe, can guide a different approach.

(1) Efforts to control the form and spread of a language have themselves a history. We must try to understand how they emerged as styles of linguistic description and of language policy. Therefore our inquiry begins with a period that preceded the definitive establishment of colonial rule.

(2) Without denying a certain fundamental importance to evidence indicating diffusion (such as a chronology of events that must have had an influence on the implantation of Swahili in Katanga), I shall adopt an interpretative frame which is *processual*. Concretely this means that I shall be concentrating less on when, where, and by what means Swahili 'arrives' in Katanga, than on why and in what form it 'emerges' in this area. Special attention will be given to the conditions in the population of a given time which facilitated (or prevented) adoption of Swahili. Specifically, I shall offer reasons for placing the pivotal period roughly between 1910 and 1920 (rather than in the 1880 s).

(3) A processual approach has two immediate consequences:

(a) Instead of seeking spots (centers of diffusion) I shall attempt to identify *spheres* or *fields of interaction* in which not 'Swahili,' but varieties of Swahili, became one medium of communication among others. There cannot be a history of Shaba Swahili except one that is attentive to multilingualism in southeastern Zaire.

(b) Notions such as sphere and field serve to stress that the problem is not so much in describing points and routes of infiltration as in identifying an arena of interplay between historical events, political decisions, and socioeconomic and even demographic and ecological conditions. Difference in spheres has of course been recognized, for instance when authors point to trade, the military, and the industrial labor force, usually as *successive* contexts and stages in the implantation of Swahili. What has not been sufficiently considered is the possibility of a discontinuous history – one, at any rate, in which no state of affairs can be derived simply from a preceding one.

(4) These aims – to identify processes, spheres of interaction, and sets of conditions – determine the selection of sources. As I noted before, the situation is precarious as far as documents in Shaba Swahili, or at least statements descriptive of that language, are concerned. Therefore, *any* sort of information about the occurrence, use, and nature of Swahili in southeastern Zaire deserves our attention. Even if a systematic search of documents and secondary literature relating to Katanga were made, little more than very general, oblique references to the use of Swahili would likely to be found. One notable exception is a small corpus of *vocabulaires* – rudimentary dictionaries, grammars and phrase books – destined for various categories of colonials.

(5) Swahili in general, and Shaba Swahili in particular, has been the subject of policy decisions and regulations since the beginning of this century. Valuable information, if properly interpreted, is therefore to be found in government regulations and in the correspondence of private employers, missionaries, and government agencies. This material is dispersed in numerous public and private archives, which could only be consulted selectively.

(6) There exist publications in the colonial press (both in the Congo and in Belgium) and in various scholarly journals in which 'the language question' was publicly discussed, frequently in the context of educational policies and in debates about the choice of 'languages of wider communication'. Swahili had a prominent place in these debates, and some valuable indirect information about the status of Shaba Swahili may be culled from arguments *pro* and *contra* offered by various authors.

(7) Finally, there is the archive kept by the people. There are the memories of participants in these developments, which could be collected in the form of oral histories. Although at the time I did not concentrate on the history of Shaba Swahili, my ethnographic material contains some information. Moreover, it indicates that people are eager to talk about the subject of language and are able to do so in subtle and articulate ways. We can also surmise the existence of archives in a more literal sense of the word. Literacy in Swahili, often quite independent of schooling in that language, goes back to the beginning of colonial rule in Katanga. There are early references in colonial sources to a voluminous correspondence among Africans. There were 'organic intellectuals' – before they were officially recognized, and controled, under the category of *evolués* – who kept records of traditional lore, of daily life, and of personal experiences in Swahili. It is reasonable to assume that most of that material, especially for earlier periods, has been lost. Only field research specifically geared to these sources could settle the question. However, we do get an occasional glimpse of the importance of such writing – as, for instance, through that remarkable history of Elisabethville/Lubumbashi compiled in 1965 by one Yav André under the title *Vocabulaire de ville de Elisabethville.*[9] The use of the term *vocabulaire* for an historical account should not be dismissed as merely quaint. It reflects the literary form of this document, in which (quasi-)genealogical lists of persons and establishments, comparable to wordlists, predominate. The choice of the term may also reflect the image, in popular consciousness, of vocabularies as accurate and authoritative depositories of knowledge. On a deeper level, it adumbrates analogies between historiography and linguistic description: both give shape to, impose a certain order on, discourse. To a large extent, my own project rests on a methodological strategy which follows Yav André's intuition from the other end, as it were: I want to approach vocabularies as *historical accounts*, not just as sources of historical information. This, however, requires some explanation.

To begin with, it might seem problematic to give much weight to vocabularies which were mostly compiled by linguistic amateurs. I believe, however, that these documents can be read with great profit if we manage to turn their vices into methodological virtues. Almost all of these language manuals are of doubtful linguistic value. They are destined for users who have limited and very specific interests in learning some Swahili – hence the attributes *petit, pratique* and *abrégé* that are sometimes added to *vocabulaire*. All in all, what we get are truncated descriptions of reduced variants of a variety of forms of vehicular Swahili. However, the same characteristics as make these manuals almost worthless as technical descriptions of a language provide valuable indicators of a communicative praxis. If properly interpreted they can be made to reveal what they hide and to release what they control, at least up to a point.

Vocabularies and other language manuals are texts. Like other texts, from government decrees to ethnographic notes, they put before the anthropologist–historian the task of historizing a record by working back from codified products of communication to the praxis and processes which produced these documents. From this point of view, which owes as much to literary theory as it does to historical methodology, there is no difference in kind between texts which advertise themselves as historical documents and those which were created for other purposes. For a literary concept which corresponds to notions of communicative fields or spheres I propose to use *genre*. Generic differentiation will then be the object of a processual approach to our source-material.

Taking each vocabulary to represent a genre (or certain dominant generic traits) will serve to place various efforts to codify and thereby control Shaba Swahili in contexts that are wider than the former colonial territory. It is true that colonial borders often defined the horizon of those who wrote about languages and language problems; but one must always keep in mind that these frontiers served as devices of administration and control, often only with partial success and in many cases with no success at all. We begin to know of more and more expressions of culture (emerging after the establishment of colonial rule) which spread through large areas of Africa without much respect for colonial borders. It is therefore legitimate and even necessary to count among the conditions that influenced the development of Shaba Swahili multilingual interaction and contact with other vehicular languages (e.g. Fanagalo/Kitchen-Kaffir), with autochthonous bantu languages, and with European languages. That such contacts existed has been reported, together with more or less anecdotal evidence, by most writers, even by the amateurs. What exactly they entailed linguistically and how they influenced language policies is another matter. One of the aims of this study is to show how a politically motivated choice between French and English, and to a lesser extent between French and Flemish, as colonial languages influenced the processes by which Swahili became the principal African vehicular language of the region.

Thinking in spheres and fields rather than territories also helps to counteract a tendency among Swahili specialists to equate distance from the East Coast with linguistic degeneration and marginality. Claims to linguistic hegemony cannot be justified on linguistic grounds alone. Centre–periphery thinking applied to language development shares with similar views in politics and economics an opprobrious logic of tautological definitions of correctness and deviance (the center is correct, the periphery deviates). A healthy lack of respect for so-called Standard Swahili comes naturally to speakers of varieties such as Shaba Swahili; it must be acquired by serious students of this and other 'up-country' languages.

Writing about the history of a language, even if it is only the history of its descriptive appropriation, requires that the writer have some knowledge of that language and some basic notions of linguistics. My study is addressed to readers who have neither. This poses problems of presentation. I acquired my own working knowledge of Shaba Swahili during almost four years of research and teaching in Shaba (Kolwezi and Lubumbashi) and during many more years when I worked on the transcription and translation of recordings made in Shaba. Most of the publications that resulted were text- and language-oriented without being linguistic in the technical sense. As I have done in earlier writings, I have included in this study foreign language items whenever this has seemed required by the argument. The illustrations that are given ask for no more knowledge of linguistics or of a foreign language than anthropological texts usually do. A few Swahili experts may read these samples with greater profit than the general reader (and would, I am sure, have liked more material of this sort). Even if some of the lists and the more detailed comments on linguistic traits are skipped, this should not affect the flow of the narrative. Occasional bibliographic inventories and many lengthy footnotes are designed to unburden the text of too much scholarly apparatus. They also point to gaps and limits of which I am aware. Much of what I have to say is exploratory and requires further research in archives, libraries, and, above all, among the speakers of Shaba Swahili.

1

Prelude: expeditions and campaigns

Swahili and Nyamwezi traders and conquistadors, through movements that were at least partly triggered by outside forces such as American sea-trade out of Salem, Massachusetts, extended the interaction sphere in which Swahili came to serve as a means of communication.[1] That it eventually included Katanga is a matter of historical record, but we know little about the kind of Swahili that was spoken there before about 1910. By that time, at least some of the residents of that region must have used the language for almost two generations. The earliest written document, and the only one known of any importance, Tipo-Tip's autobiographical account of his campaigns in Tanganyika and the eastern Congo, is a precious source but hardly reflects language use at the western periphery of the Swahili sphere.[2]

When the European colonial enterprise got under way, expansion westward through the Swahili sphere and attempts to gain some control of that vehicular language followed each other closely. On the East Coast, Protestant missionaries belonging to organizations based in Great Britain took the lead in domesticating Swahili for Western purposes. Catholic Holy Ghost Fathers in Zanzibar and Bagamoyo were among the pioneers who selected and codified a popular variety by means of writing it in Latin script, casting it into familiar categories of grammatical description, and compiling its vocabulary. Descriptive appropriation of the language accompanied its spread westward. The White Fathers (officially 'Société des Missionnaires d'Afrique') played a prominent role in this. This Catholic, largely French-oriented, order directed missionary activities from its base in Algiers explicitly toward areas 'threatened' by Islam. Père Delaunay of the White Fathers published his *Grammaire kiswahili* in the year before the Congo Free State was established (1884); his *Dictionnaire français–kiswahili* followed in 1885.[3] In the preface to his grammar, he states:

> To teach how to speak and write correctly is the purpose of a grammar. We have therefore tried in this study to formulate the rules of a pure and correct Kiswahili. A white person, especially a missionary, must not be content if he gets no farther than making himself understood. To preserve his prestige with the Blacks he must speak their language well. (1920 [3rd edition]: 5)

One may give to *prestige* a psychological or a political reading. At any rate, P. Delaunay's remarks exemplify a contention underlying this study: in descriptions of Swahili (and of other African languages, of course) 'communication and control' – the *need* to communicate and the *intent* to control – were inseparable motives. As we shall see, this raises a most interesting question: under what conditions do these motives reinforce or cancel each other out?

The year 1884 also saw the publication of *À l'assaut des pays nègres*, the logs of expeditions carried out by the White Fathers. Their travels led, in 1880, to the establishment of a post opposite Ujiji on the western shore of Lake Tanganyika. The very form of that expansion by *caravane* was not conducive to the kind of intensive study of Swahili (or of other languages encountered on the road) later recommended by P. Delaunay. This apparently caused the wrath of Cardinal Lavigerie, the founder, who, upon learning that in the second expedition only one of the Fathers understood the local language, exclaimed:

> What were the Fathers doing during the journey? From now on they should know it is my own and the Council's formal intention that study of the language be given priority among all the activities of the missionaries until they speak it perfectly. Having read their letters I was about to forbid them, under threat of ecclesiastic censure, to speak French among each other, so as to force them to speak only the language of the Blacks. (1939 [1880]: 165)

The founder's consternation testifies to the seriousness with which the White Fathers approached their missionary work; it also reveals that the element of power over, and control of, languages was not just present in face-to-face communicative situations between Africans and Europeans. Very early on, it became a matter of policy and a subject of regulations (and sanctions) in the hierarchy of organizations, religious as well as secular, which carried out colonization. The individual colonial agent was not to be left to his (linguistic) devices.

Later on we shall return to linguistic work on Swahili done by the White Fathers. Here we are merely interested in them as one of the agents and channels of Swahili in the eastern Congo at a time before the vast territories claimed by Leopold II were fully under control. The first members of the order to work inside the borders of the Congo Independent State were mostly of French origin and steered a course of conflict with the political powers as soon as they began to shift their work from groups of freed slaves to autochthonous populations. After 1890, French nationals were replaced by Belgian priests who under the leadership of Fr (later Msgr) Roelens opted for close cooperation with the agents of the Free State, at least for a certain period. In 1894, a school was opened at Mpala and the town of Baudouinville (now Moba) was founded – both on the western shore of Lake Tanganyika. Baudouinville was to serve as a basis in this area for colonization similar to the scheme of *fermes–chapelles* in the lower Congo.[4] By 1894, in other words, missionaries had begun to set up educational institutions in northern Katanga

14

in which Swahili served as the principal medium of instruction. This was twelve years before the Union Minière du Haut Katanga began smelting copper at the Mine d'Étoile near present-day Lubumbashi (1906), and more than fifteen years before Benedictines (1910) and Salesians (1911) established their first stations and schools in southern Katanga. This sequence of dates, suggestive as it is of the consolidation of Belgian colonial rule, should however not be read as reflecting the development of colonial interests in promoting Swahili. That story was more complicated and must include the Independent State's commercial and political efforts to stem Arab influence in the northeast. W. Stapleton, a Protestant missionary, was stationed at Yakusu near present-day Kisangani when he wrote in 1898:

> Kiswahili, which has succeeded in becoming the lingua franca of almost the whole of East Africa, is forcing its way into the West, and slowly but surely asserting its sway into this region. (*Missionary Herald* (Journal of the Baptist Missionary Society, London), November 1898)[5]

Enthusiasm for Swahili is expressed in the title of one of the earliest primers published in 1909 for the Catholic missions in the same area. Here Swahili is called '[the language] which is the most widely spread among the Bantu languages in the Belgian Congo'.[6]

Given the conditions around the turn of the century, one can hardly assume that the use which Catholic and Protestant missionaries found for Swahili in the vast region between Zanzibar, Stanley Falls and southern Katanga represented a concerted effort. Like the agents of the Free State, they were too much preoccupied with claiming, gaining, and maintaining territories and posts to think of long-term planning. Nevertheless, it is worth recording that this initial phase of control-through-codification was characterized by a positive, optimistic attitude toward Swahili, and by a remarkably wide geographic perspective. Undoubtedly, such thinking in large, global terms could be maintained only while colonial penetration was still in full sway (the first major Katanga expedition set out in 1890).[7] The need to concentrate on specific areas, cultures and local languages, although recognized in theory, was not yet firmly established in practice.

POLYGLOTTA AFRICANA

Such relative openness corresponded to the as yet rather abstract nature of (future) colonial projects; it was also a pragmatic response to actual communicative situations obtaining in an era of campaigns and expeditions. It is in the praxis of a 'colony on the road (or on the river)' that we can place an early genre of writing about Swahili (and other African languages) whose foremost characteristic it was to present descriptions of, and vocabularies for, *several* African languages (occasionally with glosses in more than one European language). It appears that, at least at an early period, approaches to Swahili recognized its embeddedness in a *multilingual context*. What motivated the authors of these *polyglot guides*, as I shall call the genre, can often be ascertained from remarks in prefaces and introductions. Unfortunately, information regarding the circumstances and method of compilation is hardly ever included in these publications.

Before we take a look at some of the polyglot guides, I should like to present material apt to confirm the contention that generic differences are not merely artifacts of classification *post factum*, but indicative of historical conditions and processes. I believe, if comparison with paleontology is permitted, that the polyglot guide offers to the 'archeology of Swahili' a kind of *leitfossil*. It marks a base-line or first stratum in the history of modern colonial encounters with African languages as media of communication.[8]

Such a line or pattern showed up when I tried to compile a synopsis of the principal sources that were consulted for this study. I plotted roughly 100 titles dealing with Swahili, and about 25 addressed to languages contiguous and often coextensive with Swahili, on a matrix whose axes were chronological (beginning in 1850, the publication date of Krapf's study of Swahili dialects) and geographic–political (following the regions in which authors of language guides and grammars worked). The resulting table is too unwieldy to be reproduced here, so I shall limit myself to summarizing some results. In a given colonial context (English, German, French, Belgian) polyglot guides occur at a certain time. When one compares contexts, going from the East Coast to Katanga, one finds the oldest ones in the east and the most recent ones in Katanga. Such at least is the picture if one looks at it from a distance, as it were.

However, even more interesting than continuities and similarities of language description, spanning the continent from the East Coast to the lower Congo (we shall see presently why investigations of Swahili guides cannot be confined to the 'territory' of that language) are certain breaks and deviations from the general trend.

As was to be expected, the line connecting polyglot guides in different contexts follows, roughly, the chronology of colonial penetration. But the movement suggested here is not to be taken as a simple reflex of the spread of Swahili from eastern toward Central Africa. Some of the polyglot guides were written from the perspective of an eastward movement (up the Congo river).[9] Then there is the fact of a remarkably uneven representation of polyglot guides if different contexts are compared. They are most frequent in the English and Belgian spheres (ca. 1850–1910 and 1890–1925, respectively). With one exception, I did not find any polyglot guides published in the German context, a fact which confirms that the German colonial administration had opted for Swahili as the exclusive medium of communication.[10] Authors of Swahili language guides destined for these colonies found it unnecessary to provide information about other African languages. It also appears that the White Fathers and other French-inspired Catholic mission orders based on the East Coast contributed little or nothing to the polyglot genre (with one notable exception).[11] Finally, there appears a hiatus of about twenty years between polyglot guides published in the final years of the Congo Independent State (before 1908) and guides to Katanga Swahili containing information about at least one other African language (Quinot, 1925, destined 'à l'usage des agents au Congo des Sociétés Congolaises', and Van de Weyer and Quets, 1929, published 'par les soins de l'UMHK'). This gap is bridged by a series of strictly bilingual texts, most of them sponsored or published by the Ministry of Colonies. We shall consider later how this demise of the polyglot genre is to be interpreted. At any rate, the Van de Weyer and Quets manual seems to be the last of the multilingual vocabularies (in fact it is multilingual only in that it attempts to identify the diverse sources of the lexicon employed in the work-language of the Union Minière).

It may seem crude and arbitrary to include Krapf's pioneering work. Sacleux' classic study of Swahili dialects, Stapleton's ambitious *Handbook*, and the mishmash recommended to the personnel of the mining company in Katanga in one and the same generic category. To justify this procedure we need to take a closer look at practical reasons and motives which may be taken to connect these works. Methodologically, one may treat a group of texts as a genre – i.e. as a historical – processual complex and not just as an artifact of more or less elegant classification – if one can identify common historical conditions, including political, economic, and ecological factors. Therefore attention must be paid not only to easily recognizable, if perhaps superficial, similarities (such as the fact that these writings contain items from more than one African language besides Swahili), but to significant differences between them, reflecting differences in concrete settings and communicative situations. Disregarding a number of finer distinctions which could be made, the polyglot literature contains two major sub-genres.

The first one corresponds to a complex of motives and purposes which are, at least predominantly, *scholarly–comparative*. A work which is actually outside the horizon of this study, S. Koelle's *Polyglotta Africana* (1854), might be considered the ideal type exemplifying polyglot vocabularies conceived to show genetic relationships among a bewildering variety of African languages. Swahili figures in Last's *Polyglotta Africana Orientalis* (1885), in Torrend's *A Comparative Grammar of South African Languages* (1891) and in Johnston's *Comparative Study of the Bantu and Semi-Bantu Languages* (1919). These works had forerunners (such as the famous Pallas) and they foreshadowed modern classificatory work associated with the names of Meinhof, Greenberg and Guthrie.[12]

Somewhat different in focus, but still characterized by scholarly–comparative interests, were investigations of dialect variation within Swahili and the classic dictionaries by Madan–Johnson and Sacleux (both published in 1939). It may seem to be stretching the attribute 'polyglot' if we list Swahili–English and Swahili–French dictionaries here; yet it was characteristic of these attempts to codify Swahili in a definitive manner to indicate the essentially multilingual context of that language. Johnson regularly identifies the sources of non-bantu lexemes, and the scope of

Language and colonial power

Sacleux's search for the origins of the Swahili lexicon is illustrated by the fact that he lists more than seventy abbreviations for dialects and languages contributing to the dictionary he compiled (Sacleux 1939: 17–22).

A second manifestation of the polyglot genre I shall call *military–expeditionary*. Travelers, traders, explorers, prospectors, and leaders of military campaigns are the authors and users of multilingual vocabularies destined to assure minimal communication with populations encountered along their routes. Rivers and caravan routes, rather than regions or territories, circumscribe setting and communicative situations; conquest, expansion, surveys, and pacification define political and economic contexts for these guides, which are often vocabularies in the strict sense. They only provide lists of lexical items and a few *phrases usuelles*, but no grammar and certainly no explicit cultural information (every vocabulary contains at least some implicit ethnography).

Before we take a closer look at some examples from the second sub-genre, a likely objection should be considered. Is it really justified to give generic status to a highly diverse group of writings simply on the basis of a polyglot orientation? What do the works of scholarly comparativists and the often pitiful compilations by colonial men of action really have in common? To begin with, the two roles could be combined in the same person (Barth, for example).[13] At any rate, the latter often provided the sources for the work of the former and none of the scholars collecting linguistic information during the second half of the nineteenth and in the early decades of the twentieth century could remain oblivious to the significance of their work for the colonial enterprise. Working in Freetown, Koelle established his *polyglotta* from informants, who, as former slaves, had often traveled widely (including to the New World) before they settled in Sierra Leone. For each of his 200-odd informants he gives a brief biographic note intended to elicit as much *geographical* information as possible concerning the location of settlements, rivers, and lakes, and the routes taken to arrive at Freetown. Koelle sets aside a special section to summarize information about certain routes 'obtained at the time when Lingual Specimens were collected' (1963: 22). His predecessors in the Church Mission Society linguistic program at Freetown, the famous Samuel Crowther and J. F. Schön, had participated, as linguists, in the Niger expedition of 1841 for which Edwin Norris, a scholarly linguist, had compiled his *Outline of a Vocabulary of a Few of the Principal Languages of Western and Central Africa* (1841) – certainly a work combining scholarly and practical goals.[14]

Although the genre we are trying to describe here has polyglossia as its most striking external trait, this must not be allowed to divert attention from deeper determinants. Foremost among these are the position and attitude of the compilers. 'Stationary' collectors of vocabularies (such as Koelle and presumably some of the early East Coast linguists) found their informants in a wide spectrum of ethnic and linguistic identities represented in coastal towns. These centers – Zanzibar among them – were of interest as points of depar-

18

ture and return for the caravans and expeditions, which crossed numerous political and linguistic boundaries. Neither urban nor up-country compilers of vocabularies can be assumed to have had the time or inclination to establish long-lasting contacts requiring (and creating) complex communicative competences. Most urgently needed were 'vocables', labels for objects and features of the environment, and crude social and political categories. Therefore the term 'vocabulary' was perhaps never just a label for one possible form of linguistic description; rather it was programmatic, stressing minimal *definitions* of objects and concepts needed in only those communicative situations that were of vital importance to the compilers and their readers. It is plausible that pidgin and trade languages developed without, and prior to, interference from a certain practice in linguistic description. But the history of writing about Swahili certainly causes us to look at the pidgin problem from another angle. One may ask, for instance, why *vocabulaire* continued to serve as the title for later and more ambitious texts containing sketches of grammar, 'associative' vocabularies (amounting to descriptions of lexical domains), and extensive phrase sections. In my view, this apparently innocuous convention signals the continued normative power of an orientation toward *using words* rather than *speaking*. The pidgin character which Swahili exhibited so often during the history of its descriptive appropriation has quite likely been an artifact of these normative constraints (apart from reflecting limited linguistic abilities on the part of European authors of *vocabulaires*). This interpretation will receive much support later on when I shall show that the development of Swahili guides in the Congo never followed the expected course from simple beginnings to more differentiated accounts. To be sure, modest beginnings had to be made somewhere, but as a rule one observes a limiting, constricting tendency as time went on. In this manner the description of a medium of communication followed developments in human relations under colonial rule.

SWAHILI GUIDES FOR THE ROAD

It is time we put these general considerations to the test by looking more closely at a series of guides in the military–expeditionary genre. A few titles will be included in our list which are not polyglot. They contain only Swahili items with glosses in a European language, but are in other ways clearly destined for expeditionary use. In some cases, these guides were part of a series of *vocabulaires*, each to be used in a different language area along the route. Most importantly, language guides in this genre, whether they are polyglot or not, typically make no attempt to describe a language as a self-contained system occupying a certain territory. Correctness, completeness, and ethnocultural identification were of little concern to their authors.[15]

The first example is simply titled *Vocabulaire français–kisouahili*, published in 1880 by Imprimerie Verhavert in Brussels. Instead of an author's name the Association Internationale Africaine (i.e. the predecessor to the

Congo Independent State) is identified as the sponsor. This work had a second edition in 1894 with Van Campenhout in Brussels, still anonymous but now published for the État Indépendant du Congo. Several things are remarkable about this vocabulary (in the strict sense of that term). First it was probably compiled in Zanzibar or from sources describing Zanzibar Swahili (Kiunguja). Certain indications make it likely that the compiler worked with informants. Most conspicuous are derived verb-forms which reflect the competence of fluent speakers of a bantu language. Secondly, one is impressed by the scope of the vocabulary, especially if compared to later texts. The list contains *c.* 2000 alphabetically listed French terms,[16] each with a single gloss in Swahili. No attempts are made to include synonyms or to illustrate usage, nor are any phrases given. Semantically, the lexicon is broad in scope and not limited to items of 'practical use'. The work lacks preface or introduction, the places where later authors typically formulate their claims and/or excuses. Occasional footnotes contain mostly instructions for pronunciation. This attitude of utter modesty and openness is expressed in the layout which, in the first edition, accommodates only 17 items/glosses per page and in the second edition provides a blank page facing each printed page, so as to leave ample room for notes by the users.[17] A noticeable East Coast perspective and a relatively high standard may have caused bibliographers to identify the author, mentioned as 'Docteur Dutrieux' on p. 112 of the 1880 edition, as the 'Reverend Father Dutrieux' (of the White Fathers). In reality Dutrieux, traveler, explorer, physician in the Belgian army, was exactly the kind of person who could be expected to compile a vocabulary of the military–expeditionary type.[18]

It appears that Dutrieux' long wordlist was to be the first and last 'open vocabulary' in the strict sense. In the year when its second edition appeared, Lieutenant Charles Lemaire published a *Vocabulaire pratique: Français, anglais, zanzibarite (swahili), fiote, kibangi–irébou, mongo, bangala* (1894, at the Imprimerie Scientifique Ch. Bulens in Brussels).[19] On the cover page of the second edition of 1897 the Congo Independent State is not explicitly mentioned, but its emblem, the star, and the inscription CONGO underneath, leave little doubt as to the sponsor of this publication. Apparently it had at least one more edition (1903, by Mounom at Brussels). In a note to the second edition, the author mentions that the 1000 copies of the first were sold out. He also notes the principal reason for the popularity of his *vocabulaire*: the government of the Independent State gave a copy to each of its agents. Lemaire describes the purpose of his polyglot guide in no uncertain terms:

> Knowledge of native languages (*idiomes*) is without any question of utmost importance to those who go to Africa. Every candidate for service in the Congo must study them as early as possible. The more the Independent State develops the less time it can give its agents to acquire the experience everyone needs before he becomes useful. (1897: Preface to the 1st edition)

Then follows a program of studies recommended for using 'dead time' between appointment (or arrival) and taking up service. As soon as he has been accepted for service in Africa, the future agent should learn English so that he can communicate with anglophone Protestant missionaries, Scandinavian sailors and West Africans. He should also take up Fiote, 'the language of the region of caravans'. After arriving at Boma – then the administrative base of the Free State – he may continue with other languages according to his assignment, for instance, those who go on to the region taken back from the Arabs 'will study Swahili (*le zanzibarite*) [from a section of the vocabulary] which Commander Storms was kind enough to correct and complete' (*ibid.*).

Lemaire mentions then that for those who go to the regions of 'Oubangi, Ouèllé, Sankourou', vocabularies are available at Boma and that these can be used to 'complete this vocabulary by taking care to add another column after arriving at their destination' (the last column of the *vocabulaire* was left blank).[20] The preface ends with protestations of modesty: this is nothing but an African scrapbook (*carnet d'Afrique*) without any linguistic pretensions.

If only a small percentage of the users followed Lemaire's recommendations, this must have produced quite a collection of 'completed' vocabularies, some of which may survive in various private archives. At any rate, the publishing history of the Dutrieux and Lemaire vocabularies leaves little doubt about the extent to which compiling of wordlists had become a common practice in this expansive phase of colonization.

Let us now take a look at Lemaire's text. Not counting one page of numerals, the vocabulary has about 500 French entries listed in alphabetical order, each with a gloss in the six other languages, juxtaposed in rows on the same page (pp. 6–35). This is followed by 'useful phrases' also printed lengthwise across the page (pp. 38–47). The latter part does not, for some reason, include a Lingala (or, rather, Bangala) version and the English phrases are quite amusing. Lieutenant Lemaire seems to have concocted his translations with the help of a dictionary but without any knowledge of idiomatic English (as we said before, using words rather than speaking was what these guides were to teach). One may assume that the other parts of his vocabulary suffer from similar lack of finesse. Like Dutrieux, Lemaire uses a 'French' phonetic transcription (Swahili *moja*, for instance, is written *modjia*) and the variety contributed by Storms is identified as the Swahili of Zanzibar. There is as yet no sign of a 'Kingwana' being recognized as a Congolese variety.

Compared to Dutrieux' the scope of Lemaire's list is reduced to about one fourth (ca. 500 vs. 2000 entries). Such reduction was to be characteristic of almost all the vocabularies published later. One may grant that purely practical reasons, among them the inclusion of several African languages, made it necessary to limit the number of entries. Still, comparing Dutrieux with Lemaire, one is tempted to interpret lexical reduction (together with the addition of phrases and instructions giving advice on method) as indicative of a transition from 'communication to command' (a formula coined by Ali Mazrui for the role language played in East African colonial armies).[21] Dutrieux' vocabulary evokes an exploratory phase in which the isolated European traveler or military man depended on some sort of support which

Africans would give on, and in, *their terms* (i.e. in terms not likely to be accommodated by short lists). Lemaire's guide is an instrument for colonial agents who have begun to cover the immense area of the Congo and to dictate their terms to the natives.

These observations also apply to another Independent State publication, *Vocabulaire à l'usage des fonctionnaires se rendant dans les territoires du district de l'Uele et de l'enclave Redjaf-Lado*. Quite likely it was based on one of the texts available at Boma as mentioned by Lemaire. I have seen the anonymous first edition published in 1899 by Mounom in Brussels and the 1904 edition (a 'reimpression de 1903') identified as 'Publication de l'État Indépendant du Congo', no place mentioned. The author is a certain Georges-François Wtterwulghe (*sic*) 'de la Force Publique', another officer of the colonial army.[22] This vocabulary consists of wordlists, grouped by semantic domains, in French, 'la langue commerciale', Arabic, 'Asande', and Mangbetu. About 625 French entries are translated into these languages. The inclusion of Arabic, rather than Swahili, and the author's designation of Lingala simply as 'la langue commerciale', are intriguing:

> The trade language which is understood everywhere in the Uele is a mixture of several idioms. Bangala dominates, but one finds also numerous asande, mangbetu, arabic and even bacongo words. This language was introduced by Inspector Vankerckhoven and has slowly grown by the addition of words taken from the idioms of different tribes... (1899: 3)

It is remarkable that at this rather late date the 'practical man' interested in minimal communication perceived the variety soon to be codified as Lingala (or Bangala) as still being in the process of formation in a context of *numerous* contact and vehicular languages. Unlike linguists, military authors of language guides were not interested in the classification and identification of languages but rather in their communicative usefulness – in function over form.[23]

The 'language of the region of the caravans' is the subject of an anonymous *Vocabulaire français – fiote pour le chemin de caravanes de Matadi à Léopold-ville*, published in Brussels by Van Campenhout for the Congo Independent State, no date. Although it mentions neither Arabic nor Swahili, this text (another of the vocabularies used at Boma) is included in this survey because it typifies the genre. There is still no attempt made to provide a grammar. The items on the French–Fiote wordlist are, as in the Wtterwulghe vocabulary of 1899, arranged in groups (French items being listed alphabetically in each group). In these distinctions of domains – man, animals, food, sky, earth, trade goods, time, house and furniture, etc. – we can see signs of a method approach to language learning. They also express attempts to organize vocabularies according to communicative situations. While in this respect the vocabulary appears more sophisticated, one cannot overlook further reduction in the scope of the wordlist. It contains only ca. 200 entries as vocables and 130 *phrases usuelles*. Among the latter, many consist in fact of single terms, i.e. of vocabulary items (verbs) only slightly grammaticalized as requests and imperatives. Again, this points to situations where verbal communication seems to have been limited to uttering disconnected words, probably accompanied by much pointing, gesturing, and other 'aids' to communication. Yet there are certain signs (and small signs are very important in appreciating these documents) that, in spite of much reduction, the kind of communicative impoverishment paired with arrogance we encounter in later language guides had not yet been established. For instance, an inquiry after a name is translated as 'comment vous appelez-vous?'. One should not give undue importance to the use of the polite form of address in French, but in texts published a generation later Africans are as a matter of course addressed as *tu*.

G. Moltedo is the author of a *Petit Vocabulaire des langues arabe et swahili*, published in 1905 by Mounom in Brussels. This guide is also identified as 'Publication de l'État Indépendant du Congo'. It is remarkable for its East Coast perspective. Why did an author who shows no signs of having philological interests in the influence of Arabic on Swahili find it useful and necessary to publish a polyglot guide? (And, one might add, why did the Independent State sponsor this text?) It is also worth pointing out that the Swahili spoken in the Congo is still not (yet) labeled Kingwana. Moltedo's vocabulary conforms to the generic characteristics designated as military–expeditionary. It is destined to facilitate communication with groups or categories of people whom the State agent might meet on his travels; it does not want to give an introduction to the language of an area and its population.

In other respects, the Moltedo vocabulary exemplifies an advanced form of the command situation. While the French–Arabic–Swahili wordlist is still relatively large, with ca. 600 entries, not counting numerals, its section of useful phrases (ca. 18 pp.) contains the predictable brief sentences representing imperatives, short requests, inquiries, and the like. Because this section is so brief and the phrases so laconic it gives little information about morphology and syntax except that it shows pidgin features in certain verb forms (albeit still less pronounced than in later texts).

At least one more title needs to be added to this list: W. Stapleton's *Handbook*. But before I end this chapter with some comments on this important text, it will be instructive to look at the vocabularies of this period from the other end, as it were. Instead of concentrating only on the finished (and published) products, one can seek information about circumstances and attitudes that guided compilers of wordlists. Most of the relevant documentation is buried in archives, but some is publicly available in travelogues which reported on expeditions. Many accounts actually contained sizeable vocabularies. Usually they were separated from the narrative as appendices or tables inserted in the text.[24] However, an even more interesting form of noting native terms (interesting in view of our contention that vocabularies should be approached as 'literature') is their integration into accounts of travel. Larding one's prose with exotic words was a common practice among explorers who wanted to impress their European public. In some instances it reached a degree of intensity which made these 'integrated vocabularies' comparable in scope and quality to early manuals and wordlists published as such, whereby the travelogues often have the great advantage of informing us, explicitly or by implication, about situations and settings in which the author collected his terms. It is to a particularly rich source that I want to turn now.

ON THE ROAD: LANGUAGE AND TRAVEL

Jérôme Becker, a lieutenant in the Belgian army, was a member and later commander of the Third Expedition organized by the Brussels committee of the Association Internationale Africaine (AIA). That expedition was commanded by Captain Ramaeckers and set out from Zanzibar in July 1880 with an assignment to reach the AIA post of Karema on the eastern shore of Lake Tanganyika. Its commander, Cambier, was to be relieved, the connections and interests of the AIA in the area were to be consolidated, and the possibility was to be explored of founding another post west of the lake. Nyangwe, an important Swahili base on the Lualaba river, was considered a desirable location.[25]

Apart from official reports, J. Becker wrote a 1000-page personal account of his three years on this assignment, entitled, with a mixture of modesty and authority that was characteristic of him, *La Vie en Afrique* (1887). Unlike Stanley, Becker was not a professional penman and wrote in a language he did not really consider his own (being an ardent *flamand*). Nor was he much concerned with literary form and unity. Excerpts from his diary and from documents of the AIA, political–philosophical reflections, ethnographic notes, and detailed practical advice for the traveler in Africa are loosely strung together, roughly following the progress of the expedition. This collage results in an account that is rich and complex. *La Vie en Afrique* is a healthy antidote to the impression of an *esprit borné* one is apt to get from the language manuals examined in the previous section. Becker will, in the end, conform to colonial attitudes regarding African languages. Before he arrives at his generalizations, however, and even after he has made them, his book will provide us with precious documentation. Stories like Becker's make 'the Road' as a communicative setting come alive.

Becker's account reminds us that colonial expeditions were not just a form of invasion; nor was their purpose just inspection. They were determined efforts at *in-scription*. By putting regions on a map and native words on a list, explorers laid the first, and deepest, foundations for colonial power. By giving proof of the 'scientific' nature of their enterprise they exercised power in a most subtle form – as the power to name, to describe and to classify. The sheer physical odds against which these men had to battle – Becker soon became the only survivor among the four Europeans who started out from Zanzibar – made determination their principal virtue. But not all of them were single- or simple-minded. As part of an avant-garde (in the literal, military sense), men like Becker knew how tenuous their undertaking was. They struggled with unresolved doubts and contradictions. Occasionally they were subject to fits of whimsy. Becker once reports:

> Before we went down to the camp we cut our initials into the bark of a tree-trunk... a childish thing to do! Who knows about the future? Perhaps this will be the only trace I shall leave on this formidable continent! (1887: I 115–16)

To label the hitherto unknown and to give evidence – in the form of *vocabulaires* – of mastering a strange language had an importance to explorers (and their sponsors) above and beyond 'practical' necessities of orientation and communication. Their amateurish attempts at language description may be dismissed as linguistically light weight; *pragmatically* they weighed heavily indeed.

Compilers of wordlists could collect and list items only *by writing them down*. Thus, in many instances they initiated transition from orality to literacy. In the case of Swahili, the language which interests us and which occupied Becker, that transition had happened long before European explorers arrived. By 1880, *two* forms of literacy – in Arabic and in Latin script – were in competition. Coastal Swahilis and literate Africans in the interior had to make choices between the two, and Europeans could use this situation for their own political goals. 'Colonial language policy' began before colonies were established. Becker gives a concrete illustration. During his stay at Tabora, only a few months after he had begun to learn Swahili, he took on the role of the teacher:

> Two young men, about twenty years old, sons of the Emperor Mtéça [Mtesa] have arrived here with a caravan carrying ivory. Because they want ... to spend some time at Tabora they had someone indicated to them who could teach them to read and write Ki-Souahili by means of our letters which are far less complicated than the Arabic characters that are popularized in Africa by English missionaries. Naturally, they were sent to me. Had they stayed in their own country, they pointed out, they would have received excellent lessons from a clergyman by the name of Mac Kay. This is, therefore, a matter of not being outdone by my British colleague (1887: II 49).

On the spot Becker developed a method, and he reported success before he had to move on and leave his disciples to the White Fathers, who had meanwhile established a post at Tabora (1887: II 199).

Becker leaves Tabora when Captain Ramaeckers dies in March 1882, to take up command at the post of Karema. 'On the road', he reports, 'and whenever we arrive at a stopping place I teach Sef bin Raschid to read and write Ki-Souahili in European characters' (1887: II 199). By September 1882 he notes that his Swahili associate 'now perfectly reads and writes Ki-Souahili in our characters'. He adds: 'I had just begun to teach him French' (1887: II 350–1). He is convinced that literacy in Swahili is a step on the way to Europeanization. Because this development was expected to go in the direction of French, Becker, like his predecessor Dutrieux and others, decided on an 'orthography' that would make it easier for French-speakers to pronounce Swahili. Appropriation, rather than consistency and standardization, was at issue in these days (Becker's own transcriptions were anything but consistent). In one of only three references to Bishop Steere's authoritative works[26] he explicitly states that he changed the orthography of place-names 'without taking into account the orthography of Mr. Steere, the anglican prelate-linguist' (I 402). There was politics in orthography.

Writing, as inscription and description, served as a device to establish control. Chains of hierarchical relations were thought to exist between spoken Swahili, Swahili written in Arabic and in Latin script, and the ultimate graphic fixation regarded as the 'right' one, French orthography. This was one of the many ways in which 'civilization' was expected to be victorious. Swahili was, as yet, not to be skipped in this chain. It afforded the European traveler a position at the apex or node of a great classificatory variety of African languages. Hence Becker recommends:

> For the traveler to Central Africa it is of the utmost importance to become familiar with Ki-Souahili as soon as possible. It is an altogether indispensable idiom which *dominates the whole group of Bantu languages.* Not only is hardly anything else spoken in Zanzibar and along the Arab coast, but in the smallest village of the interior, no matter which (local) dialect may be used, the European is certain always to find some native who knows Ki-Souahili and with whom he can communicate. (1887: II 50; my emphasis)

One may doubt whether this is an accurate report on the linguistic situation between the coast and Lake Tanganyika in the 1880s. What matters is the author's consciousness of the strategic importance of Swahili[27] and, it should be added, of mastering it in such a way that the service of interpreters is not needed.

It appears that Becker did not prepare himself linguistically before he went to Africa, even though he mentions 'manuels de conversation, à l'usage des voyageurs pour l'Afrique centrale' (1887: II 58). He acquired his competence during the expedition. To him, the learning process was part of his mission. Becker knew, or felt, that a language is not merely a tool but a way of perceiving, establishing, and living relations with other speakers. His account contains many observations of sociolinguistic interest and many reflections on his own competence – all of which are conspicuously absent from the language manuals of that period. It is above all these remarks that permit us to reconstruct much of the communicative setting for 'Swahili on the road'.

If one wants to appreciate the practical communication problems faced by an expedition, certain images must first be disposed of which are lodged in the minds of most of us who are not specialists in this particular aspect of colonial history. Becker was not a lone explorer pushing ahead of a small band of porters and guides into unknown territory. The expedition of which he was a part was organized with the help of coastal recruitment agencies (Indian and European) who had great experience in these matters and acted according to long-established routines. Altogether some 198 men were hired as guides, military escort, personal servants, and porters. Their ranks and functions were clearly defined, providing the enterprise with a tight internal organization. Not included in this figure is an unknown but important number of women and children who accompanied their husbands and fathers. Women took care of cooking and other household chores and made contacts with local populations along the route. The women and children were often ahead of the main caravan, scouting villages for supplies and information, and they had the dinner ready when the men arrived at a stopping-place. Becker admired their endurance and good humor, and recognized their contribution to the success of an expedition in the strongest possible terms:

> You can be certain that a traveler who returns with a rich harvest of information and of studies of customs owes most of them to the women of his escort. (1887: I 147)

Although strictly organized internally, an expedition was not clearly defined in its membership. Death due to illness or to conflict with other members or with roaming bandits who made their living along the caravan routes; desertion, sometimes temporary; occasional recourse to local porters and other auxiliaries; temporary association with other, smaller, caravans – all this made for fuzzy boundaries and, as it were, high permeability. Expeditions should be thought of, therefore, less as a certain number of people moving from a point of departure to a point of destination, than as a kind of mobile colony.[28] From a sociolinguistic point of view, the expedition can be regarded as a 'community of speakers'. It had enough internal differentiation (in terms of tasks, sex, age, hierarchical position) and it stayed together long enough to acquire its own identity. At any rate, Becker's account suggests that an expedition required communicative competences beyond bellowing commands and gathering factual information. Especially when he was for a while the only European at Karema station, he used Swahili also to confer with his own immediate household, and he must have spoken it well enough to exchange political and philosophical views with men such as Tipo-Tip and Mirambo (1887: II Chapter 28, 34ff.), to conduct gallant conversations with the 'demoiselles d'honneur' sent by the (female) chief of Konko (1887: I 167), to appreciate the artistry of a Swahili story-teller, and to instruct Africans in a number of European crafts. I shall return to these observations later on.

I called the expedition a mobile colony so as to make it clear that it was never simply 'travel'. To begin with, at the time of Becker's experiences, there was no strict distinction between the caravan and the station. The personnel for the latter was recruited from the former (especially the military), and travel did not stop once the station was reached. Even while it was literally on the move, an expedition of the type in which Becker participated was never outside an existing, if constantly changing, context of local and international political power. Its local 'environment' included the villages and chiefdoms it traversed but also other caravans. Through couriers, fairly regular connections were maintained with the home base and with centers of Arab and European colonization. There was a tax, called *hongo* and negotiable within limits, to be paid whenever the caravan moved through a territory. On one such occasion, a particularly annoying encounter with Simba, chief of Usavira, Becker notes with exasperation:

> Has he no idea of the sacred links which unite all Europeans enrolled under the flag of the *Association Internationale Africaine*? Perhaps he is not really aware of the nature of our *Oeuvre* and therefore takes us for isolated travelers devoted to science only, such as Speke, Grant, and all those who preceded us. (1887: I 247)

Becker had no illusion about his task being merely to explore an unknown world which had, as it were, been waiting in passive immutability to be discovered by Europe. Before he is half-way through the first volume he cites at length and approvingly a report by Ramaeckers to the AIA in Brussels (1887: I 175–81). This document describes the inevitable transformation, even in the eyes of its participants, of an exploratory enterprise into an imperial campaign. There was no way to stick to AIA instructions and keep out of local politics. Gradually, the whole area of the caravan routes had become militarized. Many forms of resistance against Arabs and Europeans, ranging from passive obstruction to attacks on their lives, had been organized by local chiefs and African conquerors:

> The time is gone when Arabs went from the coast to Ujiji [on Lake Tanganyika] with nothing more than a walking stick in their hands and when the Mouzoungou [the white man] was taken for a supernatural being and inspired fear and respect merely by being present in a caravan... Most of the Negroes along the road know today that the only advantages we have are our manufactured goods and the superiority of our weapons. (1887: I 312)

Given the political context it is not surprising that many of Becker's observations relate to politics and the role that language, Swahili especially, played in it. He learned his elementary lessons about language and power as commander of the rearguard between Bagamoyo and Tabora. Within weeks after leaving the Coast he observes:

> Already we begin to see the immense difficulty involved in organizing and commanding caravans of negroes who totally lack the feeling for discipline. We shall need unlimited time, enormous sang-froid, energy, and *obstination* in order to dominate our men. Even then we will see results only after *a complete study of their language*. (1887: I 85; my emphasis)

Later, when he has learned enough Swahili, he points to its many advantages and reports on difficulties which Europeans who do not speak Swahili have in dealing with local rulers. He shows himself impressed by the way in which Dr Van den Heuvel, the AIA representative at Tabora, uses his linguistic competence with the Arab governor and other prominent members of the Swahili community. Becker knows of, and cites, contracts between AIA personnel and local chiefs drawn up in Swahili (1887: I 262). He registers surprise when he meets a particularly conservative notable at Karema station:

> The august visitor does not even understand Ki-Souahili, which is fluently spoken by almost all the African chiefs along the caravan route. His vocabulary is limited to repeated *Yambos* articulated in a quavering voice. (1887: I 287)

Swahili served Becker well in what may have been his most important political mission during his three years in Africa. In February 1882 he was at Tabora when news came that the Nyamwezi ruler Mirambo might attack Karema station. As an AIA agent he was in a difficult position. The Association depended in numerous ways, directly or indirectly, on Arab–Swahili support. Far-seeing Swahili leaders such as Tipo-Tip already understood that the AIA 'scientific' expeditions were advance missions of European imperial expansion that would eventually end Swahili military and commercial dominance between the Coast and the Congo. But the time of direct confrontation had not yet come. Deep personal friendship, for instance, between Becker and Tipo-Tip was still possible (1887: II 151). The European shared the concern of his Arab allies over slave rebellions and popular uprisings in Tabora and the mounting threat of an attack on that town by the Arab's arch-enemy Mirambo (see 1887: II 81–90). But for the AIA it was essential to be on good terms with the Nyamwezi, who controlled the region between Tabora and the lake. Between his responsibilities for the safety of Karema station and his obligations to Arab allies, Becker saw only one course of action: to contact Mirambo directly and find out whether the ruler's reported friendly disposition to Europeans (or, at any rate, his hatred for Arabs) could be prevailed upon to safeguard AIA interests.[29]

On February 4, 1882, Becker secretly left Tabora. He stopped at Urambo, a station of the London Missionary Society. There he met Dr Southon, who was on excellent terms with Mirambo, and arrived in his company at the chief's headquarters at Konongo. They were well received and granted an audience. The Mwami greeted his visitors in 'Ki-Nyamouézi'. He then addressed his court in that language. Becker, who has only 'an imperfect knowledge' of Kinyamwezi, understands that he is being recommended to the good attention of the assembled dignitaries. *He responds in Swahili* (1887: II 159), and the services of an interpreter in the ensuing conversation are not mentioned. We may assume that the exchange continues in Swahili. By beginning in Kinyamwezi, Mirambo had made a political gesture intended to emphasize his independence of, and opposition to, the Swahili. Once this was made clear, the business could be conducted in their language. The principal purpose of Becker's mission was discussed, and Mirambo pledged protection and support for Karema. Then followed a long mutual interrogation which touched on many subjects – the evolution of European societies, industrialization, the political necessity of 'centralization' in this part of Africa, the ruler's ancestry and rise to power, and the complementary interests of progressive African leaders and European powers (1887: II 161–74). If their

29

actual conversation even remotely resembled what Becker noted down, the two principal participants must have been able to use Swahili with considerable competence and subtlety. Yet it is precisely in the context of this rich exchange that Becker makes one of his remarks about the *poverty* of Swahili: 'Because Ki-Souahili does not lend itself to philosophical reasoning I must interpret, rather than translate, the Mwami's speech' (1887: II 163–4).

Becker, and generations of colonials who were to make similar statements, apparently had learned to live with the contradiction between the proven practical capacity of Swahili to serve the most delicate communicative needs and its alleged linguistic deficiencies. Like a leitmotif, this contradiction turns up again and again. Because contradictions of this kind provide glimpses into the working of colonial ideology, I shall examine some other examples in Becker's account.

Becker began his study of Swahili without any formal preparation. He does recommend Bishop Steere's *Handbook* and even his *Hadithi za Kiunguja*, a collection of Swahili tales from Zanzibar (1887: II 50, 277), but it seems that he became acquainted with these books after he had returned to Europe. They are not mentioned when he lists the contents of his traveling library and of the collection at Karema (1887: I 83, 277). Before the expedition left Zanzibar, his personal servant Daimo 'appointed himself language teacher' (1887: I 14). Daimo died of dysentery at Tabora on October 25, 1880, only three months after the caravan had left Bagamoyo. Becker, in an obituary for his servant, acknowledges his indebtedness: 'Thanks to him I now speak Swahili with enough facility to be understood by all the populations I am going to come upon from here to Lake Tanganyika' (1887: I 229).

This is fast learning, and one suspects that Becker held an exaggerated view of his linguistic abilities. However, he was not usually given to exaggeration. Occasionally he estimates his competence and then also indicates its limitations. He simply put much hard and concentrated work into his apprenticeship. We get an idea of the method he followed, at least during the early days of the expedition, when he reports how he used the brief period of leisure on board an Arab *dao* between Zanzibar and Bagamoyo:

> Our black domestic servants have given themselves over to the pleasures of *far niente*. While we wait to find out how active they will eventually be, we use them as language teachers. The smallest object that attracts our attention and whose name in Ki-Souahili we should like to know is an occasion to ask them *Hii? Nini?* (This what?). And our *glossary, carefully consigned to a notebook, grows very slowly* (1887: I 42–3; my emphasis)

When he lived in Tabora, Becker even learned some Swahili from his two parrots (whom he promptly taught Flemish), which afforded him an occasion to note three of the strongest Swahili curses, 'expressions for which I don't even dare to give the milder equivalents' (1887: II 71).

From many oblique remarks we can infer that he owed much of his knowledge to his female cook and housekeeper (a 'present' from Tipo-Tip; see 1887: II 62), to his kitchen staff of three women at Karema (1887: II 224), and above all to people such as Mohamed Maskam, *akida* (a sort of non-commissioned officer) and tailor. Maskam was born of a Beloutchi father and a mother from Kilwa and he was famous as a story-teller (1887: I 340). Later in the book, Becker gives examples of his art (1887: II 240–51, 260–5) together with observations on style, delivery, and sources of Swahili ideas and customs. At one point he says:

> I have transcribed, after Mohamed Maskam's own dictation, the fable of the washerman's she-donkey which I found almost entirely in the collection of stories by Bishop Steere. I present it here as a model of the genre. (1887: II 242)

These hints and glimpses from Becker's account show that he learned and practiced his Swahili with different types of speakers, in many different situations, and most likely in several varieties of that language. It is interesting to note that he frequently mentions *Wangwana* as a social–ethnic category among Swahili-speakers but *never Kingwana* as a recognized dialect. Perhaps this should not be surprising, given the fact that he did not travel west of Lake Tanganyika, where that variety was presumably spoken. Or else the term 'Kingwana' simply was not yet used in the years immediately preceding the establishment of the Congo Independent State. It is also intriguing that Becker, usually an accurate and methodical observer and reporter, does not dwell on differences between 'good' and 'bad', 'pure' and 'bastardized' Swahili. That his own knowledge was too poor to recognize differences is not a good explanation. In a few instances he identifies correct and less correct forms, but he apparently found no reason to attribute such variation to distinct varieties such as the oppositions between coastal and up-country or standard vs. vehicular that preoccupied other writers. On one occasion he reports, for instance, a visit to Karema by Fipa fishermen plying their trade along the shore of Lake Tanganyika. Several among the visitors, he mentions, 'speak Swahili' (1887: II 292). The setting of this encounter was certainly typical of ephemeral commercial contact in which a vehicular or pidgin variety might be used. Becker did not notice use of such a form, or, if he noticed it, did not think it worth reporting.

All this is negative evidence which does not permit any definite conclusions, but, at the very least, it does not contradict the hypothesis that one variety of Swahili – the Kiunguja dialect spoken in Zanzibar – dominated and that its westward expansion was still too much in flux to have congealed in distinct up-country varieties. Other reasons for Becker's failure to dwell on variation may have to be sought on an ideological level. Europeans in Belgian service in the 1880s had *practical* aims; exact description and classification of African languages and dialects were of little interest to them. Their expeditions traveled within existing political structures determined largely by Swahili–African interaction. Becker and his colleagues were not yet in the position of later colonial administrators of the Congo for whom multilingualism, standardization, and controlled transition to literacy became practical problems of government.

Yet even Becker, the open-minded pioneer, embarked on the colonization of an African language almost as soon as he began to learn it. Apart from remarks dispersed throughout the book, there are a few pages in his account where he behaves, as it were, as a linguist (1887: II 50–8). He describes noun-classes and 'conjugates' a verb; he gives his opinion of Swahili semantics ('no abstract term, no literary turn, not one synonym', 1887: II 51) and of its syntax ('the sentence is constructed mathematically', *ibid.*). His conclusion is: 'Obviously, all this is most elementary. One or two days are sufficient to get the knack of it' (1887: II 53). He adds a few observations on lexical borrowing from Arabic, Portuguese, French and English, lists greetings, exclamations and proverbs, and ends with some more evidence purporting to show the poverty of the language. All this confirms an opinion stated at the outset of his grammatical sketch: 'The African, by the way, gets along with a very restricted choice of vocables. Three or four hundred words make up his usual glossary' (1887: II 51). A benevolent interpretation of this statement would be to assume that Becker meant by 'glossary' not a speaker's lexical repertory but the number of items actually used in an average conversation; in that case, he would have been more or less correct – for almost any language and any 'average' conversation. But nothing indicates that he wanted to make such a distinction. By its very form as an offhand, global estimate with a generous margin of error his pronouncement is characterized as a stereotype and gratuitous generalization not worth serious discussion.

What he has to say about the poverty of Swahili takes on a particularly ironic twist in view of an extraordinary aspect of *La Vie en Afrique* to which we have paid little attention so far. Becker laced his descriptive prose with Swahili (and Arabic) terms and phrases. If there is one literary–rhetorical device that permeates the whole book it is the exhibition to the reader (mostly, but not always, emphasized in print through italics and capital initial letters) of *the author's ability to name and to understand the signification of names.* Swahili words serve as points of orientation in the early chapters when Becker describes Zanzibar. Its social classes and their attire, divisions of time and space, political structure, the port and the importance of navigation, weights and measures, types of trade goods, crafts and professions, foodstuffs, domestic and wild animals, plants and features of the landscape and many other subjects, are treated as lexical *domains.* The writer thus gives proof of *dominion,* of mastering his subject-matter, in ways that recall the uses of scientific nomenclature. As his account moves on, Becker even incorporates some of the terms into his own (and the reader's) lexicon and no longer provides a French gloss.

To put these observations onto firmer ground I compiled the Swahili terms and phrases used in *La Vie en Afrique.* The results were most revealing. Becker lists about *425 items* and some *90 phrases* (this count includes types only, occurrence of tokens is much higher). Most of the items are nouns, especially generic names, as might be expected from an author whose overriding interest was in labeling the persons, objects, features and activities he found in the world he explored. Other categories, especially verbs and adjectives, are less numerous. We may assume, however, that Becker knew and used many more than he listed in his book. Even so, *La Vie en Afrique* contains a wordlist and collection of phrases that surpasses some Swahili manuals that were published or sponsored by colonials and colonial authorities at a later time.

This is not the place to analyze the many features of Becker's vocabulary that could provide further, detailed information on the ways he perceived and acquired Swahili.[30] That he cites so many Arabic terms, and quite a few terms in other African languages, situates his linguistic work between the orientations of Dutrieux and Lemaire (see above, pp. 19ff.) – that is, between a relatively open attitude, characteristic of a period of expeditions, and an increasingly closed, reduced approach that signals military campaigns and the actual establishment of colonial rule. Historically this change of attitude went together with a change of strategy and perspective. Attempts to penetrate the Congo from the east were eventually to be abandoned for bases and points of departure on the lower Congo.[31]

END OF THE ROAD

This change of perspective is documented in a last example of the polyglot genre to be examined here. The work is best introduced by citing its full title:

> *Comparative Handbook of the Congo Languages. Being a Comparative Grammar of the Eight Principal Languages spoken along the banks of the Congo River from the West Coast of Africa to Stanley Falls, a distance of 1300 miles, and of Swahili, the 'lingua franca' of the country stretching thence to the East Coast, with a Comparative Vocabulary giving 800 selected words from these Languages with their English equivalents, followed by Appendices on six other Dialects. Compiled and prepared for the Baptist Missionary Society, London.* Yakusu, Stanley Falls, Congo Independent State: 'Hanna Wade' Printing Press. Baptist Missionary Society, Bolobo, Congo Independent State. 1903.

The author is Walter Henry Stapleton.[32] The publication of the *Handbook* itself preceded Moltedo's vocabulary by two years. It seems, however, that the Swahili section of the French–Lingala–Swahili vocabulary, which is of immediate interest to us, was added and first published after Stapleton's death in 1906 by W. Millman in a second, French edition of the *Handbook* – or a portion thereof – in 1910. Millman notes in the preface to that edition that Stapleton could not carry out his plan to publish a manual of the 'language generally employed by the inhabitants of the district of Stanleyville' and that he therefore inserted the 'Kingwanya [*sic*] equivalents' to Lingala terms contained in Stapleton's vocabulary. As far as I can see, this is the first time in the series of texts examined in this chapter that Swahili spoken in the Congo is identified as Kingwana.

Stapleton's work appeared at the end of an era and marks the limits of the genre in which it is here included. It combines comparative–scholarly intentions with the expeditionary setting. Grammatical description takes a prominent place, but 'vocabularies' remain the principal manner of descriptive appropriation. Above all, it is remarkable for the explicitness with which the author describes purpose and context. Stapleton's Introduction to the *Handbook* (whose pages are lettered c–j), therefore, deserves a close reading.

The author writes as a missionary and his book is published by a missionary society. Nevertheless he leaves no doubt that his work, too, is intended 'à l'usage' of the Independent State's agents. Though one can grant Stapleton a scholarly–comparative intent it is obvious that, to him, comparison meant more than, and something different from, classificatory, taxonomic description with the aim of establishing genetic relationships between a multitude of languages. Stapleton 'compares' (and collects comparative evidence) because this reflects his own learning process and his own or his informants' movements up and down the Congo river. He also records the results of his studies in a comparative perspective because he is convinced of the didactic value of such an approach to language-learning. He is not interested in presenting his knowledge in a detached, scientific manner. He has a cause, and somehow the threads of his comparisons run together in one language, Bangala, which other Europeans at the time regarded as an ephemeral, unstable mixture of elements, not worthy of the attribute 'language'. Stapleton predicted its eventual rise because he foresaw the development of a sphere in which Lingala, or some language like Lingala, would spontaneously leap up and spread like a bushfire.

In the introduction to the *Handbook* he first takes up an objection to describing (and hence promoting) languages like Bangala. This sort of criticism must have been current at that time, especially among his fellow-missionaries. A medium which is so poor in grammatical differentiation (he does not mention lexical poverty) would seem ill-equipped for an 'exchange of thoughts' (p. c). Stapleton does not dwell on the linguistic–philosophical problem of relationships between language and thought, nor does he consider the communicative–political question of the extent to which an exchange of thoughts might be *desired* by the users of such reduced languages. He counters objections with a pragmatic postulate: 'the situation makes a common language truly necessary' (p. d). Then he goes on to demonstrate that necessity.

First, there is the 'effort of the State to impose one single administration onto the whole country of the Congo basin' (p. d). This demands common 'means of communication' which can serve to bridge linguistic diversity in this vast territory. Secondly, the agents of the State (and others, such as the captains of the Congo steamers) cannot be expected to learn all the languages of the area, nor even several of them. Even though the government has decided to employ 'Bangala' as a *lingua franca*, government agents have failed to come up with a simple, scientifically sound manual which could have assured 'reciprocal communication between Whites and Blacks, between the administrator and the subject' (p. e). Because no initiative has been taken to promote Lingala[33] it now faces a threat from a 'lively competitor' – that is, 'a kind of Kiswahili' which has emerged spontaneously in the regions formerly under Arab control (p. e). Even there, he points out, 'Bangala' is spoken by the soldiers of the colonial army (Force Publique) so that there exists in fact a sphere for that language which extends 'from the Atlantic to Lake Tanganyika and from the regions of the Upper Kasai to the Nile'. 'It is evident', he concludes, 'that the necessity of a common language is felt and that it will come' (p. e).

Having established the need for a common medium in geopolitical terms – based on a territory and its administration – Stapleton then raises the question of a language policy which will determine the choice of one language among several possible candidates. He disagrees with those who think one can solve that problem only by introducing a European language as the common medium, because 'experience has shown that the Congolese native cannot acquire French' (p. f) – especially since there are no State-sponsored schools in which this language could be taught. But 'why a European language?' he asks; ' "Bangala" exists and is here to stay.' Why don't the whites make an effort to grammaticalize what otherwise will have to remain an 'absolutely ineffective jargon' (p. f)? It is too late to make Lingala disappear by decree. Among the children of soldiers there exists already a group of native speakers of that language, and a similar situation can be foreseen for the thousands of workers who are being recruited from many different parts of the Congo (see p. g). These people begin to forget their native languages and 'speak Bangala with astonishing facility'. Unaware of the contradiction which this implies, Stapleton on the one hand expresses his conviction that use of this jargon will further limit the already narrow horizon of these people to the 'small circle of physical needs'; while on the other hand he fears that this 'movement' toward Lingala-as-spoken will make Western attempts to create a more literate form obsolete. There is only one way left by which to proceed:

> We could try to *direct* and *control* this *movement* and make of it, step by step, a language which will render important *services* to the State post, the colony, the mission school. That is to say, it will be useful to the government, the trading posts and the philanthropic societies as an effective means of establishing reciprocal exchange of ideas among the tribes so widely spread in this region of the black continent. (p. g; my emphases)

In his reasoning, Stapleton does not seem to be bothered by the fact that he started out to recommend ways of improving communication between colonial agents and their 'subjects' and ends up addressing an apparently different issue, namely communication between speakers of different African languages. The logic which keeps the two propositions together is, of course, expressive of an intent to control, using (to employ a distinction suggested by B. Heine) both 'vertical' and 'horizontal' communication.[34] Power is expressed in terms of hierarchies; and hierarchies need both dimensions to be established and to expand themselves.

The introduction ends with remarks on the history of Lingala which need not concern us here, and with another call for giving a 'little form and order to essential modes of expression' (p. j).

Stapleton's manifesto for Lingala does not seem to have caused much of a stir (as noted by Millman in his preface to the second edition of the *Handbook*). A text published in the Congo by a Protestant foreign missionary was not likely to carry much weight among those who would have had the power to implement its recommendations.[35] Still, as a document it is valuable because of the openness and freshness (perhaps signs of a certain political naïveté) with which it tackles the question of language in the colony. More specifically, it provides some important information about the state of Swahili around the turn of the century, attesting the vitality of that language. It constructs its arguments on premises which are no longer purely philological or 'practical' in the slightly insidious sense of many a *vocabulaire pratique*. Stapleton thinks in categories which nowadays would count as sociolinguistic. But, most of all, he formulates, in an exemplary manner, goals and purposes of language policy which, transformed into constraints on communication, were to determine the generic form of manuals we shall examine in chapters that follow.

Stapleton's Lingala grammar should probably no longer be included in the military–expeditionary genre, except as a borderline case. But his vocabularies, and especially the Swahili wordlist and phrases added by Millman, still reflect the communicative situations we inferred from the texts published by and for the Congo Independent State. It will be useful to make explicit some of the less obvious assumptions that underlie Stapleton's introduction. To be sure, he concentrated on Lingala, Swahili remaining at the periphery of his interests. Yet much of what he observes about the spontaneous growth of Lingala might be applicable to Congo Swahili. In the absence of comparable reflections about Swahili from such an early period, the justification given for writing the *Handbook* may be read as a model.

Stapleton regards his own contribution as the description of an existing *lingua franca* and as a project or program for the future. He feels a mission to give 'form and order' and is convinced that the linguist's contribution will serve the government's purposes, which are to 'direct and control'. A superficial reading of his text may lead one to conclude that his principal aims are the promotion and improvement of Lingala. Upon closer examination one notices that Stapleton offers a solution not to a single problem or need, but to a conflict between contradictory demands and forces. Of the two conflicting conceptualizations one is signaled by terms such as *territory* and *administration*, the other announces itself in the term *movement* which Stapleton uses when he wants to stress the spontaneous, vital nature of vehicular media such as Lingala and Swahili. Movement threatens a state of affairs (and therefore the affairs of the State). This overall conflict between (to use a nineteenth-century formula) the social statics and the social dynamics of a linguistic

36

situation covers, like an umbrella, a number of specific contradictions which remain unanalyzed.

Stapleton is, for instance, aware of 'Bangala's' living sources and of a continual flux of innovation, yet, accepting current European stereotypes, he depicts it as an artificial and deficient 'jargon'. He knows of native speakers of that language and might therefore conclude that it must be capable of providing the means of verbal communication for a growing number of Africans. Instead, he interprets the grammatical poverty of the variety known to him as a sign of the intellectual poverty of Lingala speakers. It does not occur to him that his implicit assumptions regarding language and thought/communication might have to be reexamined (of course, he should perhaps not be blamed for making assumptions around 1900 which are still held by observers of vehicular languages).

To give another example of an unnoticed contradiction, Stapleton observes that the context of Lingala is no longer predominantly trade, nor even military operations, but *work* (p. i) – incipient industrialization and urbanization – yet he states that its function is to serve as a bridge between 'tribes' (p. d). One dares not let go of the fiction (a population living in isolated tribal societies) especially when the reality (means of communication uniting the populations of vast areas and large urban centers) is so obvious.

Finally, Stapleton proposes improvement of Lingala through grammaticalization although he seems fully aware that such efforts would have little chance of keeping up with spontaneous developments. Whatever his moral–political intentions may have been (probably the best available at the time), the missionary–linguist entered the debates about colonial policies with the kind of intellectual bad faith which signals the submission of critical insight to the dictates of power.[36]

We have so far only commented on the introduction to the *Handbook*. The text itself consists of three parts, two of them devoted to a Lingala grammar, whereby the very short Part Two seems to be a sketch for, or a summary of, Part One (there is something very confusing in this composition, but this is not the place to reconstruct the history of Stapleton's text), while Part Three contains the *Vocabulaire français–bangala–swahili (kingwanya)* (pp. 60–123), two short sections on the metric system and divisions of time (pp. 124–7, both giving Lingala glosses only, most of them loans from French), and a rather extensive section with *phrases utiles* (pp. 128–43, listing first Lingala, then the French and Swahili equivalents). The grammar part is more extensive and ambitious than anything we have seen so far in this genre. The wordlist and phrase section, however, have, with one notable exception, the traits and flavor of the military–expeditionary *vocabulaires*. The exception is the length of the vocabulary (ca. 2250 items), French terms being listed alphabetically with glosses in Lingala and Swahili. In this respect it is comparable to the Dutrieux text which we examined first and took as an example of an 'open' vocabulary. In Stapleton's book, too, the wordlist is printed in such a way that

Table 1

No.	English	Dutrieux	Stapleton	Standard Swahili
1	all	Ioté; zoté	yote, wote	-ote
2	and	–	na	na
3	animal	Nyama	nyama	mnayma, nyama
4	ashes	Djivou	makala, maifi	majivu
5	back	Gongo	mkongwe	mgongo
6	bad	Mbaya	mbaya	-baya
7	bark	–	–	mguno
8	because	Sababou	amana kani	kwa sababu
9	belly	Toumbo	tumbu	tumbo
10	big	Mkouboi	mukubwa	-kubwa
11	bird	Ndégué	ndeke	ndege
12	black	Maousi	mweusi	-eusi
13	blood	Damou	damu	damu
14	blow	Kou-poliza	uvuma	-toa pumzi, -polizia
15	bone	Foupa	mufupa	mfupa
16	breathe	Kou-poumzika	toa pumuzi	-vuta pumzi, -pumzika
17	burn	Kou-oungouza, Kou-oungouzoua ('être')	choma, choma ('se')	-choma, -unguza
18	child	Mtoto, kiana	mtoto	mtoto
19	cold	Baridi	malili	baridi
20	come	Kou-dja	kuya	-ja
21	count	Hésabou	sawa	-hesabu
22	cut	Kou-kata	kata	-kata
23	day	Sikou	siku	siku
24	die	Kou-fa	kufwa	-fa
25	dig	Kou-tchimba, chimo	chibua	-chimba
26	dirty	Tchafou	–	-chafu
27	dog	Mboi	umvwa	mbwa
28	drink	Kou-niouwa	nyue	-nywa
29	dry, be	Kavou	kauka	-kavu

a wide margin remains blank for additions by users (see also the author's recommendation, p. 58). One interesting difference exists between Stapleton's Lingala list and the Swahili terms added by Millman. The latter are always single glosses, while in the former synonyms and plural forms are frequently included.

An indication of Stapleton's attitude toward lexicography appears in the 'preliminary observations' to the vocabulary (p. 58). His procedure was to collect Lingala equivalents for French terms. Whenever such equivalents were unknown to the author he resorted to terms common to a majority of the 'riverain languages', and failing that he adopted a Swahili term found 'among the Congolese who speak Swahili'. Does this not imply that he ascribed to Swahili a general currency and a hierarchical position above 'Bangala', at least as a source of lexical enrichment?

Millman tells us nothing about the sources and the method he followed when he compiled the Swahili list, at least not explicitly. In order to illustrate a contention made earlier – namely that wordlists contain much intrinsic information about conditions and circumstances, especially if compared with one another – I compiled in Table 1 a list of items from Dutrieux and Millman, together with English glosses and Standard Swahili equivalents.[37] Comparison between Dutrieux and Stapleton/Millman, even on the basis of a small sample, is quite instructive. If we disregard Dutrieux' 'French' orthography, two gaps (nos. 2, 7), and one doubtful transcription (no. 12), his vocabulary is practically identical to the Standard Swahili list in the last column. Stapleton/Millman, on the other hand, show significant deviations in more than two-thirds of the items. They are the following kinds:

1. Inaccurate or garbled transcriptions (nos. 21, 25, 29).
2. Forms showing phonological characteristics typical of Congo Swahili,[38] such as devoicing *v* to *f* (no. 4) and *g* to *k* (nos. 5, 8, 11); change of syllabic *m* to *mu* (no. 15); trace of an *i*-prosthesis in '*umvwa*' (no. 27), for *imbwa*, compared to Standard Swahili *mbwa*; change from *j* to *y* (no. 20); *d/l* alternation (no. 19); and a 'lubaized' form in *kufwa* for *kufa* (no. 24).
3. Semantic mistakes that give us a glimpse of the way these items were collected. To elicit the term for ashes (no. 4), the collector must have pointed to a fire and got two answers: *makala* (coal, embers) and *maifi*, for *maivu* (ashes). Trying to find a translation for 'because', probably with the help of a framing question, he noted the translation for his question: *amana kani* for *maana gani* (which cause?). *Uvuma* (no. 14), probably for *kuvuma* (make an indistinct sound), may have been the answer when he demonstrated blowing and his informants described the sound rather than the action.

Not documented in the list above, but nevertheless characteristic of Millman's transcriptions, is a great degree of inconsistency, which may be due to the compiler's deficiencies but also to much tolerance for variation, such as is still characteristic of Swahili spoken in Zaire. For instance, intervocalic *l*, a trait usually listed as typical of 'Kingwana' appears in *s'asseoir: ikala*, but not in *patates: kiazi* (which should be *viazi*, corresponding to the plural form of the French term). Similarly, change from *j* to *y* shows in *connaître: yuwa*, but not in *adolescent: kijana*.

That these and other 'deviations' from an East Coast standard are not just idiosyncratic is confirmed by more systematic evidence for pidginization. Noun-classes are reduced, and so are morphemes marking person, tense, voice, and derivation of verb forms. All this characterizes the syntax of the *phrases utiles* (p. 128ff., keeping in mind that the borders between syntactic and semantic – or, perhaps better, between linguistic and communicative – pidginization are fluid). Looking at the content and form of these phrases, which exemplify what is to be found in most texts of this genre, one realizes that it is vain to ask whether (poor) linguistic form determines communicable content, or whether it is the other way round. If one had to decide, one would probably have to conclude that the reduction and stereotyping of content are the determining factors in giving pidgin character to the description of a language. True, Stapleton/Millman employ the polite *vous* in French and translate colonial terms such as *boi* rather charmingly as *garçon*; these may be, as we said before, indicative of a communicative situation that has not yet been completely colonialized. But almost all the phrases listed as 'useful' could have come straight from the Union Minière lingo I heard in Katanga in the sixties. Syntactically the Lingala phrases may or may not be up to the standards set in the preceding grammatical sketch. At any rate, many Swahili phrases make a more than slightly defective impression. It is as if each sentence were an isolated, crude translation of the French equivalent, concocted without any systematic knowledge of Swahili. It is difficult to understand how an author with some linguistic ambitions could have noted down:

> j'irai à Stanleyville demain
> *mimi itakwenda kisangani kesho* (p. 132)

or

> si vous me parlez encore ainsi je vous battrai
> *kama wewe unasema na mimi ivi itakopika* (p. 134).

True, error in these two examples and many others is 'systematic', but it is certainly not enough so to decide whether linguist or informant might be responsible.

It would be tempting to analyze Stapleton/Millman's 135 useful phrases in detail. But this is not the place for a study which would entertain the linguist and fill the historian of colonial relations with disgust. To note just one detail, it takes the author more than 40 imperatives and (imperative) questions before he lists the first statement, which is

> ils avaient peur de votre fusil
> *wanaogopa munduki yako* (p. 132).

Nothing is contained in these phrases that does not belong to the command situation typical of the military–expeditionary genre; none of the curiosity for the country and its people which could still be inferred from phrases in some of the earlier vocabularies is left here. Perhaps these missionaries exaggerated pidgin-like features in trying to ingratiate themselves with the government authorities and the toughs who were running the river trade. It is certainly difficult to detect in this kind of talk the 'exchange of ideas' which Stapleton wanted to promote with his work.

These comments on the introduction and Swahili sections of Stapleton's

Handbook enable us to sketch the outlines of a development in which the military–expeditionary genre of language guides sponsored by the Congo Independent State reached its logical limits. In little more than two decades, an interest in African languages of wider communication, especially in Lingala and Swahili, developed from purely pragmatic, naked wordlists to programmatic proposals for one common language in the colony. In Stapleton's eastward perspective, Lingala was the most likely candidate for that role, although he had no illusions regarding the competitive power of Swahili. As was often to be the case later on, the analysis of a linguistic situation was bent to fit political decisions anticipated or already taken. After all, the Independent State had decided on Lingala, a choice which carried much weight with the succeeding Belgian administration. A remark gleaned from missionary correspondence in the twenties throws some light on motives (which indicate considerable conflict between the Government at Léopoldville and the interests of Katanga):

> The government is averse to Swahili. It has rejected it as the official language and chosen Bangala. The government seems to wish to isolate the Congo as far as possible from her neighbours. The less we use Swahili, the more the Government will approve of our books and work. (Alfred B. Buxton to Paul Hurlburt, April 20, 1925, British and Foreign Bible Society, Correspondence Files).

2

Questions and queries

Publication of polyglot and expeditionary guides came to a halt at about the time when the Congo Independent State became a Belgian colony (in 1908). We may assume, subject to later confirmation, that this discontinuity in the generic character of language manuals reflected changes in 'native policy' in response to major economic shifts from ivory, rubber, palm oil and other agricultural products to the mineral wealth mainly concentrated in Katanga. Administration, private enterprise, and a number of agencies which had the characteristics of both, faced the problem of having to assemble a large, stable labor force. As economic historians have shown, these efforts were not limited to the immediate needs of the emerging industrial areas. From the beginning almost, the transformation of vast portions of the rural African population into a salariat, a class of wage-earners, was envisaged. The (monogamous) nuclear family, a certain degree of literacy, a modicum of private property, good health and a work ethic of Christian inspiration were the aims (and symptoms) of such transformation; education, 'hygiene,' control of physical and social mobility and of political and religious association, and 'order' in the linguistic situation were regarded as the proper means to carry out the *oeuvre civilisatrice*. These objectives and directives, even if their practical realization did not occur right away, began to determine colonial attitudes toward language, especially toward linguistic media which appeared destined for use in supra-regional contexts of labor, administration, and military control.[1]

The Lingala–Swahili divide adumbrated by Stapleton was to become a permanent one. With certain qualifications it can be said to persist today. The border was never just a geographical one; it existed because spheres of political influence and economic interest were established before the Belgians took full control, and continued to inform relations between regions under colonial rule. Increasingly also Lingala and Swahili came to divide functions between them. Lingala served the military and much of the administration in the capital of the lower Congo; Swahili became the language of the workers in the mines of Katanga. This created cultural connotations which began to emerge very early and which remained prevalent in Mobutu's Zaire. From the point of view of Katanga/Shaba, Lingala has been the undignified jargon of unproductive soldiers, government clerks, entertainers and, recently, of a power clique, all of them often designated as *batoka chini*, people from down-river, i.e. from Kinshasa. Swahili as spoken in Katanga was a symbol of regionalism, even for those colonials who spoke it badly.

Intra-colonial rivalries and linguistic chauvinism are signs of progress in settling-in. The pioneering times are over when World War I breaks out; the colony is no longer 'on the road'. From the safeguarding of routes the tasks have shifted to the administration of territories. In the east and southeast, missionaries, company employees, and government agents presumably came to depend on Swahili as a means of bridging the divisions created by the ethnic and linguistic boundaries dividing the population under their 'tutelage' (a term much valued at the time). Such a presumption may be logical, but it does not constitute a historical explanation. The fact that Swahili was promoted in response to the need for a common language (granting for the moment that such a need existed in Katanga) is no answer to the question why people thought at the time that Swahili could fulfill that function. In our indirect approach to the history of Shaba Swahili via its colonial codification, these questions regarding the ideological background of linguistic policies are as important as the charting of dates and areas of diffusion.

To emphasize ideology in language policy is not to suggest that objective changes played no significant role. On the contrary, we must begin by realizing that the sphere of Swahili changed as the center of economic activities shifted to Katanga. By the last decade of the nineteenth century a continuous, open connection between the Congo and the East Coast no longer existed. The Swahili traders and entrepreneurs (for they were not only traders and raiders, but also agricultural producers and innovators) were pushed out, or aside, by relentless anti-Arab campaigns. The ensuing localization of *arabisés* or Wangwana in a few chiefdoms[2] is sometimes considered a main factor in the implantation of Swahili in the eastern Congo. But, as we have seen, prior to about 1900, differentiation of a Congolese dialect of Swahili had not progressed far enough to warrant use of the label 'Kingwana'. At any rate, when Swahili was again given official attention, this was in Katanga around 1910, and there it was called Swahili, certainly by its African speakers. The term 'Kingwana' gained currency among European observers, who used it to designate the Congolese variety in contrast to an East Coast Standard codified in the British territories (not to be confused with the language of educated Swahili traders that had been a model for generations before colonial standardization took place).[3]

Against the view of a continuity between eastern Congo Swahili and Katanga/Shaba Swahili also speaks the fact that proposals to promote Swahili in Katanga came at a time during World War I when a critical mass of native 'Kingwana' speakers no longer lived in that area (if, indeed, such a group ever existed around Msiri's capital).[4] Nor had recruitment of Swahili-speaking workers from the Maniema and Lomami regions to the north gotten anywhere near its peak. In sum, we have no evidence for spontaneous or directed diffusion of 'Kingwana' southward into the language areas of Luba, Lunda, Sanga, Lamba and Bemba. For that reason, the northeast remains by and large outside the horizon of a history of Swahili in Katanga. At any rate, a high degree of mutual intelligibility and of multilingualism in this area of the 'kingdoms of the savannah'[5] makes it implausible that Swahili could have taken 'naturally' a dominant role as a language of wider communication. If such a spontaneous process went on prior to effective colonization, why did it stop somewhere near the Congo–Rhodesia border, which cut right through several ethnic and traditional political areas?

And yet, for the years during and immediately following the World War, documents leave little doubt that Swahili was, or was to be, the common language of Katanga. What brought about the turn to Swahili? It is this gap in our knowledge that first caused me to think about the problems of this study. As I see the situation now, at least three series of events and decisions contributed to create the effect of a sudden and massive emergence of Swahili around 1920 in southern Katanga. The first one was the belgianization of Elisabethville and of the personnel of the largest employer, the Union Minière du Haut Katanga (UMHK). Prior to that period both had been oriented toward the south, and English had had a strong, sometimes a dominant, position. How and why Swahili should have become linked to policies regarding a European language will be explained in some detail. Another factor was changes in the recruitment policies for African workers, which brought sufficient numbers of Swahili-speakers, actual and potential, into the area to make official adoption of that language feasible. A third factor, intimately linked to those already mentioned, was the use of Swahili as a language of education by most of the urban missions. Cooperation in this matter between employers and educators was not without conflict, especially over the kind of Swahili to be promoted, but a degree of harmony was certainly reached by the end of the period covered here (around 1938). Three sorts of question occupied linguistic 'planners', if this is not too strong a term for the time: legal, empirical – administrative, and political. A section will be devoted to each of these.

A QUESTION OF LAW AND RIGHTS: LANGUAGE AND THE COLONIAL CHARTER

We must begin with what may seem an onerous detour, examining Belgian attitudes toward language policy at about the time when the Independent State was transformed into a colony. The *Charte coloniale* of October 18, 1908, was a sort of constitution for Belgium's African possessions. Its Article 3 formulated rights and regulations with respect to the use of languages. This is not the place to discuss the law in a wider context, such as the parliamentary and other public debates in the decades prior and subsequent to 1898, when the utilization of French and Flemish in all branches of government was decreed by law. Here we must focus on the colonial angle of the *question linguistique/taalkwestie.* M. Halewyck's informative and authoritative commentary on the Colonial Charter, which addresses some of the instances of parliamentary struggle and some of the obvious sources of conflict between legislators and colonial men of action, will serve as a basis.[6]

But first the text of the law in a free translation:

> *Colonial Charter Article 3*
> The use of language is optional. It will be regulated by decree such that the rights of Belgians and Congolese are guaranteed. These regulations will concern only activities of public authority and judicial affairs.
>
> In these matters, the Belgians in the Congo shall have the same guarantees as those of which they are assured in Belgium. Respective decrees will be published later, during the five years which follow the promulgation of this law.
>
> All regulations and decrees having a general character must be formulated and published in the French language and in the Flemish language. Both texts are official. (Halewyck 1910: 109)[7]

The commentator's remarks may be summarized as follows. The Colonial Charter would not have had a separate article concerning language had it not been for the 'language question' in Belgium. The text that was originally proposed to Parliament said nothing about the issue, and the present Article 3 goes back to an amendment proposed by the Government, roughly equivalent to the first paragraph of the final text. A group of representatives led by M. Henderickx – obviously acting in Flemish interests – asked for a second amendment which caused the second and third paragraphs of Article 3 to be included. The final version was a compromise worked out by the Minister of Justice (Halewyck 1910: 110–12). The commentator does not explain why and how the 'rights of the Congolese', which were mentioned neither in the original proposal nor in the Henderickx amendment, came to be part of the ministry proposal and the definitive text. Perhaps a link existed with another amendment proposed by M. de Brouchhoven de Bergeyck which was rejected by the Chamber. Its intent was to give teeth to Article 3 by demanding that five years from the promulgation of the Colonial Charter no one could be appointed to judicial, administrative, or military service unless he had given proof of knowing Dutch and French 'besides at least one of the principal languages of the Congo'. No one should be allowed to serve in the Ministry of Colonies (then still the Département des Colonies) without advanced knowledge of Dutch and French, and both languages should have equal status in the examination of candidates for colonial service. Only persons who had been in the service of the Independent State at the moment of transfer were to be exempt from these rules (see Halewyck 1910: 112).

The commentator goes on to deplore the haste with which Article 3 was formulated and voted into the Colonial Charter. In his view, it was futile to try and export the Belgian language question (i.e. its legal 'solutions') into the colony because in the Congo there existed a *fait accompli*: the Congo Independent State had used French as sole official language for a quarter of a century and could not have done otherwise because it needed to recruit its agents from other nations who could only be required to speak a 'world language' (Halewyck 1910: 113; nothing is said of Lingala having been declared the official African language by the Independent State administration). In Halewyck's opinion the whole question is pointless, since in practice all candidates for colonial service speak French, and if one wanted to apply legal principles the law should also include German among the official languages (it being spoken by '145000 Belgians, among them by 30000 exclusively').

Another serious objection to the exclusive use of French is disposed of in a similar tongue-in-cheek manner. Defenders of Flemish argued that privileging French as the language of administration would also mean that it became the one European language to be adopted by the Congolese. That, Halewyck says, could be corrected by making Flemish obligatory in schools run or subsidized by the State. But 'no one thought of making such a proposal' (1910: 114). What surpassed imagination around 1910 became reality at a later period.

Article 3 of the Colonial Charter was a 'transplantation' of Article 23 of the Belgian constitution. It granted the freedom to use languages which are 'usually employed' (*usitées*) in Belgium. M. Renkin (later Minister of Colonies) told the legislators: 'You are going to grant the freedom of languages used in Belgium – a freedom which concerns only 2500–3000 persons in the Congo. What about the millions and millions of negroes who don't seem to preoccupy you in this regard?' (Halewyck 1910: 115). This intervention was, apart from the Flemish pressure toward recognition of bilingualism, a reason why the formula 'freedom of language for all inhabitants of the Congo' was included in the final version.

Apart from stipulating that official documents be in French and Dutch, the law did not regulate the use of language(s) in colonial practice. The Ministry's interpretation of the sense of Article 3 in this respect looked remarkably broad. Failure to speak French should be no obstacle to colonial service in the Congo. Agents should be entitled to make their administrative and judicial decisions, according to their nationalities, 'in French, Flemish, German, Italian, Norwegian or Swedish'. In fact, 'if they should fancy the use of Arabic they could not be said to act against the law' (Halewyck 1910:116). Note the implication in this statement that French and Flemish correspond to different nationalities and the conspicuous omission of English, which was to be more of a problem than Flemish. It is also remarkable that Arabic should have been mentioned, even if it was meant as a *plaisanterie*.

The commentator had no use for such vague liberalism, and gives us on this occasion a precious view behind the scenes, as it were, of Belgian political reasoning: true freedom in the use of languages would mean in practice that 'hierarchical' relations between agents and agencies (*fonctionnaires, juridictions*) would become impossible (Halewyck 1910: 116). Given the ambiguity of Article 3, Halewyck invokes the legal principle of the overriding rule (*règle supérieure*), which he recognized in an Independent State decree of 1886 stipulating that 'local customs' and 'general' juridical principles must be followed in the absence of explicit legislation. They must determine 'which idiom should serve to express decisions by the representatives of authority' (1910: 117). What this means is clear to him: 'For a quarter of a century French has been, without interruption, the official language of Congolese administration and justice' (*ibid.*). At any rate, Halewyck thinks that the detailed regulations announced in Article 3 would have to follow the Belgian model, which recognizes *three* language areas: Wallonia, Flanders, and the 'mixed region' of Brussels. From this he derives rules concerning bilingualism for each of the three branches of government, arguing that the situation in the Congo is analogous to that of the Belgian capital (see 1910: 118–22). Halewyck then goes on to apply this reasoning to legal matters (distinguishing between criminal and civil law) and points out with scarcely hidden satisfaction that in the highest Belgian court (*cour de cassation*) 'French is the only language admitted. Therefore it will continue to be the only language used in the superior council of the colony' (1910: 123).

Yet another occasion to defend his cause he finds in the absence of precise instructions regarding the five-year deadline set for implementing Article 3. He rejects the interpretation that everything must be accomplished by 1913. Such decrees as will come forth can be applied only 'within the limits of what is possible' (1910: 124). He cites again Renkin, who (in a debate on August 13, 1908) expressed the same opinion, and adds that there must first be 'an examination of the situation' (1910: 125). As we shall see in the following section, such an examination was carried out by the colonial administration a few years later.

Who decides what is possible? The government which runs the colony. After some back-and-forth tracking about practical ways in which Flemish might be given at least a nominal status, Halewyck sees a chance to clinch his argument. The complexities of implementing the law with regard to French and Flemish are nothing compared to those arising from the *idiomes Congolais* (1910: 127). The relevant passage is worth quoting here:

> How can you ask of candidates applying for a vacant position in the colony – candidates who present themselves in insufficient numbers – that they know different languages which change from one region to another? How should decrees and other Government documents be published in a variety of dialects which are difficult to enumerate? How can you require judges to formulate their sentences in a primitive idiom which is not organized to express juridical notions...? (1910: 127)

If the provisions of Article 3 were really to become formal law, it would be legislation that could only be applied 'on the island of Utopia' (1910: 127).

Whatever the ideals were that guided the legislators who voted Article 3, the commentator has by now 'proved' that 'practical possibilities' must determine what really happens. In the next-to-last paragraph of his commentary he formulates a sort of practical program for mastering the problems of African multilingualism:

47

> The Government must assure good interpreter's services to the Blacks; we must promote the teaching of our national languages; the Government must require agents and judges to take, before their departure to the Congo, courses in the four principal idioms of the colony, 'Kikongo, also called Fiote, Bangala, Kisuaheli, and Kiluba-Kasai' (see 1910: 128, note 1).

Halewyck's footnote may be one of the earliest semi-official statements of the French-plus-four-languages formula which is still adhered to in today's Zaire.[8]

The direct relevance of the Colonial Charter to the history of Swahili in the Congo may seem doubtful. One may generally question the value of such legal documents and ask specifically whether there was ever much consistency between political goals and ideas held by Belgians in the home country and political action on the part of colonial administrators. Still, Halewyck's commentary is a precious source, documenting some of the unspoken and therefore all the more powerful principles of language policy in the Belgian Congo.

What Halewyck's more than slightly biased interpretation of Article 3 shows is not that Belgium's linguistic problems were exported to the colony (certainly not anywhere near the time he wrote). Even at the home front the positive attitude toward freedom of language use expressed in both the constitution of 1831 and the Colonial Charter was little more than a gratuitous gesture, made easy for a French-speaking elite which felt superior and held the power. What *was* exported to the Congo with this and other legal texts was a special brand of hypocrisy. There is hypocrisy in a way of reasoning which appears to grant Flemings and Africans the right to use their languages while in reality it maintains and reinforces the supremacy of French with appeals to a sense for the practically possible. At times, spokesmen for this view give themselves away, as when Halewyck argues that candidates for colonial service would at any rate have to be cultured enough to speak French (1910: 112). Language was not the only issue, to say the least. When he invokes practical needs and necessities, Halewyck does this in ways that already reveal models and arguments which were to be used in later debates and are *en vogue* among sociolinguists up to this day. Three of these are easily discernible:

(a) *Multilingualism is a threat to order.* Use of many languages is equated with confusion; in fact two languages already make the orderly exercise of government difficult.

(b) If disorder cannot be removed by radical 'unification' (exclusive use of one language), there must at least *be established hierarchical relations among languages.* Freedom of coexistence, interaction, and perhaps competition would be a threat to authority. This is why French comes out naturally on top as the exclusive language of the highest levels of the administration (see Halewyck 1910: 116, 123). The same concern for hierarchy is in my view behind the promulgation of four 'principal languages' at a time when reasonably good linguistic descriptions, let alone sociolinguistic surveys of language use, were not available. As envisaged by the colonial administration, Kikongo, Lingala, Tshiluba and Swahili were, each in a circumscribed geographical region of the colony, to constitute intermediate levels between the official European language and the autochthonous languages.

(c) Finally, *thinking in terms of order and levels invited appeal to 'laws' of linguistic evolution.* What Article 3 calls 'languages' turn in the commentator's discourse into 'idioms' (1910: 117, 127), 'dialects' (126), and ultimately into a 'primitive' speech incapable of expressing higher notions (127). For someone who saw relations between French and Flemish in terms of levels of culture, equal rights granted by law to African languages could not have meant more than their right to be 'developed'.

Order, hierarchy, and evolutionary distance – these were the basic assumptions which determined language policies throughout the colony's existence, and beyond. Agreement or disagreement with views such as those expressed by Halewyck were to determine positions in the ensuing debates.

A QUESTION OF FACTS: LANGUAGE IN AN EARLY GOVERNMENT SURVEY

Halewyck was right when be observed that with regard to the choice of an official language the colony inherited a *fait accompli.* Article 3 did not cause scruples among colonial administrators and company managers, nor even among the missionaries. French was the official medium of exchange among colonial agencies. Only in the field of education did problems become visible early on. Although the system, prior to World War I, was rudimentary and restricted to grade and trade schools for Africans, situations began to develop which made it impossible to leave the language problem to philosophical discussions or to limited practical solutions. If education was to contribute to the 'evolution' of the colony, then the language(s) in which and into which the young were educated would have to come under some sort of control.

There is evidence that the initiative in this matter came from the metropolitan government, not from the Governor General at Boma. Why this should have been so is perhaps explained by the following document. The Governor General had established a *comité consultatif pour l'enseignement.* In 1916 it consisted of three members, the Révérend Père (Rufin), Supérieur de la Colonie Scolaire (at Boma), Monsieur Dufays 'de la Justice', and A. Pièrot, teacher at the École des Candidats-Commis (at Boma). These gentlemen met on November 10, 1916, at Boma and issued a report based on an examination of results obtained in the first semester of that year at schools in Stanleyville, Léopoldville, Lusambo (Sankuru), Buta (Uele), Tumba (District des Cataractes) and Boma. This document – two and a half typewritten pages, double-spaced – contained no factual information whatsoever, only generalities characterized by a spirit of resignation. So far, it says, our efforts have neither been a total failure nor had much success. The reasons for this must be sought among the Africans. The black student has a good memory 'and nothing else'. His brain, 'lacking the elements necessary for the operations of the mind, tires much more quickly than that of our children'. In sum, 'for a long time to come teaching in the Congo will give the educators no pleasure or consolation except the thought of having worked for humanity and the Fatherland'. Although there is talk of pedagogical 'techniques', language is not mentioned at all.

Presumably this report was transmitted to the Ministry of Colonies (the copy of it from which I quoted I found in a ministry dossier, see below). It is also likely that it was one of the reasons which caused the Ministry to move on the question of education. Clearly, government officials had no use for philosophical resignation; they wanted practical results. Six weeks after the report of the *comité consultatif* was written – that is, a few weeks after it was received – the Ministry decided to put the 'question' of education on a firm empirical basis by conducting a survey.[9]

Much information about language and attitudes toward language(s) is contained in the returned questionnaires, as are certain details about the language situation in Katanga, which will have our special interest in the fifth section of this chapter.

Two drafts (typed, with copious editing in handwriting) and what looks like the final version of a letter by the Minister to the Governor General at Boma, all dated London, December 30, 1916, show that much work and thought went into formulating the purpose of this survey: not to satisfy scientific curiosity, but to provide 'precious elements' for the implementation of policies. No doubt is left about the latter. A passage in the first of the three versions says: 'We must, at least in the near future, give to our teaching *a utilitarian tendency*.' This is replaced by a more general statement in the second draft, but the final version expresses the idea in no uncertain terms:

> The lower-echelon white personnel [in the Congo] is very expensive and produces mediocre results. If we could replace it with black clerks and craftsmen it would be an enormous progress from a financial, political and economic point of view. We must pursue this aim without delay...

The Minister refers to several earlier exchanges on the subject of education and suggests that the enclosed draft of a questionnaire could be improved on by the *comité consultatif* with regard to technical questions. Three types of questionnaire should be printed and sent to missionaries, government agents, and the heads of private companies respectively. Finally he asks for 50 printed copies to be distributed among colonial personnel on leave and heads of business companies in Europe. Five months later, with a letter dated Boma, May 7, 1917, the Governor General sends out 60 copies of the printed questionnaire (15 for missionaries, 20 for administrators and 25 for heads of private firms).

Preserved in the archives are only about 50 completed questionnaires and a few letters by persons who did not want to answer the questions separately. Responses range from a laconic Yes or No to lengthy disquisitions of precisely the kind that the Minister tried to discourage. Each of the three target groups was given a different questionnaire. Businessmen, administrators, and missionaries–educators were given four, five, and twelve questions respectively on language. Persons in the first two categories were asked mainly about policy; factual information was expected to come from missionaries and teachers.

The office of the Governor General was not inhibited by scientific rules for the construction of questionnaires. Most of the questions are loaded and leading; they themselves constitute an important part of the historical information to be gleaned from this survey. It appears that the discussion about language policies in the Congo had crystallized around three categories and their corresponding positions: the national languages (really meaning French; the plural only gives ceremonial recognition to bilingualism in Belgium), vehicular trade languages (*langues véhiculaires de commerce*), and native languages (*langues indigènes* as opposed to *langues européennes*). The respondents were asked to express their opinion regarding the actual role and future prospects of each for the exercise of government and for (economic) development. It is clear that the Governor General had taken a position on the issue. He conveyed it to the addressees of the questionnaire in, among other ways, the order in which he lists his queries (national languages first, native languages last) and through the formulation of the questions (see below). Furthermore, the Government increased the chances for having its position confirmed by keeping the three linguistic concepts deliberately ambiguous. The national language problem is bypassed by never mentioning French or Flemish, let alone asking for a choice between the two; the term 'vehicular trade language' is made to apply to the kind of language one would expect, e.g. 'Bangala', but also to European languages which could have a vehicular function; native languages, as is clear from the responses, could include autochthonous as well as vehicular languages, provided they were of African origin.

Although they were formulated in an ambiguous conceptual frame, questions such as the following left little choice to respondents:

> Don't you foresee that, as trade languages, the native languages will sooner or later give way to European languages? (Questions 13 to businessmen, and 25 to administrators)

So that no doubt may be left about the expected answer, the following question asks:

> Would it not be better to promote (*pousser*) through education and, as much as possible, in everyday practice, the adoption of a European language as vehicular trade language, rather than the 'Bangala jargon'? (Questions 26 to administrators, 14 to businessmen, adding 'or another' to 'Bangala jargon')

51

Further motives are revealed in an additional question posed to administrators:

> Do you think there is a danger in promoting the spread of a European language in the Congo? (Question 28)

Questions on language to missionaries and educators were divided into two groups, one relating to elementary, the other to trade, schools. Only this group was asked which language(s) it used in teaching and in what area this language was spoken. The Government obviously knew that, with few exceptions (such as the *colonie scolaire* at Boma), African languages were used, for the fourth question asked whether the present staff could 'teach the native language without too many difficulties'. What follows expresses again the Governor's position in favor of promoting a European language, a position which was in conflict with the policy followed by most missions. Two examples may illustrate how this survey was used to make the government's preferences known and to prepare opposing groups for the measures it planned to take:

> Would it be very inconvenient to postpone the teaching of the native language given to a limited number of students until the day we have black teachers? (Question 5)
> Don't you think it would be more in the interest of the blacks, of the administration, and of the Europeans who live in the colony, if the natives were taught exclusively one of our national languages? (Question 8)

Three questions were posed under the heading 'Trade Schools', but only two of them seem to belong there. Both relate to the problems of technical terms, the name(s) for *matières premières et objets fabriqués* (materials and products). The Governor asks support for his opinion that these terms ought to be learned in a European language and uses this occasion to pose the only question which directly asks for the choice of a specific language (Question 11). The last question to missionaries and educators (Question 12) is similar to Question 28 posed to administrators, except that it is more explicit:

> Do you see an inconvenience, *political or other*, in the teaching of a European language? (My emphasis)

Given the ambiguous and tendentious manner in which all these questions were posed, one is not surprised to find in the responses mainly expressions of opinion and declarations of loyalty to the Government's (presumed) position. There is little information about linguistic situations or daily practice.[10]

At this stage in the organization of the colony, and owing to circumstances connected with the War, the respondents had a rather diverse background. Their answers to the Government's leading questions were less uniform than one would have expected. Clearly, there existed as yet no common opinion on these matters and there was little prospect for a unified and effective language policy as long as the colonial administration could not control opinion among its own employees, let alone among businessmen and missionaries.

By contrast to the impression of vagueness and indecision one gets from many of the returned questionnaires, at least two of the responses – one from the Kasai, the other from Katanga – give an assessment of a situation and express strong opinions about a specific course of action. The latter will have our attention later on, but first the positions taken by the majority of respondents should be summarized and illustrated with some of the more colorful statements.

RESPONSES FROM BUSINESSMEN AND ADMINISTRATORS[11]

Generally speaking, the Governor General got a majority of them to agree with the plans and preferences implied in the questions. One also gets the impression that the businessmen were closer to the Government's positions than the government agents. Beginning with Questions 12 and 24 respectively, most business respondents agree that promoting the national languages will be good for commerce. No one seriously considers that both languages should be introduced; several state explicitly that Flemish should not be taught. To try that would be 'puerile' (Compagnie du Congo Belge). J. Cousin, one of the more prominent respondents, wrote for the BCK/CFK railway company and explained his positive answer: 'Because in this way the culture of the White Man would be more easily accessible to the Black.' The representative in Africa of the Huileries du Congo Belge wishes that French *and* English should be spread, so that 'not only relations between natives and Europeans, but also those among natives and the many people from the [East] coast could be made easier.' The respondent for the Chemin de Fer des Grands Lacs adds to his positive answer the remark that first of all the whites should be required to know the national languages of Belgium: 'I have at CFGL five Scandinavians with whom you can only talk in the native [i.e. African] language.' Among those who responded negatively to Question 24, the UMHK leads with a laconic 'We don't think so,' echoed by several other respondents. Probably on the basis of their own experience, Société Belgika fears that widespread use of a European language will create unfair advantages to those traders who can communicate directly with Africans in their languages.

The administrators are divided in their opinions about the usefulness of a national language in government. A majority expresses a positive attitude, provided that this national language be French. 'A bilingual Colony would be an irony', observes the district commissioner of Tanganyika–Moero. Kasai voices most strongly opposition to the diffusion of European languages in any form; Kwango warns that only a small elite among the Africans will adopt a European language (which will thus create problems); Kivu makes the distinction that French will facilitate administration, while an African language will be better for trade; Sankuru reminds the Government that 'official native languages' already exist ('Bas-Congo', 'Bangala', 'Kiswahili', 'Kituba' and 'Sango (Ubangi)'), the implication being that these languages rather than a European language are, and will be, functional in government and trade.

Some confusion existed because Questions 24/12 could be interpreted either as soliciting a statement of fact or an opinion about policy. Question 26/14 clearly asked for a statement of policy. Most of the business respondents agree that a European language should be promoted as a general vehicle of economic relations. UMHK, which had answered the factual question negatively, now comes out on the positive side: once the Government has decided which European language should serve the purpose it should be taught quickly and in a practical manner. The respondent for the Syndicat d'Études et d'Entreprises au Congo suggests that blacks are morally entitled to speak a European language. Only one writer, representing the Comptoir des Exportateurs Belges, sees the problem as one of communication in both directions: natives should be taught French, and Europeans should know the language of the area in which they live. He adds, however, that the latter should be limited to 'practical knowledge without entering into all the subtleties of native grammar and all the complications which this brings about'. Some of the negative responses are of interest because they may illustrate the difference in perspective between firms oriented to trade (and rural areas) and business exploiting resources with the help of a sizeable African labor force. Belgika states that promoting French as a commercial language will not be in their interest because the trader who speaks a native language will always have an advantage over the one who must use a European language. The representative in the Congo of Huileries du Congo thinks that the question is moot; in their area relations with African workers are so temporary that it would be impossible to try and teach them French (the European respondent for the same company sees things differently). Pragmatic opposition to promoting European languages as vehicular idioms is perhaps best illustrated by an answer from Congo Oriental Cie.–Intertropical Anglo-Belgian Trading Cie.: the Swahili and Bangala jargon is firmly anchored throughout the colony. It is easy to learn for Europeans as well as for natives. It exists; why needlessly look for other difficulties? There are so many things that are more interesting to teach the natives than European languages. (It is safe to assume that 'interesting' refers to the colonizers' perspective, not to the Africans'.)

Administrators are again divided on the issue. For them, the relevant question (Question 26) is formulated more precisely. They are asked not only whether a European language should be promoted as vehicular in general, but whether this should be done through teaching and in daily practice and whether the European language should be pushed 'rather than the Bangala jargon'. Obviously, Lingala was already in a strong position. The district commissioner of Lac Léopold II notes that 'Bangala' has been used for many years; why change that? The only problem is that many Europeans speak that language badly. Haut Uele says nearly the same and deplores that a good grammar and vocabulary of Lingala are 'not available' (in 1917?). For Sankuru, the district commissioner and his *adjoint supérieur* lean to a similar formula, specifying Kituba[12] as their choice. Kivu strongly recommends

Swahili as a language spoken 'from the Nile to Rhodesia and all the way to Zanzibar and Madagascar'. The *adjoint supérieur* of Tanganyika–Moero expresses himself in similarly glowing terms for Swahili. The acting district commissioner for Lulua is in favor of Tshiluba. Only one respondent (district not identified) explains his opposition to promoting French with the remark that it would cause their (European) employees to neglect the study of native languages and would make it difficult to control their African collaborators.

Between the questions of fact and policy regarding the usefulness of a European language in administration and trade or industry, the questionnaire includes ones which elicit opinion about the survival chances of African languages in a situation of contact or conflict with a European language (Questions 13 and 25 respectively). Once again the formulation suggests the expected answer: do you not expect that, as trade languages, the native languages will sooner or later give way to European languages? All the respondents could be counted on as holding strong opinions about 'laws' of evolution, but agreement on this issue is not as clear as one might expect. Among the business respondents, the UMHK sets the tone for a majority of positive answers: 'It is evident that the colony of the Belgian Congo will be subject to the same law of evolution as the old colonies in Africa, where, in commercial matters, a European language replaced native languages.' Others share this view but insist that such will happen only in the long run. The respondent for Comptoir Commercial Congolais points to active resistance against foreign languages among the Bayaka (in the Kwango region); Compagnie du Congo Belge thinks that this will happen in the big centers only. Only the representative of Géomines declares that he does not believe it will happen and one (Comptoir des Exportateurs Belges) even challenges the theory on which the question is built: predictions about relative success could be made only if one European language were in conflict with one African language, which is not the case.

The time factor invoked by some of the business respondents was foremost in the minds of the administrators who gave their estimate of future developments. They, too, are convinced of the superiority of European languages and hence of their superior survival chances, but they are pessimistic about the speed of evolution. A well-established consensus must have been behind repeated references to a 'remote future' (*avenir éloigné*). Kivu thinks that an African trade language will prevail: one only needs to look at neighboring colonies with massive European settlement. Tanganyika–Moero (in the person of the district commissioner) expresses concerns which will occupy us later: certainly, a European language will win, but we must watch that it will be ours (although the intruder is not named, the reference is clearly to English). Only three respondents do not profess faith in an evolutionary law and think that the vehicular language will always be African.

One would assume that answers to the next questions (15 and 27 respectively) – should native languages be taught, and what could be their practical use? – would largely depend on positions taken on the preceding issues. Such is apparently not the case. Both company representatives and administrators find reasons to advocate teaching African languages, despite their views on linguistic evolution.

Most business respondents take a (qualified) positive position on this issue. The Géomines representative gives a concise reply:

> In order to know, understand and command the native – I am speaking from the industrial point of view – one must possess knowledge of his language. It is always going to be very difficult for the European to exercise authority over natives if he does not possess their languages. By 'possess' I mean understand them when they speak among themselves.

Several companies repeat earlier remarks on the advantages of being able to communicate with trade-partners in an African language, but some also take a more philosophical attitude when they point to the spiritual value of being educated in one's own language (e.g. Mercantile Anversoise). Comptoir des Exportateurs Belges recommends teaching the natives 'their own languages transformed into a grammatical written language'. Among the negative respondents, J. Cousin of the BCK/CFK reiterates his theoretical position. The only use of teaching one African language in the whole of the Congo (which was one of the many ways in which the question could be interpreted) would be to facilitate relations among the different 'Congolese races'. But

> the same result will be reached, a little more slowly, if one replaces teaching of the native jargon with that of a European language. From the point of view of relations between whites and natives, it is preferable to go resolutely toward teaching a European language. This point must be given utmost importance because civilization must penetrate into the Congo through the whites as intermediaries.

Administrators are no more united on this issue than on others. Responses also show that the wording of the question caused confusion. Who should be taught native languages, the natives or the Europeans? The district commissioner of Sankuru expresses an opinion shared by several: 'If we want to teach a people well (*avantageusement*) then it is natural, demonstrated by history and agreed upon by educators, that the mother tongue should be the basis of education.' But the opposite position is also taken: do not teach them native languages; these are the only ones they speak among each other, and this is in the way of their evolution (*Adjoint supérieur*, Lac Léopold II). Several respondents signal yet another ambiguity in the phrasing. Does 'indigenous' refer to autochthonous or vehicular languages? Some distinguish between the two and reject native-language purism in favor of those practical solutions that already exist. Haut-Uele opts for 'Bangala', noting that certain missions in the Aruwimi region have tried to adopt 'Kingwana' in their prayers and conversations. But the Bangala orientation is so strong that none of their adepts converse in Kingwana. Two respondents come up with yet another variant of the 'official' African language formula. Tanganyika–Moero lists 'Bangala, Kiswahili, Kiluba', which should be promoted and also used in correspondence. Kwango refers to the trade languages 'Kikongo, Bangala, Kisuahili', which will be picked up without formal teaching by the natives if they see an advantage in it. Sankuru prefers Kituba over Tshiluba 'taught by professors'. Lulua pushes Tshiluba (and it is of interest that Tshiluba rather than Swahili is said to be the dominant vehicular medium in the Lomami region from which a good part of the working population of Katanga was recruited). Kivu, as might be expected, looks east toward the German and British examples and strongly recommends the teaching of Swahili. Only a few soldiers speak Bangala in this district, and they adapt quickly to Swahili. The District Commissioner then provides some interesting detail:

> All the foreigners of Asian origin speak [Swahili]. Even the Europeans: Englishmen, Germans, Greeks; and we employ that language when we do not understand each other in our European languages. This is the volapuk of the country. All the native chiefs understand, speak, and some of them, write, that language. Swahili is taught in the missions and in the coranic schools (*classes mahometanes*). In the villages visited by Europeans all the children understand Swahili.

Finally there is Question 28 to administrators, which has no counterpart in the forms distributed among business representatives: is there any danger in promoting a European language in the Congo? There is indeed, in the opinion of a small but vociferous minority among the respondents. D'Hemptinne, *adjoint supérieur* at Haut-Uele, thinks:

> It would be a mistake to promote a European language in the Congo. We shall all be exposed to indiscretion by the blacks, who can be counted on spreading what we would like to be kept secret. We will have to be careful all the time that our conversations won't be overheard (there are so many which must remain secret), or that certain documents which they should not know get into the hands of the blacks we educate. I have the impression that we don't sufficiently know the soul of the native and that we still have a lot to study before we confide in him.

The District Commissioner of Kasai summarizes a lengthy statement by one of his aides in a covering letter:

> The quintessence of his documented exposé is: teach the black to read French and he will give himself over to revolutionary and pornographic French papers and he will be after all the novels and other immoral books published in the French language. And this gentleman concludes: go on teaching French to the Negro and you'll morally destroy the race while at the same time preparing the revolution which will chase you – which, by the way, is what you deserve. – I share his views.

Other administrators show that they know of this opinion (which must have been quite current at the time), and they take care to reject it. One declares, tongue-in-cheek, that of course any conversation between educated Europeans must be fit to be overheard by Africans (District Commissioner,

Sankuru). Others think that censure of the press and a good postal service will take care of the secrecy problem (Kwango and Kivu). That speaking French makes blacks 'conceited' is affirmed by one respondent and dismissed by another, who points out that what conceit there is will vanish as more and more Africans speak French.

Several take this question as an occasion to signal 'danger' for the national languages from internal conflict and from other European languages. Kivu cites a case of Flemish resistance to French, and Tanganyika–Moero reiterates an earlier warning:

> This is our colony; the natives must speak our language. If we don't watch it, it will be the language with a reputation of being universally accepted as a trade language which will impose itself and seriously damage our prestige among the natives.

Since he recommended Swahili earlier, that language can only be English. English was perceived as a real threat to Belgian 'authority' in the eastern regions of the colony. Why this should be so, and how it bears on the major theme of this study, will become clearer when we examine the reaction from Katanga in the fifth section of this chapter.

RESPONSES FROM MISSIONARIES AND EDUCATORS[13]

Missionaries and educators were given twice as many questions about language because it was they who were most immediately concerned with the subject of the survey. The wording of the questionnaire also suggests that the Government expected them to be both better informed about actual linguistic situations and more set in their opinion about the role of language in education. Question 5 especially shows that strong opposition was anticipated to plans for promoting a European language as a general vehicular medium: would it be very inconvenient to postpone teaching a native language to a limited number of students until the day we have enough black teachers?

The first four questions relating to elementary schools solicit information on the language actually used in teaching, on the area in which that language is spoken, on whether this language is used to promote literacy, and on whether currently available personnel is capable of teaching (in) the native language. As presumed in the questions, all respondents report exclusive use of an African language, with the exception of the government school at Boma, the Redemptorists of Thysville–Matadi, who already taught French (in French) in an upper class, and the Methodists in Katanga, who used, besides 'native languages', French and English. But which 'native language'? Outside Katanga this problem was apparently solved: Kikongo on the lower Congo (Redemptorists), Lingala further up the river (Scheutists at Umanye-St Pierre and Nouvelle Anvers, and the Heart of Africa Mission in Haut-Uele) (notice that the term used by the Catholic missionaries is 'Lingala', not 'Bangala').

Only the Reverend Studd, responding for the Heart of Africa Mission, uses 'Bangala', as did all the administrators and business representatives. 'Kiluba' was used in the Kasai by the Scheutists, and 'Tshiluba...spoken in the districts of Kasai, Sankuru, Lulua and Lomami' was taught at the government school at Kabinda. Swahili was the choice at the government school of Stanleyville. The respondent describes it as 'a Bantu language understood everywhere east from a line running through Gombari, Kole, Basoko, Isangi, Tshofa, Ankoro. It is the language which the natives employ and even the whites'.

In Katanga, the situation is much less clear. In the north, the Catholic mission of St Joseph l'Alleud (Pères du St Esprit) uses Swahili, the Pentecostal mission only Kiluba. In Elisabethville and the south, the Salesians teach in Swahili and Bemba, explaining that 'Kibemba [is spoken] along the Luapula, Swahili [is the] vehicular language.' The Methodists name four languages, reflecting the huge territory they are trying to cover. In Bishop Springer's rather peculiar spelling these are 'At E-ville [Elisabethville] Chivenba [Bemba] and Chibuba-Sanga [Luba-Sanga] at Kambove, at Kabongo, Chibula [Kiluba?] at Kapanga, Luanda [Lunda].' Neither Bishop Springer nor the Reverend J. A. Clarke of the Garenganze Evangelical Mission mentions Swahili at this point. There are reasons to believe that this represents a deliberate attempt to play down its importance.

The response from Katanga to the first four questions suggest three conclusions. (a) By the end of 1917 Swahili was not yet the sole candidate for a vehicular African language in this area. (b) The Protestant missions ignore Swahili (and mention English), reflecting their orientation to the English-speaking colonies to the south. (c) This orientation, together with the absence of an obvious candidate as a common African language (comparable to Tshiluba in the Kasai, or Kikongo in the lower Congo), was bound to cause concern in the Belgian colonial establishment in Katanga. We had a glimpse of that in responses from administrators and will have the suspicion confirmed in the following section.

Question 5 (quoted above, p. 58) tests opposition to plans for giving priority to a European language in education. Several respondents prefer not to answer that question, others react negatively. Among the reasons cited is the fact that they consider their teaching missionary work geared toward training native catechists and propagating Christianity (not, by implication, Western education in general). With the Reverend Burton, they consider 'the [native] language...the key to the native'. Apparently, in 1917 many missionaries had not yet accepted their role as educational agents in the service of the colony.

The next two questions seek opinions about the practical value of teaching an African language – for the natives themselves, for administration, and for trade with Europeans. Several respondents express their belief that good education must be given in the mother tongue; one flatly states that 'to develop teaching (in) the native language is to develop civilisation' (Scheut, Nouvelle

Anvers). Several attest the degree to which literacy has already been established in an African language:

> One reads, one writes, one corresponds in Lingala. (Umanyi St Pierre)

> Most of our students learn only the mother tongue. They write letters to family and friends, they read their Bibles, hymn books, and other books in their language. (Bishop Springer)

> Such training [in the native language] is even necessary because of the exchange of letters (*correspondance épistolaire*), especially in our region where trade intensifies and where the villagers send their merchandise by railway to their 'receiving agents' in all the centers. (Redemptorists at Thysville-Matadi)

The survey contains hints from respondents in Kasai and Katanga that Africans have taught themselves to read and write in French or an African language. This suggests rather more enthusiasm for literacy (and success in obtaining it) than could comfortably be admitted by colonial agents who sought to control this kind of process by 'promoting' it.

Missionary respondents reacted positively to the suggestion that native languages might make good vehicles for administration and trade. They regretted the low level of competence in these languages among Europeans. The Redemptorist from the lower Congo cites the Portuguese as a counter-example, and Bishop Springer points to the British colonies, using this occasion to plead for autochthonous rather than vehicular languages: 'The kiswahili spoken here in Katanga is not a native language but a mixed patois like the "Kitchen Kaffir" in South Africa'.

The Reverend Burton considers Swahili sufficient for the purpose of commerce. This brings us to Question 8, in which the Governor General gets to the touchy point: would it not be better for all concerned if the natives were taught only one of our national languages? Here, too, the wording leaves some scope for alternative interpretation. Should a European language be the only medium of instruction? Or should only one of our two national languages be the medium of instruction? Given the fact that many missionaries came from Flanders, such ambiguity invited a wide range of responses (of course, even for those to whom the question was not ambiguous the phrasing 'one national language' (*une langue nationale*) meant that French was going to be obligatory). The superior of the Scheutists in Kasai avoids taking a position and declares that it is too early to be thinking about such a project. The London office of the same order comes up with a particularly elaborate response. First, it invokes the existence of

> at least *five* principal 'classic' dialects, which are, in order of importance: Ngala and Swahili, Luba, Nkundu [Mongo], Nkongo (if the three missions in the lower Congo – Scheut, Jesuits and Redemptorists – reach an agreement to *unify* their three dialects). Under these conditions a single native official language would seem utopian; five, on the other hand, too much.

One could therefore suggest 'patronage' of one or two of them as commercial and administrative languages. But why, in this case, not a

European language? The respondent then gives reasons for such a solution. Every nation, he points out, imports its language to its colony. But the Belgians have two. Should the Congolese be afflicted with that problem? Before he finally asserts that Flemish must get equal treatment because it is the language of most Belgians and of most Belgians in the Congo, and will be the language of most of the future settlers in the colony, he considers an interesting way to solve the bilingualism problem. Should French perhaps be taught in the north of the Congo, contiguous with French possessions, and Flemish in the south, bordering on South African and Boer territories?

The Redemptorists propose as a solution two languages, one native, one national. The Salesians take a pedagogical attitude when they inquire whether it is not easier simply to teach the native reading and writing in his own language, and ask (an especially interesting point), 'should they not confront the European language with their own language so that they may grasp it?'. The Reverend Burton opposes the term 'only' (*exclusivement*), and adds, in shaky French, 'pour ma part je ne veux pas enseigner même une langue européenne. Aussi je ne pense que ce n'est pas courtois d'enseigner une autre langue que francaise en Congo Belge'.[14]

Bishop Springer is less diplomatic and continues his campaign for English:

> In Katanga [the natives] wish to learn English, because many *boys* here come from Rhodesia where many among them read and write English. Those have the good positions and get high salaries and, on top of it, most of the Belgians always talk English with their *boys*.

(This passage, incidentally, was marked as important by an official who studied the responses.)

Question 9 – can natives at elementary school learn the elements of more than one European language? – is not answered at all by the Salesians, with a laconic 'yes' by others, and with a negative guess by Scheut in Kasai. One gets the impression that most of the missionaries are irritated by the racist implication of this query.

The last three questions are grouped under the heading 'trade schools' (*écoles professionnelles*). Questions 10 and 11 regard the necessity of using a European language as the source for technical terms. Almost all respondents agree that borrowing from a European language is necessary. Only the Reverend Burton thinks that, if terms are lacking in Kiluba, then Swahili could provide them. Brain l'Alleud only puts a question mark. When asked which European language should be used for this purpose, the Salesians propose French and Flemish, Bishop Springer opts for English, and all others think it must be French.

Question 12, although not separated in the questionnaire from those refering to trade schools, is really of a general order: do you believe that to teach a European language would be in any way inconvenient, politically or otherwise? In contrast to several administrators, the missionaries and educators see no inconvenience (that is, danger) at all. Umanyi-St Pierre states that pushing a native language to the detriment of a European language would 'rather limit the number of black intellectuals' (a remarkable term for the time, especially since it is not used ironically). The Reverend Burton puts the fears that underlie the question into words: many whites do not want a native who can understand their private conversations.

File M 645 also contains a six-page memorandum, dated Boma, November 1917. It is addressed to 'M. le Directeur de la Justice, Congo Belge, Gouvernement Général' and signed by B. Hautefeld, 'Chef de bureau Iᵉ classe'. Apparently the Government also solicited in-house opinions. The one it got from Hautefeld was remarkable for its clarity; but it was not likely to please the authors of a survey whose major purpose was to prepare policy decisions rather than clarify an existing situation. Here is a courageous administrator who begins by challenging the whole enterprise: 'Almost all the rubrics of the questionnaire presuppose that there exists in the Congo a system of education which functions normally. . .' The fact is that 'the colony does not have a single school where the six years of study are given which are indispensable for any elementary education'. In reality, 'education in the Congo has not yet emerged from the period of timid beginnings, experiments, searching, and adaptations. It is far from being organized. Under such conditions it seems impossible to talk of the fruits reaped by the natives from their schooling'. Hautefeld then gives what he considers theoretical answers. First of all, one should not fix details before one knows what actual situations require. Public education in the Congo will, in his opinion, develop 'with the economic conditions' and will necessarily be modeled on education in Belgium. 'The methods will be the same because the capacities of acquisition, elaboration, and retention are identical under all latitudes.' He then outlines the basics of a program which he thinks should be the same as in the rural schools of Belgium. In connection with trade schools, he notes that he has observed that white craftsmen generally refuse to train African apprentices (which makes State-run schools all the more important). Better schooling would also produce African candidates for the lower ranks of civil service.

Turning to the question of language, Hautefeld confesses that his position has changed since he has lived in Africa. For several years he believed that teaching in a foreign language would hold up intellectual development and, above all, the education of the children (his view attesting the fact that the mother-tongue dogma so widespread among missionaries was an import rather than the product of local experience). The latter is of great importance: 'Instruire le nègre, sans l'éduquer c'est en faire un malfaiteur'. He now believes that nothing speaks against the adoption of French as the vehicular language in the large urban centers (he cites the successful experiment at the Colonie d'Enfants at Boma). Elsewhere, choice of a vehicular language will depend on the goal. If you want to keep the natives in their villages, an indigenous language should be used, with French as second language (but taught well enough for the students to be able to speak it when they graduate). In trade and secondary schools French should be the vehicular medium.

If Hautefeld was not an accommodating respondent he was a useful one. Being practically minded and remarkably free of the kind of vague racial and ideological prejudice visible in the reactions of businessmen, administrators, and missionaries, he sketched a course of action to be taken by those who wanted results – cheap, well-trained African employees.

A QUESTION OF POWER: WARNINGS FROM KATANGA

As far as I can ascertain, none of the responses analyzed so far contain an explicit reference to Article 3 of the Colonial Charter. Presumably it is in the mind of those who defend Flemish; others show knowledge of its idealistic provisions – granting 'freedom' to both national and native languages – and qualify these with the same term used by Halewyck: utopian. File M 645 contains one response which in this and other respects stands apart from the rest and must now be given special attention. The respondent (in the category of heads of private firms) is A. de Bauw, signing for the Comité Special du Katanga (CSK).[15] Although he roughly follows the questionnaire, he develops his opinion in a lengthy memorandum, of which the File contains several versions.[16]

De Bauw, first of all, wants to alert the Government to an alarming situation which should be 'terminated' by 'radical measures'. English has become established as the dominant European language in southern Katanga. 'Kitchen-Kaffir', together with English, is used by most as the vehicular medium of communication with Africans. Even workers recruited by the Bourse du Travail from northern regions (Sankuru and Lomami) 'answer in Kitchen-Kaffir or English to questions they are asked'. This, de Bauw insists, is a very dangerous development because, in the eyes of the natives, Belgians lose prestige, not being able to impose their language in their own colony. The danger is political since 'the language is one of the most powerful means of [colonial] penetration'. Examples from other colonies are cited, leading up to the following passage:

> We must, with all the means at our disposal, fight the spread of any European language other than French. Among these means I suggest the following: (1) Prohibition, by way of legislation, to teach natives any European language except French. (2) Inspection of all schools by agents of the State, so that the nature and tendencies of education can be safeguarded. Obligatory licensing of all teachers, white or black. (3) Revocation of all contracts between Europeans and natives drawn in a language other than French or a dialect of the colony.

If blacks are to learn a European language, de Bauw continues, it should be French. But he would prefer that Europeans should learn indigenous languages. Because Belgians learn a native language more easily than the other way round, it is 'logical that one tries to spread among the whites, who are in the minority, the language of the majority'. Not enough is done in that direction, except for the publication, by the Ministry of Colonies, of a few 'vocabularies and grammars'. One should organize courses in the native language and make them obligatory for all colonial agents and employees of the large companies. One should introduce language diplomas for various functions connected with recruiting and supervising the African labor force, as is done in some other colonies. The memorandum ends with another appeal to combat English and an example of the kind of 'establishment' which cannot possibly be of interest to the colony: a Methodist mission at Kambove (Bishop Springer, see above pp. 59ff.) teaching Congolese and other blacks in English.

De Bauw's political tirade is of entirely different caliber from similar expressions of fear and complaints voiced by other respondents. He speaks as the (former) director of the Bourse du Travail, the most important recruiting organization in Katanga, and as head of the para-governmental CSK. Both were set up to serve the one major Belgian interest, exploitation of the region's mineral resources. De Bauw, therefore, has economic as well as political objectives in mind when he formulates certain principles of language policy. Foremost among them is a sort of *cujus regio, ejus lingua* doctrine, asserting the colony's linguistic autonomy. Less obvious, but more important, is the one-way-rule he formulates when he says that Europeans should learn the native language rather than teaching Africans a European language. The spirit, if not the letter, of this rule was to guide language policies of the large companies throughout colonial times. The catch lies in the meaning of 'to learn a native language'. Which one, and how well? One may safely presume that de Bauw fully shared the outlook on communication expressed by the respondent from Géomines. From the 'industrial point of view', one must speak the language in order to know, understand, and command the native – this being an order of priorities which, in practice, may be reversed.

It is against this background that we must consider the role of Swahili. While it is not explicitly mentioned in de Bauw's memorandum, Swahili is inevitably part of his argumentation. In his call to combat the tandem English–Kitchen-Kaffir he undoubtedly envisaged a policy of promoting French and Swahili. No other available medium could have fulfilled the political requirement of, as de Bauw states, orienting Katanga toward the north[17] and away from the British-dominated south while at the same time satisfying the need for a reduced, controled command-language which could easily be learned by the European personnel.

On the basis of our documents it is not possible to determine exactly how important de Bauw's memorandum was in influencing the choices and developments which led to Swahili becoming the *lingua franca* of Katanga. The representative of the UMHK, one of the major agents in this process (by its eventual decision to use Swahili as a work-language), responded to the government survey in very general terms. That de Bauw's report made a strong enough impression on the colonial administration can be inferred from the following passages in Vice-Governor Tombeur's covering letter to the Minister of Colonies:

I especially call your attention to the question of an expanding influence of English in the mining region of Katanga which is signaled by M. de Bauw, Director General of the Comité Special du Katanga and by others. I believe with him that the Colonial Charter should be revised so that certain corrections may be made with regard to freedom of teaching and use of language. In a colony like ours, which is just being organized, it is dangerous to grant equal rights to citizens of the ruling country and to foreigners. Education is among the most appropriate means to propagate and extend the influence of the Europeans on the minds of natives...

SOME GENERAL CONCLUSIONS

Generally speaking, there can be no doubt that the 'language question' – as a *political* and *practical* (i.e. economic) question – was perceived as the central theme of the survey on education.

As returns on the questionnaire were received at Boma they were transmitted to the Ministry, apparently without first being analyzed locally. But two items of correspondence in File M 645 (both covering letters) show that ideas about the principal result of this inquiry were taking shape. In a letter dated Boma, July 5, 1917, and received in London on August 17, 1917, the Governor General, E. Henry, writes:

I call your attention, M. le Ministre, to the unanimity with which the personalities who have so far responded to the questionnaire envisage the use of French as a vehicular language of teaching in our schools.

A rather curious conclusion from a record that was, as we have seen in the previous sections, everything but unanimous (unless one is to read *personnalités* as 'persons who count', e.g. Cousin of the BCK/CFK).

In a second letter (dated Boma, July 2, 1918, received in London, August 19, 1918) the Vice-Governor General, writing for the Governor General, makes the same point again. He quotes the Vice-Governor in Katanga:

As the questionnaires are coming back, I am more and more inclined to have an official program and inspection of education adopted, and to reserve, in Katanga, an important role in it for the French language. I remind you of my earlier reports and correspondence relating to this matter, especially those that concern the missions and foreign influence.

Meanwhile the colonial Ministry was already working on a project to put education in the colonies onto a more uniform and efficient basis. The question of subsidies for, and control over, Catholic and Protestant missions was foremost in the minds of those involved in formulating policy. This is exemplified in the draft of a typewritten memo in File M 645 (identified, in handwriting, as 'note sent to Scheut and the Jesuits in January 1918, by the Minister'). Apart from formulating proposals for financial subsidies and remuneration of African teachers, the document specifies certain minimal demands regarding the curriculum. Among these, French takes a prominent place: 'Our education must make a more profound impact on the natives.

65

Among the peoples of the Congo it must provide cohesion through a national vehicular language... The schools of the Protestant missions will have to follow the same program. Teaching in a foreign language [i.e. other than French] will not be subsidized with public funds'.

The project of organization announced by the Ministry was not to be realized until 1925. During that period, enthusiasm for French as the principal medium of education was tempered by 'practical' considerations of the kind we encountered in several responses from administrators and missionaries. To cite one more document from File M 645, the Governor General submitted a report to the Ministry (dated Boma, August 24, 1920) which, apart from matters relating to subsidies, addresses once again the language question. It refers to inquiries on education and 'special missions' on this subject (citing a mission Cambier' and a 'mission du F. Marcel, Visiteur des Écoles Chrétiennes'), but regrets that the results of these inquiries have not been communicated to the Government in the Congo (in other words, no official evaluation of the 1917–18 survey had been circulated by 1920). It then states that the problem of a vehicular language was examined and that a detailed report 'has led to the adoption for our colony of the indigenous language (Lingala or one of the four *langues commerciales*) as vehicular languages of education. French should only be taught in the upper classes, i.e. in the sections of the [*école*] *normale* and in the sections [destined for the training of] clerks'. A remarkable turn-about from conclusions drawn a few years earlier (but one that is in agreement with the opinion expressed by UMHK and CSK in response to Question 4).

This is confusing only if one fails to learn the principal lesson from the documents studied in this chapter. In Article 3 of the Colonial Charter equal rights were granted for all languages, as long as everyone recognized in practice that French was more equal. And when a challenge was put up by English (and not by Flemish) the liberal mask was dropped and calls for changing the Colonial Charter and abrogating freedom of language use as defined in Article 3 quickly came to the fore.

Multilingualism (now including African languages) was to the Belgian colonizers above all a matter of order and control. Principles of evolutionary status and hierarchical precedence were to govern relations among European and native languages. In spite of initial enthusiasm for French as a general medium of education, it was eventually decided to adopt the 'four trade languages'. This must be evaluated in the light of the above-mentioned principles as a decision to restrict access to higher and better-paid positions while at the same time assuring that education served the paramount economic objective of training a cheap labor force.

The government survey on education was ostensibly to determine facts about current practice in administration, private enterprise, the missions, and a few government schools. If one looks more closely at how the questionnaire was formulated (and how the responses showed it was understood) one finds that the metropolitan Government used the inquiry to announce, propagate, and perhaps test ideas of a hierarchical linguistic policy as part of a tightly controled educational system. Returned questionnaires contained little specific information, but all the more expressions of opinion and prejudice. All respondents, even those who dissented from the majority, accepted as a fact the network of power and controls which began to cover the colony. Their views, too, could be made to serve colonial goals. No matter whether propagation of a European language was advocated so that the blacks should not be condemned to intellectual isolation, or whether the native language was declared the only proper means to develop a person, no one seriously doubted that government controls on means of communication were necessary. With the possible exception of a few trading companies who saw advantages in a two-way traffic and exchange, linguistically as well as in other ways, an overwhelming majority of the respondents had only propagation and command in mind when talking about language. Together with strong opinions went a great deal of insecurity. Just how firm was Belgium's grip on its colony? The threat of English coming from 'foreign' Protestant missions and from territories bordering the Congo to the east and south preoccupied many respondents. No one voiced this concern more urgently than the Director of the CSK, a powerful agency which could be certain of the Government's ear. De Bauw's memoranda allow us to reconstruct the political situation in which decisions about the future of Swahili in Katanga were to be taken.

It bears repeating that File M 645 is fragmentary and incomplete. Furthermore, only part of the survey, addressed directly to questions of language, has been given attention in this chapter. It may therefore be useful to report in conclusion some of the overall impressions one gets from these documents. If the inquiry was to mirror facts and opinions in the colony, it was a mirror crack'd. There are faults in the image and oddities in some accounts, and these may tell us as much about communication in the colony as some of the well-formulated responses.

To begin with, the situation created by the War most likely accounted for a slow, unsystematic execution and evaluation of the project.[18] It may also explain an atmosphere of fear and defensiveness occasioned by a subject one would think most people would be able to write about with academic detachment (especially when it concerned an educational system that was yet to be set up). If the 'language question' had everyone's interest it was because it was recognized as a prime factor in the training of a native labor force. The wording of the questionnaire, above all of those questions we have not commented on, left no doubt that 'education' meant 'education for work' (in industry and to a lesser extent in trade and administration). But precisely on these issues many responses show a good measure of insecurity and apprehensiveness. Foremost among them was the fear that 'promotion' of certain languages would mean loss of control over vital areas of communication. Paradoxically, it was feared *both* that the natives might avail themselves of technical knowledge and use it for their own practical aims (thus becoming

67

competitors) *and* that they might use their schooling for non-practical purposes, such as exchange of ideas, access to literature, and developing idle hopes for intellectual equality. This contradictory predicament, so typical of colonial policy – having to develop a country to make it profitable but having to retard it at the same time so that it stays under control – is visible in attitudes toward linguistic development. Incidentally, many of the respondents had a less than perfect grasp of the French language (especially of its orthography). This lends an ironical twist to their pontificating about the need to promote that language.

There were reasons to be afraid. This can be deduced from a few glimpses one catches now and then through the generalities and banalities which made up the larger portion of responses to the questionnaire. Most interesting among them are open and veiled admissions that there existed conscious, active resistance to colonial language policies (still) and what one might call spontaneous literacy in French and in African languages (already). The former is reported from the Kwango area (citing the case of the Bayaka), the latter is known from the lower Congo[19] and reported from the Kasai and from Katanga. For instance, the respondent of Géomines answers to Question 8 (Have you, at your own expense, organized a school to train craftsmen?): 'There is no school, most of them learn to read and write at their own expense in order to increase their wages'. The respondent for Scheut in London (speaking as someone who has had experience in the Congo) notes that teaching Africans to become literate in their own language is 'surprisingly easy. There are many natives who have the desire to learn and who, with a few private lessons taken from a catechist or a friend who is farther advanced, have learned to read by themselves. To write, that is, to form letters, is more difficult without a teacher'. Outside the section on language the questionnaire contains some information on wages paid to African workers and craftsmen. 'Schooling' (presumably the ability to read instructions and designs and to make calculations) was a factor that could double or triple wages.[20] The market value of competence in a European language and of a certain degree of literacy was established, and means to procure these assets had been found, *before* the Government took over the 'promotion' of languages and the organization of schooling.

On the other hand, the desire to control was often far ahead of actual situations. An example of this is very early and glib references to 'official' African vehicular languages – as if that matter had been settled – together with a failure to agree on their identity, number, or area, or even on exact terms and their orthography. Of special interest to us is that those colonials who were directly concerned with Swahili did not refer to it as 'Kingwana' (that was done only by two respondents from other areas). Remarkable is the choice of Kituba in Sankuru. Is this a survival from the Independent State practice? What was Kituba, anyway? Why is the obvious popularity of Kitchen-Kaffir (also called Kitembele, but not Fanagalo or Chikabanga,

which must mean that these terms were not yet current at that time)
acknowledged only by two respondents?

Around 1917 linguistic etiquette was not firmly established. This makes
Bishop Springer naïvely plead for English, giving fuel to allegations that
Protestant missions were agents for foreign interests. It also accounts for a
certain lack of inhibition in using an African language as *lingua franca* among
Europeans. The response to the questionnaire in which this is reported is clear
and specific enough to be taken seriously. Such disregard for hierarchical
levels of communication would be impossible in later years, except among
members of the 'Mediterranean' population (Greeks, Italians, Portuguese),
where it only demonstrated their relatively low social position in the colony.

That foreign Protestant missions were a source of concern is obvious from
the documents. Allusions to conflict of interest with Catholic missions are less
frequent. Nevertheless, those that one finds are quite revealing. Most likely,
anticlericalism was involved (but to make sure one would have to know on
which side of the Catholic/liberal fence a given writer stood). There was also
the determination, apparently still alive among some missionaries, to convert
rather than 'educate' the African. This caused government and missions to
take different views on the language(s) to be used in elementary and
professional instruction. Missionaries tended to value the native language for
its own spiritual and intellectual worth; the Government had little use for such
romanticism. The final choice (by 1925) of African vehiculars as primary
languages of instruction may be seen as a compromise between the advocates
of the mother tongue and those who wanted to go straight to French.

We may conclude this chapter on 'questions and queries' with a somewhat
cynical observation. The fact that the linguistic situation in the Congo was
said to constitute a problem (*la question des langues*) which remained a topic
for debate throughout the period of colonial rule, may be taken as an
indication that most of those who participated in the discussions, and
certainly the organizers of the survey on education, had no questions about
it – only answers derived from political and economic objectives.

3

Settling in: colonization and language

Two issues emerged from the survey on education which the Belgian Government conducted in the Congo around 1917. The missions, especially the Catholic missions, played an important part in the school system, such as it was. Their role was to be extended as the Government decided to develop and sponsor elementary and trade schools in the colony. The 1917 survey was not so much preparatory to, as expressive of, such a decision. It may seem unlikely that a metropolitan government in exile and a local administration troubled by lack of personnel and internal unrest should seriously have been concerned with education for Africans. However, the colonial planners, at least those who operated on the highest levels, where contacts with commercial and industrial interests determined policies, were not moved by vague designs of civilizing the natives. That kind of talk, to be sure, never ceased during colonial times, but what really counted was a growing need for skilled and (moderately) literate manpower. This was most urgent in the mining industry and its attendant services; it was also felt in the administration, especially as its fiscal and judicial functions, its transportation, medical and municipal services, and the need for police and military expanded. Some planners also saw far enough to realize that an African 'middle class' of clerks, teachers, craftsmen and small entrepreneurs was beginning to emerge and that this development had to be controlled politically as well as encouraged for economic reasons. Eventually, the colony was to be 'valued' (a term often used in colonial discourse) as a reservoir of manpower and resources *and* as a potential market for industrial and agricultural products.

These two colonial projects – an educational system entrusted to the missions and the creation of an African salariat – significantly determined attitudes towards African languages. This is perhaps obvious as regards the choice and promotion of certain languages and the formulation of policies justifying choices. It may at first seem to have only remote connections with the study and description of these languages. Yet the production of language guides on all levels, from wordlists to grammars and dictionaries with scientific ambitions (and merits), was determined by the same practical concerns, though this is not to say that these goals were pursued uniformly and without debate and factional maneuvering. To explore in a general way the role of education and the missions in colonizing African languages is the purpose of this chapter.[1] Connections between labor and language, with a more narrow focus on Swahili in Katanga, will occupy us in the remainder of the book.

MISSIONS, EDUCATION AND THE *OEUVRE CIVILISATRICE*

Responses to the 1917 survey showed that no consensus existed with regard to the question of choosing between African and European languages, or, among African languages, to selecting those that should officially be adopted as vehicles of administration and education. There was, however, one area of agreement: English, and African languages associated with British interests (especially in Katanga), were to be kept under control. This issue may serve as a first illustration of the interplay between missionary and political interests, because it found its way into the *Instructions aux missionnaires*, a sort of official code regulating, among other matters, missionary involvement in education. It says under, 'languages of education':

> The superiors [of the missions] think that, as a general rule, only the mother tongue of the children should be employed in their rural schools. They will make exceptions, for serious reasons, if they think it opportune, for instance, in order to counterbalance foreign influence, trying to spread a language other than one of the Belgian national languages.[2]

The more bewildering the linguistic situation appeared, the more urgent became the need to create order, either by imposing 'vehicular' languages that already existed, or by promoting certain local languages to vehicular status. Various projects, directives, and debates were soon addressed to problems of linguistic planning, and at least the outlines of that aspect of colonial control are known. It should be noted, however, that the use of *véhiculaire* in colonial documents (for instance in the *Projet d'organisation* of 1925) differed from current linguistic usage. In most of the early texts, 'vehicular language' designated a function, usually as the language in which teaching is done or in which government documents are formulated. French, therefore, could be *langue véhiculaire*. By 1948 this was still the case, but French had now its firm place at the apex of a hierarchy of languages, so that the term *lingua franca* was used to refer to vehicular functions of African languages, notably of the four 'official' *linguae francae*.[3] This reflects development in linguistic usage, which now opposes vehiculars to vernaculars as different kinds of languages (different, that is, in terms of structure, not only of function). Obviously, the different meanings of vehicular are historically connected.

How did missions and missionaries, acting presumably with religious aims, bring their convictions and purposes to bear on language in the Belgian Congo? Such a question meets at once three major difficulties. One lies in the qualification 'presumably,' another in the generalization 'missions'; a third problem is that of periodization. Too much social-scientific pontificating about the role of the missions has relied on fanciful imputation of motives and ideas and on indiscriminate lumping together of missionary organizations which, even if they belonged to a strongly centralized institution such as the Roman Catholic Church, usually represented a wide spectrum of intellectual, social, and political orientations. Recently, anthropologists and other social scientists have become more sophisticated in these matters.[4]

Missionary attitudes toward African languages did not remain the same during the 75 years of Belgian colonial rule, although there was a remarkable continuity in the way in which the problems were perceived. Most of the observations to be made here are valid for what might be called the period of 'settling in' which followed the exploratory stage (and did not occur at the same time everywhere in the colony). Whereas in the earlier period much pioneer work was done by Protestant missionaries, especially in the lower Congo and in Katanga, Catholic missions took a dominant role in a series of arrangements which culminated in the formalization of the role of missions in education. A convenient date for the beginning of that period could be 1906, the year of the treaty between the Congo Independent State and the Vatican (see below); 1925, the year when the Ministry of Colonies published the first *Projet d'organisation* (Ministère des Colonies 1925), could be counted as its culmination. At that point the lively debates on the 'language question' which occurred in the 1930s and 1940s (and which were resumed after World War II) fall outside the scope of this chapter. They cannot go entirely unmentioned, but they changed very little as to their basic terms, which were set by 1925.[5]

In the Congo, European missionaries had worked in regions close to the Atlantic coast since the sixteenth century, but the modern era began with the establishment of colonial rule in the last quarter of the nineteenth century. Depending on one's views, the presence of missionaries in Africa may be seen as a response to a religious calling, or as a mere concomitant of the gradual implantation of a European regime. Perhaps one can avoid a fruitless debate between 'internalist' and 'externalist' explanations and better appreciate the practical and specific contributions made by the missions if their role is understood as having been crucial in helping the colony 'enter the world system'.[6] The missions fulfilled that role by helping to set up a colonial mode of production – that is, those economic, social and political conditions which prepared the colony for profitable utilization (mostly through the extraction of natural resources, secondarily through the creation of new markets) by the Belgian State and the country's ruling class (both of whom had their international connections and ramifications).

Imperialist expansion, Christian evangelization, and the development of modern linguistics and anthropology have not been merely coincidental. Each of these movements – economic, religious, scientific (and all of them political) – needed a global perspective and a global field of action for ideological legitimation and for practical implementation. To object that individual colonial agents, missionaries and field-anthropologists/linguists were mostly quite limited in their political horizons and in their subjective consciousness does not discredit the 'world-system' or similar notions as heuristic tools in writing history. What counts is the factual existence of conditions allowing global circulation of commodities, ideas and personnel.[7]

No matter how problematic relations between the Catholic Church and the often liberal (in other words, militantly anti-clerical) ruling powers in Belgium may have been,[8] in the colony cooperation between them was put on firm ground. Already in King Leopold II's Independent State[9] missions were part of the famous triad – together with administration and private companies – which sustained Belgian colonial rule throughout its tenure. Cooperation from the missions was assured by a simple device. The colonial Government, which held exclusive claim to the land and its inhabitants, gave to various missionary orders land concessions within circumscribed territories. On that basis, mission posts as centers of religious but also of agricultural, commercial, and small industrial, activities could be established. In exchange – although it was not always put in these terms – the missions agreed to set up, staff, and run more or less the entire system of education in the colony. This arrangement was finalized in a convention between the Vatican and the Congo Independent State, signed on May 26, 1906. Each mission post was to be given at least 100 hectares of arable land, provided the following four conditions were met:

1. Each post agrees to establish 'if possible' a school in which indigenous children are to receive elementary and manual instruction.
2. The curriculum will be submitted to the Governor General, and the subjects will be fixed by mutual agreement.
3. Apart from elementary instruction, the curriculum comprises instruction in agriculture, in forestry, and in the manual crafts.
4. Teaching the Belgian national languages will be an essential part of the curriculum. (Missions Catholiques du Congo Belge 1910: 34–5)

It would be a mistake, however, to assume that the practical implementation of this arrangement was always as simple as its basic terms. Many complicating factors intervened. Individual missionaries saw and resented their dependence on the colonial government. Certain missionary organizations with an international orientation and personnel were not easily integrated into the Belgian *oeuvre civilisatrice*. There was competition between Catholic and Protestant missions, as well as among Catholic missions. Belgian liberals began to fear that the payoff from this arrangement for the Christians was too high. Finally, there existed several contradictions internal to the Belgian colonial enterprise, to which we must now turn our attention.

The most pervasive of these was between projects to industrialize and modernize the colony so that it would become increasingly self-supporting and profitable for metropolitan interests, and the need to control these developments in such a way that a take-over of the system by the colonized could be prevented or at least delayed. As B. Jewsiewicki has argued convincingly, this contradictory situation made it imperative to create and maintain 'symbolic power' on which 'civilization as a way of life and system of education, Christianization, racial superiority, technological superiority, modes of consumption, styles of political life, and so on all come to bear' (1979: 32–3).

This real contradiction in the economic and political dynamics of colonization invited cultivation of an ideological contradiction, especially in the later phases. It was expressed axiomatically as a radical difference between uncivilized (and uncivilizable) and civilized Africans. At first this distinction tended to coincide with those between rural areas and European centers, later more with an opposition between an elite of evolués and the masses. At any rate, a dualist outlook on 'civilization' became a permanent fixture in Belgian colonial thought, and 'education' was to be the glue of an *oeuvre civilisatrice* ridden with contradictory demands.

To distinguish between civilized and non-civilized might have expressed ideas of progress to which the projects of Christianization could easily have been tied. But colonial practice soon revealed that the distinction was promoted as one between those parts of the population which were of interest primarily to private enterprise (as cheap labor and later as consumers of industrial goods) and others which (mainly through agricultural production and taxation) paid for the maintenance of conditions favorable to private enterprise (food, health care, transportation, public order). Being involved in education, to the point of having a near-monopoly in it, the missions worked indirectly, and often also quite directly, for the promotion of private commercial and industrial interests. That collaboration was systemic, independent of assent on the part of individual missionaries or even missionary organizations.

As education was vital in creating and maintaining symbolic power, so also was control over, and choice of, the linguistic medium of education – not so much on instrumental grounds (such as whether or not a given language was capable of serving as a medium of instruction) as for symbolic reasons regarding the value and prestige of a given language. In this respect, too, the situation was characterized by oppositions and contradictions, some of them imported from the political scene in the metropolitan country. For example when linguistic rights were legally defined in the Colonial Charter of 1908, the relevant article liberally stipulated that the use of languages should be 'optional,' specifying only that official documents were to be in French and Flemish. Belgians and Africans alike were to be guaranteed rights, but all details were left to regulation by administrative decrees.

As we have seen in the preceding chapter, the liberal tone of the text was to appease advocates of linguistic equality on the home front. As regards the colony, it was little more than a cover for a pragmatic position long established and never adandoned: French was to maintain its superior position over Dutch and certainly over African languages. When missions had to decide on languages to be taught, and in which to teach, they always faced contradictions between constitutional rights and established administrative practice, and very often between their own cultural allegiance (most of them were Flemish-speaking) and the dictate of a ruling class to which few of them belonged.

MISSIONARY LINGUISTICS

The contributions by missionaries to the study of African cultures and languages in the Congo are a matter of record. Missionaries were the most active participants in ambitious projects of monographic description conceived during the Free State era, and received the highest praise for their work.[10] Numerous linguistic publications had appeared by 1925, when the first of several government directives was published in which regulation of language use in the school curricula had a central place.[11] Missionaries also taught African languages at institutions where colonial agents were trained, and they dominated scholarly linguistics throughout the period of colonial rule.

How narrow and formal cooperation between government and missions was is illustrated by the draft for a standard contract found in the Brussels colonial archives. The text is not dated, but an accompanying memorandum places it before 1925, and a marginal note suggests that it was submitted for approval to Minister Renkin on May 21, 1919. The relevant passages are:

> Between the congregation of ... and the colony of the Belgian Congo, represented by M. the Governor General, the following has been agreed:
> ... 3° The colony will pay a sum of 1000 frs. for every indigenous dialect, unknown, of which the mission will furnish, in manuscript, the grammar, the vocabulary, a sketch indicating the area of diffusion, and a collection of useful phrases, with translation in (a, the?) national language.
> The Government will be entitled to print these works or to have them printed at their expense.
> The mission will do the work of proofreading.
> 100 copies of the work will be given to the mission without charge ... against cession of author's rights by the mission to the colony.
> A sum of 500 frs. will be paid to the mission for each handwritten monograph on a subject whose usefulness will be determined by common agreement, following the method which the Government will consider the most practical one.

By the time this contract was drafted, the Ministry had officially sponsored a number of dictionaries and grammars compiled by missionaries (of Kikongo, Kiluba and Swahili, among others; see below, pp. 84ff.) and continued to do so in later years. Closer examination of this linguistic literature reveals certain expected patterns, such as modest beginnings and later improvements. But I doubt that these developments simply reflected an accumulation of empirical knowledge and an increase in technical and theoretical sophistication. Missionaries did not describe (or even learn) African languages simply because 'they were there'; their linguistic, scholarly work was embedded in a communicative praxis which had its own internal dynamics. In very broad terms, it was characterized by a gradual shift from descriptive appropriation to prescriptive imposition and control. Learning from the natives, collecting words and useful phrases, and noting a few grammatical observations, these were the principal activities during an initial phase of settling in and establishing contacts. Knowledge of African languages was considered important enough to become the subject of detailed regulations. Just for the White Fathers, who are of special interest to us, many texts could be cited. Article VI of this order's *Directory of Constitutions* treats of 'knowledge required of a missionary'. It begins with 'perfect command of native languages', qualified as a 'grave obligation'. It goes on to give detailed instructions, including recommendations about methods of learning. These are even further developed in later documents, such as the Instructions by Msgr V. Roelens, for many years the leader of the White Fathers in the Congo.[12]

Vocabularies and grammars came first. Translations of liturgical, doctrinal, and biblical texts, initially destined for use by the missionaries in their oral work of evangelization, rather than for their as yet illiterate African converts, were soon to follow. It is at least imaginable that these efforts to transpose the Christian message through translations into African languages should have remained the principal preoccupation (as it did among certain Protestant groups). But we begin to see very soon how concern with spreading the content of the message became overshadowed by attention to formal and normative matters such as the exact classification of languages, the standardization of writing, and the teaching of correct grammar.

Much of the linguistic work on African languages was dictated by the demands of literacy. In a general survey of education in Africa which, given the date and place of its publication (Berlin 1934), is a remarkable study, H. T. Becker had some astute observations on this subject. For the educational policies of the European powers, he noted, literacy was not only a goal, it was a prerequisite and condition. The school-system to be imported had historically developed around a core of written texts (originally around the Bible). Because such a situation did not exist in most African societies (excepting those under the influence of Islam) it had to be created. Missions were essential in providing this prerequisite for imposed schooling (*Beschulung*), even though colonial governments and the colonial economy eventually profited most from it. A second condition was related to the first one: a social class had to be created for which literacy would become a guarded privilege and which in turn could become an instrument of power and control. Only when the early wild growth of missionary schools had produced members of such a class in sufficient numbers (toward the end of the nineteenth century) did colonial governments begin to 'regulate' education, very much as the governments of European countries had done between the seventeenth and nineteenth centuries.[13]

Work toward literacy found its institutional expression in the establishment of print shops and presses, which became an important aspect of missionary activities. A special significance attaches to the recommended policy of publishing inexpensive literature for African consumption in the form of small pamphlets and brochures. Such an important aspect of missionary work could not have escaped regulation. In the general *Instructions* of 1920, for instance, missionaries are not only required to produce elementary textbooks for teaching, but also 'other *small* books, as *numerous* as possible' (Missions Catholiques du Congo Belge 1920: 38; emphases in original). The *Rules* of the White Fathers are more explicit. Paragraph 3 of Article VI recommends the 'apostolate of the leaflet, the pamphlet, and the book' (Société des Missionnaires d'Afrique 1914: 345). Many missionary organizations, Protestant as well as Catholic, had acquired great experience (and a good portion of the market) in popular mass-publishing on the home front. At home as well as abroad, they were crucially involved in 'taking charge of the laboring classes' (Raison-Jourde 1977: 639).

Undoubtedly, mass-publication was a practical way of making reading-matter available to Africans who could not afford expensive books. At the same time, it established in the colony a mode of literary production and patterns of mass-consumption comparable to working-class mass-literature (dime novels, pulp magazines and pious pamphlets) throughout the industrial world. Among the specific ways in which the Congo was linked up to the 'world system' this was certainly one. For most missionaries the form of this literature was not really problematic. They feared other aspects of the world system, as is illustrated in a statement by a Protestant missionary linguist, E. Nida (a statement to which most Catholic missionaries would have subscribed):

> There is a danger that in making a people literate and then leaving them without constructive material, we shall be guilty of making such people the bait for subversive propaganda, and there are plenty of agencies who have discovered the importance of the printed page for influencing opinion. (Nida 1949: 15)

That Africans were passive objects of literacy has been one of the most widely shared beliefs among colonizers – and anthropologists.

Given the vastness of the territory and the artificiality of its external borders and of many of its internal divisions, a 'levelling of differences' (Jewsiewicki 1979: 33) became imperative for the colonial administration. The missions had tied their fate to colonial rule by accepting the monopoly in education. They had to participate in these centralizing efforts no matter how much they may have come to identify themselves with local cultures and regional interests. This added another dimension to normative concerns in matters of language. Missions were involved with projects to control multilingualism and with the selection of those languages which were to be given privileged status in school curricula and administrative practice.

'Education' was *the* field in which criteria had to be formulated for choosing among African languages and between African and European languages. Missionary schoolmen, representing different regions in the colony, usually had practical interests in defending their choices and in preventing government interference as much as possible. The Government's position was strong in these matters, especially when, in addition to land grants, another form of dependency was established through cash subsidies for schools satisfying government regulations and standards. On the other hand, the administration had to rely on missionary cooperation for information and especially for scientific legitimation of choices. Missionaries were expected to deliver the theory fitting colonial practice. In the debates we find, therefore, that each advocate for a specific solution of the 'language question' invoked linguistic laws (usually of an evolutionary type supposedly demonstrating the superiority of certain languages) and 'universally accepted' pedagogical principles. These demanded that at least primary education (but probably intellectual formation in general) ought to be given in the mother tongue. Otherwise, it was argued, one would have to expect serious damage to the minds of young Africans.[14]

In sum, the same missionaries who promoted 'modernization' of African languages through codification in writing, standardization, and diffusion of printed texts also used language to defend traditional culture. Throughout the history of Belgian colonization disputes were carried out between two ostensibly opposed factions: 'indigenists' advocating the preservation of African culture, and 'assimilationists' recommending Europeanization ('ostensibly opposed' because both positions can be seen as contributing to the maintenance of civilized vs. non-civilized dualism such as was essential to Belgian colonial rule). It was no accident that leading assimilationists represented regions such as highly industrialized and urbanized Katanga, whereas indigenists tended to work in predominantly rural-agricultural areas. Because they were locked in debate over an ideologically necessary contradiction, one faction could not do without the other. Indigenists stressing the importance of 'tradition' delivered, as it were, the material for modernization; assimilationists producing 'uprooted' évolués gave proof of the need to maintain links with the tradition so that the emerging elites could be kept in place. From the beginning of the twentieth century, the opposing positions were often characterized as evolutionary vs. revolutionary.[15]

RELIGIOUS AND SECULAR COLONIZATION: COMMON GROUND

How and where did 'normativity', as revealed in missionary linguistic work and language policy, articulate with normative notions informing secular colonial concerns, private and public? Focusing on the 'language question' helps to narrow down a vast area of overlapping as well as conflicting interests. Here the notion of discourse is of methodological value. The assumption is that ideas and ideologies expressing as well as informing colonial praxis are formulated and perpetuated (and occasionally changed) in ways of talking and writing about the *oeuvre civilisatrice*. In interpreting this sort of talk as discourse one is less interested in the truth value of specific statements, in the question, for instance, whether a certain author really expressed his convictions, gave an accurate report of facts, and so on. Instead, one seeks to appreciate the documentary value of a 'style' by discerning key notions, rules of combining these and theoretical devices used to build arguments. In short, one concentrates on elements which determined the shape and content of colonial thought irrespective of individual intentions. A point of special interest for this approach (which is in part based on the work of M. Foucault)[16] is to identify those devices which make it possible for an issue (or a kind of experience, a certain constellation of values) to pass from one discourse into another – from, say, religion into politics. Belgian colonial discourse constituted such a field of passages, of crossing and criss-crossing ideas.

When one examines colonial pronouncements about language one can identify certain ideological operators. These are concepts which assured agreement in form and content between religious, missionary thought and secular, political and economic ideas, irrespective of explicitly concluded agreements such as contracts and concordats.

Perhaps the most fundamental of these common notions were certain conceptualizations of space. When examining sources and documents which formulate missionary projects in the second half of the nineteenth century one is struck by an all-pervasive proclivity to express the proclamation of the Christian message in spatial categories and metaphors. To be sure, some spatial notions are logically implied if a religious institution wants to bring its message to the world. But it is another matter when this is expressed in terms of military conquest and penetration.[17] Do such images necessarily flow from the tenets of Christian doctrine? Is the well-known concretization of the missionary calling in spatial terms that is already found in the Gospels (e.g. Mark 16, 15) a sufficient explanation?

To find such an explanation we must seek it in deep-going transformations of religious ideas through political notions, such as the territorially defined nation–state and its imperialist extension into colonies, *and* through what Foucault called the episteme of natural history. Territorial thinking helped to cast religious thought into categories of 'geopolitical' space; natural history made of space an element of rationality itself and a prime concern of scientific pursuit. No wonder, then, that missionaries encountering African languages should approach them as strange regions to be explored, as bounded systems to be monographically described, as the possessions of territorially defined groups (so that linguistic, ethnic and geographic labels could become interchangeable).[18] From the same sources came a fascination with movement in space – with migration and diffusion – and more subtle preconceptions such as the idea one finds implied in much colonial writing that the same social space could not normally be occupied by more than one language. Displacement, rather than exchange or transformation, was under these circumstances the 'natural' way to think about both the nature of colonization and the task of evangelization. Thus assimilationists predicted and indigenists feared that European or 'bastardized' vehicular idioms would eventually replace vernacular languages.

Deep convictions about time – about the things time was thought to accomplish through progress and evolution, about the time needed to carry out the work of civilization, about the right time for Africans to be civilized and, above all, about the 'ages' that separated childlike Africans and adult Europeans – were inextricably bound up with those spatial notions. However, even to begin to relate them to the issues at hand would lead us too far astray.[19]

Another undisputed assumption held that education offered to Africans was to be *total*. It was not just to convey skills and kinds of knowledge; it had to form and transform the whole person in all respects, religious as well as secular. Commonsense tells one that such aims could never be reached. But actual, literal realization of the idea did not have to occur, because its real significance lay in the realm of ideology. It postulated that the 'unit' – psychological, cultural, and very soon also economic – which the educational system was to produce should be an 'individual'. Now, Africans were individuals whether or not they went through missionary education. The point was that the colonial system needed a type of individual who, separated from a traditional context, derived strength and continuity from symbolic vehicles of identity such as the *langue maternelle* and had the personality traits expected of wage-earners, consumers and supporters of nuclear families (based on monogamous stable marriages). Total claims on a person arising from religious convictions, and total claims made by a socioeconomic system on its human 'units', may contradict each other in content; they are formally analogous. In the Congo, missionaries saw education, in religious terms, as inculcating Christianity through teaching impressionable children in the mother tongue. Those, representing secular interests, for whom neither African tradition nor Christianity constituted intrinsic values, could support missionary education in native languages for purposes of their own.

Formal analogies were not the only indicators of common interests. What gave them substance and an inexhaustible source of ideological justification was the idea of *work*. It would be difficult to find in colonial discourse a value more often affirmed, or a 'problem' more often discussed. The ease with which the religious rhetoric of 'mission' could be adopted by politicians in pursuit of secular ends may be illustrated by the following pronouncement from Maurice Lippens, Governor General of the Congo. Addressing government officials, he wrote:

> You will put yourself to work in aid of agriculture, commerce and industry. You will be *apostles of labour which you will preach constantly* everywhere, not of an

accidental labour which is content with paying taxes, but a persevering labour which is the basis of all prosperity, development and civilization. (Quoted in Buell 1928: 539.)[20]

Collaboration between missionaries and colonial administration in the area of work is not a matter for conjecture. Missionaries ran trade and professional schools for government and private enterprise and they participated in the formulation of policies. Almost as soon as the Congo became a Belgian colony, a standing 'Committee for the Protection of Natives' was formed. Initially it consisted of missionaries only and was to have a watch-dog function. Later, members of the administration and representatives of other interest groups were added and the committee became advisory to the Government in matters of native policy. Throughout its existence (eight sessions took place between 1911 and 1947), 'protection' really meant direction and control of those socioeconomic processes which transformed Africans into wage-earners. Private property (on a modest scale), monogamous marriages, nuclear families, stability, sobriety, and 'hygiene' were seen as the means to protect a reservoir of manpower. Bureaucratic division of labor, incidentally, kept the issues of language and education by and large outside the discussions in the Protection Committee; other departments had to see to these matters. Keeping things apart was a way to keep them under control.[21]

A problem was created by the fact that indigenist ideology promoted utilization of vernacular languages while socioeconomic development called for languages adapted to a colony-wide working class and, as markets and consumption became more important, to an incipient *petite bourgeoisie*. In such a situation another ideological operator was needed to maintain contradictory demands in a profitable equilibrium. This was the idea of *hierarchical order* or, more exactly, the equation of order with hierarchy; it has long been recognized as a characteristic of the Belgian 'platonic' approach to colonial policy. Thomas Hodgkin, who coined the term, already pointed to its religious origin in Catholicism (see 1957: 48ff.).

Hierarchy certainly was 'religiously' observed by the mission church. It also determined the paternalist outlook of administration and private companies on access to positions, property, and political offices. To understand it more fully we must appreciate its logical power which endowed it with 'scientific' authority. Most proposals for a colonial language policy coming from missionary linguists and schoolmen were based on the logic of the taxonomic tree.[22] As a figure of thought and discourse it was used to express notions of inclusion and subsumption. It encouraged 'ordering' languages in terms of branches and levels. In most of the arguments one finds in the colonial literature, the lowest level of the tree or pyramid was occupied by the mythical 200 'idioms' supposedly spoken in the territory. It does credit to the critical spirit of Fr Hulstaert, himself a towering figure among missionary linguists, when he asks: 'Why go on always proclaiming the existence of about 200 different languages in the Congo if one has not yet made their inventory, has not studied them, nor examined the degree to which they are related?' (1939: 88). Ten years later another prominent linguist, Eugene Nida, stated: 'For its size and population the Congo is probably the most homogenous linguistic area in Africa' (1949: 14).

Whether the count of 200 languages was correct or not did (and does) not really matter. Any enumeration of distinct languages will be an artifact of linguistic classification rather than an accurate indication of communicative praxis. Language typology and classification, valuable and respectable as they may be from a philological, historical point of view, encourage equivocation between language and communication (aggravating the confusion created by equations between language and thought, linguistic structure and intellectual capacities). At any rate, without any empirical research to speak of on mutual intelligibility, multilingualism and spheres of wider communication, and sometimes against better knowledge, this classificatory diversity of African languages was declared a problem for the African and an obstacle to civilization. After all, everyone knew that, before the arrival of colonial rule, the Congolese had been living in isolated little tribes, only sometimes united in kingdoms that quarreled among themselves. Later historical research has shown this to have been wrong. Like 'hygiene' (the control of diseases often introduced or spread by colonization), 'vagabondage', and alcoholism, the language question belonged to those problems of largely European making whose real importance lay in the fact that they legitimized regulation from above. The myth of a Congolese Tower of Babel provided arguments for promoting those supra-regional languages which offered, in the eyes of the powers concerned, the best prospects of serving the needs of the colonial system.[23]

In addition to French, four African languages (occasionally five, when Sango was added in the north, Bemba in the south, or Mongo in the center) had been singled out for supra-regional, 'official' use by the time the Congo became a Belgian colony: Kikongo, Lingala (mostly referred to as Bangala), Tshiluba (also called Kiluba) and Swahili. By the logic of the classificatory scheme, one of them (or, as it turned out to no one's surprise, French) was expected eventually to occupy the tip of the pyramid. Abstract as it may have been as a logical principle, hierarchy was used to produce concrete results.

While such a taxonomic scheme of language planning formally satisfied the requirements of hierarchical order expressed in levels of increasing modernity and official recognition, it required some double-think in other respects. An almost universally held low opinion of vehicular languages as *langues passe-partout* had to be reconciled with their high status as vehicles of supra-regional communication in commerce, industry, administration, and education. As 'total education' was imposed on individuals (without consulting the Africans involved, or their families and communities) so were reglementation and 'improvement' of vehicular languages reserved to the Europeans, especially missionaries, without much attention to the users of these languages. The 1925 edition of government regulations for subsidized schools still asks 'But which indigenous dialect should be given preference?' and makes the vague recommendation to use a local *langue commerciale* (Ministère des Colonies 1925: 5). The 1948 edition speaks of a 'law of the four linguae francae' (and complains that this law is often not respected). It gives a definition of *lingua franca* and rules that 'these idioms shall be determined in agreement with the missions' – not a hint of possible consultations with the people concerned (Congo Belge – Service de l'Enseignement 1948: 33, 35).

The literature is replete with caricature-like exaggerations of certain features in these languages considered degenerate, vulgar and generally deficient. All this was used to justify intervention and various projects of grammatical and lexical improvement. With regard to language as well as to religion, missionaries, especially the early missionaries, knew better than the stereotyped images used in colonial discourse. Pagan religions did not consist of superficial, ill-assembled superstitions and barbarous ceremonial, or of timeless myth and ritual (admittedly, descriptions oscillated between the two); nor did native languages exist in hopeless dispersion and confusion (dispersed in space and mixed-up logically). The work of evangelization and that of linguistic appropriation – let us call it grammaticalization – were therefore not, and could not have been, to elevate what was low, to develop what only existed in traces or to illuminate what was in the dark. On the contrary, the real, practical task soon became, if not to eradicate and replace, then to take control of, direct and regulate what was there.

Control interests expressed themselves in the very terms and concepts that were used to describe the task: Christians brought religion and spoke a language. Africans held superstitions and talked in idioms (*parlers, dialectes*). Where it went wrong in the eyes of colonizers, colonization resulted in syncretist cults and separatist movements, concocted by Africans who had adopted vehicular and mixed languages, pidgins, sabirs, and other degenerate forms of expression. These figures of speech demonstrate analogies in the perception of religious and linguistic dynamics. But there was more than analogy. 'Language' in the practical sense of speaking and in the even wider meaning of communicative praxis was felt to be vitally bound up with those ultimate conceptions and concerns we call religious. This is why the involvement of missionaries in the control of language was no coincidence, nor just a side-effect of their role in education. The aim of colonial rule was to establish and maintain power; to be able to do this on the level of 'symbolic' power was vital to that rule's success. Missionaries were essential in this. Watching over the purity of Christian doctrine *and* regulating correctness of grammar and orthography were intrinsically related as two aspects of one and the same project. This is not just a matter for conjecture. It was seen by those who were concerned:

> [The linguistic works written by the White Fathers] give to the different idioms a fixity which prevents the dialects from splitting up indefinitely. From now on, orthography, lexicon, and syntax will have rules that are certain. The sense of words and idioms will be precise. Religious works, more than others, will serve

to make these barbarous languages more refined and to elevate them – languages which hitherto lacked almost everything that expresses ideas of a moral and spiritual order. The severities of orthodoxy will make it necessary to observe in expressions those fine distinctions which they require. (Monchamp 1904: 10)

LANGUAGE GUIDES AND TEACHING AIDS

Government and missions agreed on common, long-range goals in native education. African languages were recognized as having a crucial role in implementing these plans, and so were the prerequisites for that implementation: description, standardization, and choice of languages. However, practical applications of these agreed-upon policies, as far as we can judge from documented results in the form of language guides and other educational materials, were slow to appear and anything but coordinated. Order and hierarchy may have been favorite topoi of colonial discourse; they are not conspicuous in the publication history of linguistic texts during the period which we are trying to cover in this chapter.

Much was said and written about the pedagogical necessity to provide education in the vernacular language on the one hand, and to equip Africans for tasks demanding knowledge of French and languages of wider communication on the other. The Government, in consultation with the missions, took steps to reconcile these often contradictory demands (see the *Projet d'organisation* of 1925, discussed earlier). But programs and projects were just that: 'on the ground' there remained much conflict and confusion, especially with regard to our subject, Swahili. This was expressive of changes which affected communicative setting and situations. Such changes, as we have argued before, resulted in generic differentiation in the descriptive literature.

Serving as guides for or on 'the road' ceased to be the major function of State-sponsored vocabularies. To be sure, the time of 'exploratory', usurpatory expeditions was followed by an equally long period of pacification and punitive campaigns aimed at securing Belgian rule within the internationally recognized boundaries of the colony. This entailed a change from 'open' vocabularies to closed, greatly reduced manuals reflecting above all relations of (military) command. Pacification preceded and accompanied the setting up of a territorial administration: the colony began 'to settle in'. Relations between colonial agents and populations under their 'tutelage' became more frequent, regular and lasting (which is not to say more direct). The need for the polyglot guide to several languages along expeditionary routes disappears. Those multilingual texts that were still published began to reflect regional multilingualism.

A territorial outlook also characterized the missions, who continued to play the leading role in the descriptive appropriation of African languages. Various mission orders and their linguistic work became associated with regions, with ethnic groups and with the creation of 'literary' forms of vernacular and vehicular languages.

84

Table 2 *Guides for languages other than Swahili (1908–28)*[24]

No.	Author	Language	Place/Date	Publisher/Sponsor
1	Bentley, M.	Kongo	Brussels 1911	Ministry of Colonies
2	Buttaye	Kongo	Roulers [1909]	De Meester/Mission (SJ)
3	Buttaye	Kongo	Roulers 1910	De Meester/Mission (SJ)
4	Calloc'h	Sango	Paris 1911	Geuthner/? Mission
5	Courboin	Ngala	Antwerp 1908 Paris 1908	Forst/? Challamel/?
6	De Boeck	Ngala	Turnhout 1920	Proost/Mission
7	De Clercq, A.	Luba	Brussels 1911	Polleunis & Ceuterick/ Mission (Scheut)
8	De Clercq, L.	Yombe	Brussels [1921]	Goemaere/Bibliothèque Congo
9	Dolan	Zande	Averbode 1912	Abbey/Mission (O. Prem.)
10	Gabriel	Luba	Brussels 1921	De Wit/Ministry of Colonies
11	Gabriel	Luba	Brussels 1921	Ministry of Colonies
12	Gilliard	Lontomba	Brussels – Elisa- bethville 1928	Editions de l'Esso- rial/? private
13	Giraud	Sango, Kongo, Zande	Paris 1908	Challamel/?
14	Guillerme	Bemba	Malines 1920	?/Mission (P.B.)
15	Hurel	Rwanda	Berlin 1911	?/Mission (P.B.)
16	Hurel	Rwanda	Algiers 1921	Maison-Carrée/ Missions (P.B.)
17	Hurel	Rwanda	Algiers 1926	Maison-Carrée/ Missions (P.B.)
18	Jenniges	Luba	Brussels 1909	Spineux/Ministry of Colonies
19	Kuypers	Haya	Boxtel 1920	?/Mission (P.B.)
20	Ménard	Rundi	Algiers 1908	Maison-Carrée/ Missions (P.B.)
21	Ménard	Rundi	Roulers 1909	De Meester/ Mission (P.B.)
22	Ménard	Rundi	Algiers 1910	Maison-Carrée/ Mission (P.B.)
23	Samain	Songye	Brussels [1923]	Goemaere/Biblio- thèque Congo
24	Seidel & Struyf	Kongo	Paris 1910	J. Groos/commercial
25	Vandermeiren	Hemba	Brussels 1912	Ministry of Colonies
26	Vandermeiren	Hemba	Brussels 1913	Ministry of Colonies
27	Vanheusden	Bemba	Kafubu 1928	École Professionnelle Salésienne/Mission
28	Verbeken	Luba	Brussels – Elisa- bethville 1928	Éditions de l'Esso- rial/? private
29	White Fathers	Tabwa	Algiers 1909	Maison-Carrée Mission (P.B.)

Publication activities in the field of language manuals are best illustrated by the given in lists Tables 2 and 3. Table 2 contains works on languages other than Swahili and is representative rather than exhaustive. Only titles that appeared during the twenty years following the Belgian take-over of the Independent State in 1908 are mentioned. Furthermore, the list is restricted to guides based on French and clearly destined for use in the Congo and Rwanda–Urundi (former German colonies that came under Belgian 'mandate' in 1918).

The table confirms expectations of a generic change from polyglot to bilingual guides, corresponding to an advanced stage of settling in. The only exception is a manual (no. 13) covering three languages used as vehicular media in the northwestern part of the colony; it was probably aimed at the French Congo. Among the languages covered, most are media of wider communication, both vernacular and vehicular. Apart from Kinywarwanda and Kirundi, two languages with clear territorial demarcations, the list includes the 'official' languages Kongo, Ngala and Luba, and two additional 'candidates' noted before among the responses to the 1917 government survey, Sango and Bemba. Regionalization is most pronounced in the Luba group. Three varieties are specified for the Kasai (Tshiluba, 'Lulua' and Songye); Katanga and the northeast are represented by Kiluba (no. 18), Hemba, Tabwa and Haya. Kiyombe (no. 8) is a vernacular variety of Kongo. As to place of publication, more than two-thirds of the guides appeared in Belgium or the Congo, the rest in Paris, Berlin and Algiers. Looking at dates, it is immediately obvious that World War I caused a break. Not a single title was published between 1914 and 1919, sixteen came out before, seven immediately after the war.

All but six or seven of the authors are missionaries. Explicit sponsorship by the Ministry of Colonies is limited to six titles (five of them by missionaries); two appeared as part of a semi-official series (Bibliothèque Congo),[25] one, possibly three (no. 24 and perhaps nos. 12 and 28), can be qualified as commercial; on a few there is not enough information (nos. 6 and 13), and the rest come from missions with the White Fathers making most of the contributions.

Table 3 includes only works on Swahili. It covers the same period as the first, except that the cut-off date is 1929 (with the publication of Van de Weyer and Quets). Furthermore, it is exhaustive (with one qualification to be made later) as far as can be determined from bibliographic sources and search in several libraries and archives. It only covers material for use in the Belgian colonies.

This list of Swahili manuals differs in several respects from the preceding one. Only twelve of the authors are missionaries, and sponsorship by the Ministry of Colonies is now more pronounced (twelve titles, two of which, nos. 14 and 15, have not been verified; but at least three others, nos. 9, 10, 12, should probably be added as coming from persons/organizations close to the Ministry). Most of the rest were published by missions. Among these titles,

Table 3   *Swahili guides and primers (1908–29)*

No.	Author	Place/Date	Publisher/Sponsor
1	Anonymous	[Brussels, before 1917]	Impr. Industrielle et Financière/Ministry of Colonies
2	Brutel	Brussels 1911	C. Marci/Ministry of Colonies
3	Brutel	Algiers 1914	Maison-Carrée/Mission (PB)
4	Buttaye	Roulers 1909	De Meester/Mission (S.J.)
5	Colle	Brussels [before 1912]	Ministry of Colonies
6	Colle	Brussels [before 1912]	Librairie Coloniale R. Weverbergh/Ministry of Colonies
7	Colle	[Brussels, after 1912, before 1928]	Ministry of Colonies
8	Colle & Thielemans	Brussels 1928	Ministry of Colonies
9	Hautefelt	Brussels 1912	J. Vanderhoeven/? private
10	Hautefelt	Dison [after 1912]	Impr. Disonaise/private
11	Jesuits	Kisantu 1915	Pères Jesuites/Mission
12	Labeye	Brussels 1928	R. Louis/Union Coloniale Belge
13	[Leplae]	Brussels 1912	Impr. Industrielle et Financière/M. of Colonies
14	Quinot	Brussels 1925	Schicks/? Ministry of Colonies
15	Quinot	Brussels 1926	?/? Ministry of Colonies
16	Quinot	Brussels 1926	Librairie Coloniale R. Weverbergh/? Ministry of Colonies
17	Salesians	Elisabethville 1916	Salesian Press Capetown/Mission
18	Salesians /Sak & Verboven	Lubumbashi [!] 1921	Impr. des écoles professionnelles officielles pour indigènes/Mission
19	Soors	Brussels 1927	?/Ministry of Colonies
20	Van de Weyer & Quets	Brussels 1929 ['Fourth Edition']	Impr. Industrielle et Financière/UMHK
21	Vicariat de Buta	Averbode 1909	Abbey/Mission (O. Prem.)
22	White Fathers	Albertville 1929	Procure des Pères Blancs/Mission
23	Whitehead & Whitehead	Wayika 1928	Mission

nos. 17 and 18 were almost certainly sponsored by the mining company (UMHK) which is also responsible for no. 20. Protestant missions contribute only one entry on this list, no. 23 on 'Kingwana'. That Protestant organizations working in Katanga should not have contributed to the description of local Swahili (this also goes for periods before and after the one covered in this list) is no surprise if our earlier observations were correct (see above, p. 61). Swahili 'as spoken in Katanga' is for the first time specified in manuals published during this period (explicitly in nos. 1, 13 and 20; Katanga is mentioned in the titles of nos. 6 and 7, but the variety of Swahili described there is not typical of Katanga). Needless to say, the polyglot genre has almost disappeared, nos. 15 and 16 being the only examples (with Lingala and Tshiluba in addition to Swahili).

Table 3 shares one limitation with Table 2: it only contains manuals based on French (at least primarily) and destined for use in Belgian possessions. In addition, however, it includes some monolingual texts (nos. 9, 17, 18, 21 and 22). These are primers and grammars for teaching Africans in Swahili. This part is by no means exhaustive; it merely exemplifies yet another genre that is associated with advancements in settling in and in building up a system of schools. With the exception of no. 22 (about which more will be said later) these texts are adapted to lower-level trade and rural schools.[26] Needless to say, teaching aids of this sort were also published in languages other than Swahili. Two titles (nos. 4 and 11) require special explanation, because it is not obvious that they treat Swahili, and because the region for which they were published would make it unlikely that they did. I shall comment on them in Chapter 5. That brings us to place of publication. All but one of the guides (no. 3) appeared in Belgium or the Congo. Publication dates show more or less the same pattern as the one observed for guides to languages other than Swahili. The War reduced activities, but two or three titles did appear (nos. 11 and 17; 3 may have come out just before the War). A significant number was published between 1925 and 1929.

COLONIAL LANGUAGE TRAINING IN BELGIUM

Language guides were printed to be sold or distributed. Who were the buyers and recipients? In the absence of exact information on the market in colonial language aids, this question can only be answered by informed guesses. It is safe to assume that missionaries were as important as consumers of this literature as they were as its producers. Through the school system they were, after all, in the frontline of communication with Africans. Linguistic skills, however, were also required of military men, administrators and commercial agents, of employees of industry and even settlers. Already in the Independent State era some sort of language training (in Belgium) had been part of preparing future 'colonials'. There arose a number of educational institutions specializing in colonial training which had one or another sort of language course in their curricula. Some of these owed their existence to private initiative; eventually the missions and the Ministry of Colonies became the major sponsors. The history of training for colonial service in Belgium has not been written, and the exact relations among the institutions that were involved in it remain confusing. In order to throw at least some light onto this question an attempt was made to locate as many course programs as possible. Eventually thirteen of them, published by six different institutions between 1895 and 1928, were found.[27]

The information obtained from these programs is summarized in Table 4. Even though it is fragmentary, to compare this list with those on the publication of language guides is inviting and interesting. Apart from the first entry, which dates from the Independent State period, and the last one, which cannot be dated at the moment, these course programs cover the same period. World War I is again marked by a gap in publication dates. As might be expected, a few names occur both as authors of guides and as instructors (A. de Clercq, Thielemans, Labeye). Among the instructors, Fleury (Belgian consul in Zanzibar) and de Permentier[28] were former Independent State agents; A. de Clercq, A. Foncé and J. Bruynseels were Scheutist missionaries; Thielemans (co-author of Colle) was a White Father. The affiliation of J. Watteyne, also a Catholic missionary, is not specified. Of the remaining three, J. Tanghe, G. G. Van Langenhove, and 'Lieutenant Colonel' Labeye, the latter was a former police commander in Katanga (see below, Chapter 6). It is known that Fr Colle's Swahili manual originated from his work in teaching and remained a standard text for many decades. The major difference between language description and language teaching as it appears in these lists is one of scope. The number of described languages was relatively high and grew with the years; the languages taught at colonial training schools were limited to Swahili and Lingala, with the early and odd exception of Sanga and a conspicuous absence of Luba and Kongo, the other 'official' languages. One may assume that this division of the territory, as it were, between Lingala and Swahili reflected tensions between eastward and westward perspectives, i.e. between Léopoldville and Katanga.

As colonial rule consolidated after World War I, it required agents to move within and between territories if they wanted to rise in the hierarchy. Preparation for a specific language prior to a definite assignment had always been a problem; it now became almost impossible to solve. Therefore, course announcements begin to speak of *langue indigène*, using a general term even if a specific language was still meant. The most striking case of such usage is Labeye's 1928 Swahili manual, which obviously came out of his teaching for the Union Coloniale Belge in 1927 (see Table 4, no. 9), but the practice showed up as early as 1912 (no. 2) and continued until 1922. The Colonial University in Antwerp first listed 'bantu linguistics' among its required courses. Claims for Swahili or Lingala as dominant vehicular languages were made throughout the period covered here, while at the same time the trend toward more and more general approaches grew stronger. By 1928, 'general linguistics' appears as a separate subject next to bantu linguistics. Both were

Table 4 *Language and linguistics courses at some colonial training schools (1895–1928)*

No.	Year	Institution/Sponsor	Language(s)	Instructor
1	1895	École Coloniale, Brussels Société d'Études Coloniales	Swahili	Fleury
2	1912	Union Coloniale Belge, Brussels	'langues indigènes' (choice of Bangala or Swahili)	A. De Clercq
3	[1913]	Cercle d'Études Coloniales, Club Africain d'Anvers, Antwerp	'langues congolaises' (Lingala, Kiluba–Sanga, Swahili)	R. de Permentier
4	1914	Union Coloniale Belge	'Lingala (Bangala commercial)'	A. Foncé
5	[1920]	École Coloniale Supérieure d'Anvers	'langues indigènes' [announced, not given in first year]	A. Foncé
6	[ca. 1921–3]	École Coloniale Supérieure d'Anvers	'langue indigène' (not specified)	J. Bruynseels
7	1924	École Coloniale Supérieure d'Anvers	'Lingala (Bangala commercial)'	J. Bruynseels
8	[1925]	Université Coloniale de Belgique	'Lingala'	J. Bruynseels
9	1927	Union Coloniale Belge	'langue indigène' (= Swahili)	Labeye
10	[1927–8]	Université Coloniale de Belgique	Swahili Linguistique bantoue	Thielemans Van Langenhove Tanghe
11	1928	Université Coloniale de Belgique	Lingala, linguistique bantoue Linguistique générale Swahili	Van Langenhove Thielemans
12	[after 1928]	Université Coloniale de Belgique	Linguistique générale Swahili Lingala, linguistique bantoue	Van Langenhove J. Watteyne J. Tanghe
13	[?]	École Coloniale de Liège	Swahili, Lingala	?

aimed at equipping students at a fairly high level with elements of general understanding that would allow them to master the languages in the regions to which they would eventually be assigned. This approach was maintained at Antwerp throughout colonial times, its classic text being a work by A. Burssens (1954).[29]

Leaving aside the question of how well the trainees for colonial service absorbed the language teaching that was offered to them, it is interesting to note a connection that was felt by instructors and planners of curricula: as the need increased for colonial agents who were *broadly* prepared for their future tasks, the necessity arose to push language instruction, as it were, to ever higher taxonomic and theoretical levels. What J. Becker had claimed, intuitively and programmatically, for Swahili – that it would be the key to all other bantu languages – was now expected from bantu linguistics. Both claims rested on the idea that African languages were to be confronted from some point above the multitude of different media of communication.

4

Labor and language in Katanga

Looking at descriptions of, and policy statements about, languages in the Belgian Congo, we have begun to sketch the background and some of the conditions under which media of wider communication emerged. The procedure was mainly to reason from texts to context. This explains the importance ascribed to 'vocabularies'. We take generic differentiation in this (pseudo-)linguistic literature to correspond to changes in communicative situations. Both aspects, literary form and social context, need to be examined if the history of appropriating a language is to be understood. This methodological perspective is not to be abandoned now, although, as we narrow the scope to Katanga (to southeastern Katanga, to be accurate), information about changes in socioeconomic conditions affecting communication, and consequently language policies and manuals, becomes more plentiful.[1] Therefore, documented labor history now moves into the foreground until, in the following chapter, we return to examining linguistic documents.

The beginning of the period to be covered here is marked by the start of copper-mining at the Star Mine (Mine d'Étoile) near Elisabethville and by the chartering of the Union Minière du Haut Katanga (UMHK), both in 1906. The story ends, as far as we are concerned, around 1938, when, under the auspices of the UMHK, A. Verbeken's authoritative introduction to Swahili was published. These dates are convenient points of departure and arrival for an account of practices in the recruitment and management of African labor in Katanga. This is not to suggest, however, that they frame a stage in a process of continuous development.

LABOR IN KATANGA: A COMPLICATED STORY

The period on which we are about to concentrate was an eventful one. In the second decade of this century mining grew from an exploratory phase to operations on an industrial scale. As a consequence, it became necessary to develop supporting services such as transportation, housing, food supplies, and a growing array of auxiliary industries (chemical factories, coal mines, and power plants). The railroad link to southern Africa was established in 1910; Elisabethville became a boom town and was incorporated in 1911. A world war, a global epidemic, a world economic crisis, and technological developments in mining and metallurgy were among the factors that caused major changes in labor policies, which in turn affected the social conditions under which Katanga Swahili took shape.

As far as documentation is concerned, the period to be treated remains comparable to earlier ones. We still lack first-hand documents for Swahili as *spoken* by the people – that is, by African workers and their families and by a growing urban population not directly linked to the mining industry. (It must be borne in mind that, especially during the early decades, nothing happened in Katanga that was not in some way initiated and controlled by mining interests.) We must therefore continue to base our story of Katanga Swahili on points and structures of articulation between colonial powers exercising control and imposing decisions on the one hand, and a medium of communication about whose linguistic nature and practical use we only have indirect evidence on the other.

In a situation such as this one naturally looks for guidance and useful heuristic concepts in the growing field of pidgin and creole studies[2] – only to find that not much help can be expected from that quarter. Shaba Swahili – that is, the present form of it – is now generally qualified as a creole, but theorizing about this type of language is heavily dominated by work on Caribbean creoles and consequently by contexts specific to that area. It is doubtful that there ever existed conditions in Katanga which could usefully be compared to those that obtained in a plantation economy based on slave labor. To begin with, a situation where a majority of multilingual African workers faced a small but relatively stable, monolingual group of white employers did not exist in Katanga during the time when 'creolization' of Swahili must have occurred. During the Independent State era, colonial activities consisted of military expeditions and prospecting, preparatory to 'opening up' mineral resources which constituted the main interest of this region. B. Fetter notes that between 1892 and 1900 'there were never more than six Belgians in Katanga', and that the Comité Special du Katanga (CSK) – the agency *de facto* governing Katanga – never had more than 100 agents prior to 1910 (1968: 8, 18). When Europeans began to live in Katanga in numbers that might have been sufficient to justify considering the white population a significant 'partner' in language contact, they were a highly unstable, multinational group. French and Flemish had claims to be the official languages, but English dominated in practice, and speakers of other European and non-European languages probably shifted their allegiance according to their own work-situation and social networks.[3] Table 5 gives a vivid picture of the situation in Elisabethville in 1912–13:

Belgians made up 42% of the reported white population in Elisabethville in 1911 and 58% in 1912 (the increase in percentage being partly caused by departures by members of other nationalities). This did not represent a trend

93

Table 5 *White population of Elisabeth-ville, by nationality, 1912 and 1913*[4]

Nationality	January 1912	January 1913
Germany	41	26
USA	8	6
Great Britain	127	—
Argentina	1	85
Australia	8	3
Austria	3	3
Belgium	430	557
Canada	—	2
Denmark	4	3
Egypt	2	5
Spain	2	—
France	19	21
Greece	81	55
Netherlands	2	3
Hungary	2	—
Italy	100	58
India	3	3
Luxembourg	2	—
Norway	2	5
Portugal	2	1
Rumania	9	8
Russia	57	45
South Africa	86	27
Sweden	6	—
Switzerland	6	12
Turkey	33	28
Totals	1036	956
(Women	140	160)

Table 6 *Percentage of Belgians in the white population of the Belgian Congo and of Katanga, 1912, 1917 and 1922*[5]

	1912		1917		1922	
	Congo	Katanga	Congo	Katanga	Congo	Katanga
Whites	5465	1760	5719	2180	9597	3963
Belgians	3307	907	3109	971	5493	2119
% Belgian	60.5	51.5	54.3	44.5	57.2	53.5

in Katanga as a whole as can be seen in Table 6 (which, incidentally, also shows that the percentage of Belgians in the white population was consistently somewhat lower in Katanga than in the Congo as a whole).

The African population of Elisabethville was estimated at close to 7000 in 1912. Fetter's figures for 1923 are 12,650 and 30,000 for 1928–9 (1968: 131, Tables 3, 7). The world economic crisis, which led to a reduction of the labor force employed by the UMHK, brought a temporary halt to urban growth.[6] Work in the mines was not the only thing that brought Africans to town. With the years a growing percentage of the African population of Elisabethville lived outside the company town and other quarters provided by white employers. Already in 1912 these settlements were organized as *cité indigène*. In 1921 an inspection by Governor Lippens signaled an alarming rate of growth (as well as 'disgusting filth') of that township. The decision was taken to stop this development by razing the existing quarters and rebuilding the *cité* close to the UMHK compound, 'following the example of Johannesburg'.[7] Recruitment of industrial labor was carried out and regulated by a rather complicated organization (some of the details will have to be given later on). Even though labor was, during several decades, procured in ways that differed little from slavery,[8] and even though workers, in the majority male and single, lived under conditions approaching internment, one must remember that industrial operations and workers' settlements were situated in an environment of pre-industrial rural societies and of emerging urban centers. Workers in the labor camps had close cultural affinities with both. From the beginning, most of the labor was recruited at a considerable distance. Colonial administration and mining company justified this practice with reports that southeastern Katanga was virtually unpopulated or, at any rate, did not produce people capable of heavy industrial work. As we begin to understand more about the economics of labor during that period, we suspect that some of this may have been misrepresentation devised to hide the true reasons for long-distance recruitment. Workers could be gotten cheaper and more readily in distant regions (especially when taxation in the target areas made wage labor a necessity). Undoubtedly, the fact that workers hired for short terms, far away from their home regions, were more easily controled must have crossed the minds of those who made labor policy. Long-distance recruitment may thus be an indicator of the vitality of political resistance in the population of this area.[9] It is intriguing to note that in 1923 the workers' camp of the Union Minière counted 3290 inhabitants, that of the military (Force Publique) 1750. That ratio went down by 1929, when the respective figures were 6765 and 1672 (FP and Police Urbaine). Added to these figures must be an unknown number of industrial guards and company police. The 'forces of order' were certainly an important element in the urban scene (even if troops were kept apart from the population and many of them were deployed up-country).[10] The very least one can say is that African workers/immigrants to Katanga faced not only European employers and supervisors, but also rural societies *in situ* and a sizeable urban population which had only indirect links with mining. All this

95

created communicative situations for which 'contact' is not an adequate label.

If we must abandon the idea of (relatively) simple initial and sustained contacts between various groups of colonials and Africans in Katanga during the first decades of this century, it follows that diachronic models of contact-language development that postulate evolutionary sequences from simple, reduced pidgins to more complex creoles lose their plausibility. This does not seem to affect their tenacity. Evolution from primitive beginnings to higher forms – where 'evolution' is understood both in the intransitive sense of a natural process and in the transitive one of improvement – has been such a powerful figure of colonial discourse, political and scientific, that it must be regarded a major obstacle to historical understanding. Even if this appears to cause a cumbersome detour in our account, we must therefore first demythologize the 'evolutionary' view of colonial labor relations in Katanga before we can again concentrate on what happened to Swahili during the first three decades of this century.

The first point to be made is that the quantity and quality of labor supply did not increase in any way even approaching a steady, linear process (although it is obvious that, at the beginning of this period, we find a relatively small number of workers and a low degree of specialization). Perrings (1979) has shown that the changes and developments that occurred were dictated by the necessity of choosing between alternatives or adopting regressive measures whenever the decisive goal, profitability, was endangered. Most important among these choices was the decision to mine only high-grade ore deposits. This could be done through low-technology manual procedures, with the prospect, however, of a relatively short life for each site. Mining low-grade deposits would have required a technology of concentration, leaching and electrolysis, and consequently a long-term perspective on capital investments. While the needs of the former could be satisfied with short-term recruitment of able-bodied workers, the latter system (necessitating supplies of chemicals, caloric and hydro-electric power, and maintenance of installations and machines) could only be run with a more stable, skilled labor force. That was not an immediately attractive alternative because, unless skilled jobs were opened to *Africans* (an idea for which the time had not yet come), it would lead to an additional increase in the cost of production.

Alternatives were chosen on the basis of cost and profitability, and the availability of both high-grade ores suitable for direct smelting and cheap African labor (and *not*, or at least not only, the low degree of development of African workers, as was officially maintained) favored the low-technology solution in the first decade. However, by 1913, only seven years after starting the first operation at the Mine d'Étoile near Lubumbashi, the UMHK local management was ready to take the direction of mechanization, high technology, and the training/employment of skilled African workers. This was delayed, again, not by a slow adaptation or evolution of African workers, but by an external event, World War I. Demands on production increased suddenly, the long-term perspective required for major investments and technological changes was lacking and therefore the African labor force almost doubled, from 3869 in 1914 to 7500 in 1918. This sharply increased need was met by long distance recruitment, with additional demand being generated in 1918, when about 1000 workers died from the Spanish flu and a similar number deserted. Only with the help of the military could greater losses due to desertion be avoided (see Perrings 1979: 34–5, 40). The high-technology alternative was delayed until the twenties; and a sizeable *stable* population of workers (and their families) which, given requirements for inter-ethnic and inter-generational communication, would have been likely to employ a language such as creolized Swahili did not exist before the mid-twenties. This does not mean that a Swahili creole could not have developed before that time – there is evidence to the contrary to be discussed later – but only that its origin *must not be sought in the compounds of the mining company.*

Procedures and targets of labor recruitment did not develop in any straightforward correlation with demand either, and this also has a bearing on the question of Swahili in Shaba. It adds plausibility to the hypothesis suggested by documents examined in Chapter 2: namely, that the 'choice' of Swahili as the work language of Katanga is not to be explained by its actual preponderance in preindustrial southeastern Katanga, or by the arrival of important numbers of Swahili-speaking workers from some other area, but as part of a political strategy.

It is impossible to draw a simpler picture of this situation: too many kinds of conflict and tension within and between the various agencies characterized the first two decades of mining in Katanga. Contradictions arose, for instance, between an official, liberal doctrine of freely accepted contracts for African workers and the impossibility of satisfying labor demands on that basis in practice (practice meaning economic feasibility). The dirty work of recruiting by various means of direct and indirect coercion (through traditional authorities, through taxation generating need for cash, to name only the cleaner ones) and the even dirtier business of transporting the recruits cheaply over long distances (with much attrition due to death and desertion) were farmed out by the mining company to private operators. Most of these had gained their experience, and maintained their bases of operation, in the British and Portuguese possessions to the south of Katanga. This further contributed to conflicts between Belgian and Anglo–South African interests. Although the Belgians had the political sovereignty – a claim that still had to be made good by measures of pacification until 1917, when the Luba paramount chief Kasongo Nyembo was defeated (see Fetter 1968: 63–4) – South African and Rhodesian technicians, skilled workers, supervisors, but also tradespeople and suppliers of various kinds dominated the scene in Katanga, especially in Elisabethville. This northward migration, perceived as a threat by the Belgians, was greatly facilitated when the railroad connection from the south to Elisabethville was established in 1910 (while the link from Katanga to Port Franqui, and, via the Congo river, to the capital of the colony, was only made in 1923; see Perrings 1979: 44–5).[11]

Already in the Independent State era the (private) Compagnie du Katanga was chartered by Leopold II (in 1891) against the British threat (Fetter 1968: 7). When in 1899 Tanganyika Concessions Ltd (TCL) was founded by Robert Williams on the initiative of Cecil Rhodes, the Belgian King responded (in 1900) by buying out the Compagnie du Katanga and setting up the para-statal Comité Special du Katanga (CSK). Eventually the principal industrial interest groups came to an understanding (reflected in substantial participation by TCL in the UMHK). But the pull to the south continued to be a problem for the Belgians, especially for those whose primary attachment was to the spreading colonial administration. Also concerned was an emerging group of legal practitioners and businessmen not directly employed by the mining company. A labor agency with official status, the Bourse du Travail du Katanga (BTK),[12] was set up in 1910, but it could not meet the industry's needs; its main function appears to have been a supervisory one in the area of recruitment policies, and especially the control of wages.

In spite or because of these political and organizational complexities, the business of private recruiting companies throve. Operators were eager to respond to fluctuations in demand and supply, having an eye on quick profits and not being bound by any long-term political considerations. As a result, the labor force in Katanga during the early decades of this century did not become ethnically homogenous, nor was it dominated for any length of time by ethnic groups, although opinions about the suitability of certain 'races' for industrial labor were as strong in this region as in other colonies. In the absence of demographic data, the often repeated Belgian claims that southeastern Katanga could not supply sufficient numbers of physically strong, well-fed workers remain doubtful. They do, however, have a certain ecological plausibility. The highly mineralized soils of the savannah which constituted the immediate environment of mining operations did not support large populations, certainly not large enough to provide both labor and the agricultural products necessary to feed the work force. But, as Perrings has pointed out, the densely populated Luapula valley was nearby and could have become a steady reservoir. However, under the pretext of controlling the spread of sleeping sickness, the British South African Company closed the border to Katanga as early as 1907 – a move that was obviously made to protect the resources of the Luapula region for its own labor market.

In search of workers for Katanga, recruiters turned to the South (to Moçambique, Nyasaland and Angola), and, by 1909, also to the Lualaba valley to the north of the mining region (see Perrings 1979: 18). But the population in that area lacked (as yet) the incentive to earn cash by wage labor. The reason for this is an interesting one. In part it was the fact that the Belgians had not developed the instrument of taxation to the same perfection as their southern neighbors. More importantly, the rural population in the north had been able to choose the alternative of earning cash by supplying the industrial regions with agricultural products. Strong competition from colonial agricultural enterprise did not exist (and never developed to the degree that was characteristic of the Rhodesias) and, prior to the establishment of rail connections, importation of foodstuffs from distant areas was not feasible. A system of porterage was required as soon as mining operations started. Already in 1908 two-thirds of the food supplies had to come from sources 100 miles or more away from the mines (see Perrings 1979: 13). Porterage, a *constant* movement of goods and persons between rural and industrial Katanga, contributed to the establishment of an interaction sphere comprising mining operations and agricultural producers. Such a sphere, rather than actual migration of Swahili-speaking workers from the north to the south, was in all probability a factor in the rise of Swahili as the common language of industrial Katanga. However, Belgian authorities would not tolerate an agricultural supply system over which they had no direct control and from which they did not directly profit. A first reaction was to encourage, against earlier policies, the immigration of European farmers. By 1909 the first farms were producing (Perrings 1979: 19), and we shall, in the following chapter, present evidence that the language used to communicate with African agricultural workers was Swahili.

Eventually European producers provided part of the supply for the mining area, but there never developed in Katanga a class of white agricultural capitalists. If we accept Perrings' findings, it was also more profitable for the industry in Katanga to encourage direct and constant links between its workers and their rural areas of origin than to 'detribalize' their labor force and thus create a true urban proletariat. Continued ties with a village home base made repeated, short-term engagements possible and helped to save some or all of the cost of (sick) leaves and, at a later period, of pensions. A village to return to was the substitute for a system of social security.

After World War I, the high-technology option of mining low-grade deposits became again more attractive, and the existing recruitment system and labor policies were reassessed. Eventually this resulted in the famed 'stabilization' of the labor force in Katanga. As long-term contracts for married workers, accompanied by their families, were encouraged, labor camps turned into company towns modeled upon similar institutions such as had been typical of industrial expansion in the West during the nineteenth century. Because stabilization proved to be such a success – eventually it created a self-reproductive labor force, making recruitment virtually unnecessary – Belgian accounts of it are usually self-congratulatory and rather summary.[13] Perrings' analysis, especially of the early phases of stabilization, stresses the selective and 'unstable' character of measures that were taken to implement the scheme. From government and company sources one gets the impression that the program was directed at the colonial labor force at large and that it had 'humanitarian' aims which went beyond economic considerations. In reality, objectives and directives remained closely tied to short-term utility and profitability. Above all, stabilization was not meant to result in cutting links between workers and their regions of origin. On the contrary, to maintain economic, but also social, cultural, and

99

emotional, ties with traditional life was thought to be essential if the emerging working class was to remain 'healthy'. It even justified expenses such as paying or advancing bridewealth for bachelor workers who wanted to obtain wives from their native region. Such a practice was strongly encouraged in order to prevent inter-ethnic marriages, a source of 'trouble' that could have undesirable effects on productivity. In other words, the same policy as succeeded in tying part of the labor force to industrial employment for longer periods of time was also calculated to assure maintenance of ethnic identity and eventual return to rural areas.

What we do know about labor history in Katanga during the period which must have been crucial for the emergence of Katanga Swahili supports our contention that it cannot simply be envisaged as diffusion from a center. Rather it was a process occurring in a large interaction sphere. Both rural and urban environments, and considerable movement of persons, goods, and ideas between them, were part of that sphere during the earlier phase of recruited labor, as well as under the policy of stabilization. Swahili no more 'migrated' from, say, some location in the rural north to the compounds and towns of the south than did the workers. A major characteristic of the labor force in Katanga was its 'existence' (in the literal sense of subsistence as well as in the symbolic sense of cultural orientation) in both rural and urban environments.

SWAHILI AS A SYMBOL OF 'REORIENTATION':
CONSOLIDATION OF BELGIAN RULE IN KATANGA

We can be virtually certain that Swahili in Katanga did not 'evolve' from some pidgin form. Otherwise one would have to postulate that first a pidgin Swahili was spoken not only by Europeans (as it undoubtedly was) but also among Africans (for which there is no evidence). Furthermore, such a theory would not explain why a pidgin form of *Swahili* rather than of French or English, or the readily available Kitchen-Kaffir became the starting-point. Some sort of simplified English and French *petit nègre* were certainly used in communication between Europeans and Africans, but a European-language-based creole never appeared in this region. At any rate, frequent change in areas of recruitment, expansion and contraction of the labor force, reversals and revisions of stabilization policies, and a high degree of mobility between urban and rural environments make it impossible to envisage social conditions conducive to the slow, continuous development of a contact language *in situ*.

Diffusion of Swahili from a local center in the region of the mines, or its migration to that region together with a group or groups of speakers who would have been dominant enough to impose the language on others, do not provide alternative explanations either. The former – let us call it the Msiri/Bunkeya hypothesis – is weak enough in itself, and further weakened by the well-documented policies of isolating recruited workers from the local population. The migration hypothesis would make sense only if one could identify a group of immigrants for whom Swahili was already the principal language and symbol of identity. Arab Swahili influence in the north was strong enough to produce significant numbers of speakers, but it did not create Swahili ethnicity.

If explanation by slow growth or displacement is not sufficient, what is? It must be a type of interpretation which considers *simultaneously* local, creative response to communicative needs *and* restrictive intervention from above motivated by a resolve to control communication within and with the labor force. 'Resolve to control' may be presumed to have been a constant in colonial relations. To be exercised, however, it needed specific objects and had to respond to variable situations. Some of these were created by events, others resulted from slower processes such as the introduction of schooling and professional training. Furthermore, only a few communicative situations could be controled directly, the most obvious examples being instruction and command at work and the administration of workers' settlements. Nor should one forget that a considerable portion of the labor force, while necessary for operating the mines, was not under the direct control of the mining company. Persons working for (sub-)contractors, agricultural producers, and merchants were by and large free to communicate as they wished, and that was even more true of their dependants. These people, and an undetermined number of day-laborers and self-employed Africans (for instance, those that supplied fuel and transportation), constituted an urban population of some stability even before hiring of married workers, family-housing, and medical and social services became characteristic of UMHK labor policy.

The preceding enumeration of targets of control roughly corresponds to an order of increasing difficulty in finding historical documentation. Historical events, if they are known at all, are fairly well documented; much less is known about early institutional settings for the use of Swahili; only indirect and circumstantial evidence can be mustered for the role played by Swahili as the medium of expression of a growing urban working class and an embryonic *petit bourgeois* culture.

Apart from events which made Katanga part of the Belgian Congo and a region of industrial activity, nothing was more important for the future history of Swahili in this area than a series of political decisions which found their expression in a company ordinance issued on April 12, 1918, 'under which compound managers had to be able to speak at least one of the languages of the Africans in their charge' (Perrings 1979: 43; see also Fetter 1968: 71–2). As Perrings notes, this was interpreted to refer to languages of the Congolese Africans, and Fetter is probably right when he mentions only Swahili (although a certain element of indecision in this document, expressive of a multilingual situation, should not be overlooked). At any rate, it appears that the warning and recommendations from the Director of the CSK, on which we commented in a previous chapter, were taken seriously and implemented less than a year after they had been voiced (in September 1917).

Of course, the adoption of Swahili as quasi-official language cannot be traced to a single ordinance. This is significant because it allows us to make connections between a multitude of considerations and decisions. First of all, links can be established between the 1918 ordinance, the De Bauw letter of 1917, resultant correspondence between the local colonial administration and the Ministry of Colonies (see Perrings 1979: 158, note 55), and a context that was wider than the local mining industry. Mining interests were too vital to Belgium to be left to the attention of managers and administrators in Katanga. Among such wider considerations were those that called for the elimination of English and Kitchen-Kaffir (Chi-Kabanga) from areas vital to labor management. This was a measure designed to dramatize political sovereignty at a critical moment in the history of Katanga. So urgent was this move perceived to be that its advocates recommended revoking constitutionally granted linguistic rights.[14]

The immediate occasion for the ordinance was a move to oust the firm of Robert Williams and Co. from its dominant position in labor recruitment and management. Since the early days, Robert Williams had had a major role in recruiting workers, especially from Angola and the British possessions to the south.[15] It had its agents in the target areas, organized transportation, and took care of 'administrating' (i.e. housing and feeding) workers in company settlements. Relations between the Belgians and Robert Williams had their ups and downs through the years. In particular, the increased needs for labor during World War I prolonged close association of the firm with the UMHK. Around 1917, Belgian opposition (outside the UMHK) to Robert Williams and the system of labor recruitment he represented grew to the point where action was required. I consulted three different accounts of the events that led up to the break (UMHK, Fetter, Perrings): each of them suggests a different issue as being central, but in such a way that the three reports may be taken as complementary rather than contradictory.

There is, first, the somewhat hagiographic official history of the UMHK (see UMHK 1956: 124ff.), which notes concern expressed in 1917 by the CSK to the Minister of Colonies about the low proportion of Belgian nationals among management and staff of the company (the Director General at that time was the American P. K. Horner). We are told that E. Sengier arrived in Katanga on April 28, 1918, as the representative of the metropolitan *conseil d'administration*. His task was to reorganize the head office in Africa. The success of his mission is summarized in a laconic statement: 'At the end of the year the percentage of Belgians had risen to 42%'. In the manner of chronicles, this is followed, without a connecting statement, by a passage worth quoting here:

> It was at that time also that M. Scraeyen [Director General of the CFK] decided to let Blacks drive locomotives, and this decision was the point of departure for a policy tending to give to blacks work that previously was done by whites. (UMHK 1956: 126)

The account continues with an anecdote reporting a conversation between Sengier and General Smuts (Sengier had taken the usual route to Katanga, via

South Africa) about the possible danger such a policy might pose to the 'color bar'. Smuts is said to have approved of the innovation. After that, the story of policy decisions taken in 1917/18 ends with a carefully worded allusion to

> [expressions] of some unrest among the white personnel in that time of war. These had been provoked mainly by agitators recruited in South Africa, who, having kept contact with the trade unions of Johannesburg, demanded that the European personnel in Katanga become members of the white unions of South Africa. They had no success. (UMHK 1956: 127)

This is an incomplete story, to say the least, but in reporting on the success of Belgianization, on the decision to put blacks into skilled jobs, and on the failure of white labor leaders to organize successful action, the UMHK account touches on several important issues. The first one – mounting Belgian resentment against South African-dominated policies at the UMHK – is given much attention by Fetter (see 1968: 68ff.). He also provides an account of the prehistory of Sengier's mission, in the form of protests culminating in an official investigation into working and living conditions among African workers in the mines. This investigation was conducted by Martin Rutten, then an attorney general (Fetter 1968: 70–1). Compound managers were accused, but also black supervisory personnel, who were mostly of Rhodesian and Nyasan origin. Calls for Belgianization could therefore be joined to demands for improving the lot of Congolese workers, both being declared matters of national interest (see Fetter 1968: 71). In this context Fetter notes that

> several Belgians recommended that Congolese workers receive the same treatment as those from British territory and that Europeans from the south be forced to speak to work gangs in Swahili rather than in Karanga (Shona). (Fetter 1968: 72f)[16]

Perrings cites chapter and verse of the 1918 ordinance, but puts it into a yet different context. Those changes in policy of which the directive to use Swahili was a manifestation on the surface had deeper causes. It had become necessary to modify production methods and accordingly to adjust demands in quantity and quality of African labor (see, for the following, Perrings 1979: 41ff.). As we noted earlier, geological conditions in Katanga had made it possible to exploit deposits by surface mining of high-grade ores. Supplying a large proportion of low-skill, short-term labor for these operations had been the principal role of Robert Williams and Co. As soon it became foreseeable that extensive mining of high-grade ores would greatly limit the life of the industry, alternatives were envisaged. These involved either concentration of low-grade ores by physical means (flottation) or the process of leaching with the help of chemicals, to be followed by electrolysis. The latter process was recommended as early as 1916 but would have required years of planning and construction during which selective mining had to be continued. That in turn involved the danger that the smelters might run out of high-grade ore; eventually, therefore, it was decided to build a concentrator (in February 1918). Robert

103

Williams and Co. had supported the leaching–electrolysis alternative because that meant that for some time they could keep on running labor recruitment and management as before. According to Perrings:

> This conflict was inevitably carried over into the field of labour management, since the matching of the requirements of production techniques and labour supplies depends on the unity of control over both. Horner [the director of the UMHK] was at pains to stress this point, arguing that the UMHK could far better utilize its labour if it had direct control over it, bypassing the labour contractors, the BTK and Robert Williams and Company. (1979: 41ff.)

In search of independence from official and private recruiters, the UMHK had already begun to investigate potential sources of labor to the north and especially in the Kasai. What was sought with these attempts was less an expansion of existing resources than an alternative – a different kind of worker, as required by imminent changes in production methods. It may not have been entirely coincidental that preparations to break with Robert Williams and Co. and protest against this firm, as reported by Fetter, occurred at the same time. Finally, however, it was not Sengier but the foreigner Horner who

> succeeded in May 1918 in reorganizing the management of labour to exclude Robert Williams and Company altogether, although the actual transfer of compounds only took place the following year. But revocation of the agreement turned out to be not enough. In April 1918 an Ordinance was issued under which compound managers had to be able to speak at least one of the languages of the Africans in their charge. Interpreting this to mean a language of the Congolese Africans on the mines, the state then moved against former Robert Williams and Company employees who had been retained as compound managers in order to wipe out totally the influence of that company on labour policy. (Perrings 1979: 43–4)

The high symbolic value given in the official UMHK publication to the decision to train blacks as engine-drivers links the 1918 ordinance to yet another issue, namely the high cost of white labor and the problems it posed to management. The latter were brought home to UMHK in a series of strikes and attempts at unionization in 1919–20. Euphemistically, these were referred to as 'unrest' and blamed on foreign *meneurs*. Perrings' analysis shows that these actions not only proved connections between the expatriate labor force in Katanga and labor struggle in South Africa; the strikes also responded to local conditions. Above all, the post-War devaluation of the Belgian franc meant a loss of income for employees, who counted on repatriating their earnings in other currencies (see Perrings 1979: 51). Demands for compensation from these employees made replacing them with Belgian personnel, hired on relatively short-term contracts and paid in francs, more and more attractive. Prospects of higher profit and national interest nicely converged and gave additional impetus to proposals for Belgianization. But this was not all. Belgian personnel were also expected to offer less resistance to a policy of giving to Africans many of the skilled and supervisory functions hitherto reserved to whites (Perrings 1979: 53).

In sum, the reorientation of Katanga away from its dependence on the south, a change in which Swahili was to play such an important role, was motivated by technological and financial considerations. This detracts nothing from the importance of political goals and measures. Because the linkage French/Swahili, as opposed to English/Chikabanga, is so crucial to our argument it will be instructive to take a closer look at some documents reporting on unrest among white personnel in the years following the War. Perrings describes the swift and decisive manner in which the management of the UMHK dealt with the strike of 1919. The South African leaders E. J. Brown and J. M. Keir were fired, and the colonial administration was approached to issue expulsion orders. But, while the metropolitan Government was ready to respond to demands from the industry, relations with the Vice-Governor in Elisabethville were apparently such that actions could not be perfectly synchronized. A copy of a letter from Vice-Governor Tombeur to the Minister of Colonies, dated Elisabethville, June 11, 1920, shows that Brown had not yet been expelled by that date. More than that, even though the Ministry urged the local administration to use all legal means to remove the strike leaders (a decree of March 3, 1913 was cited, authorizing expulsion on the grounds of a suspected threat to public order), the Governor in Katanga hesitated because Brown, in his opinion, had not (yet) been a threat to public order. To him, labor discipline and public order were not identical.

Another reason that the provincial administration hesitated to intervene is given in a report on the second strike (in 1920). The author reminds the Minister of Colonies that a problem encountered during the first strike continued to exist. If unrest got serious, the Vice-Governor General would have to send black troops against white strikers – something for which the time clearly had not yet come.[17] Other documents – including a report from the Belgian Consul General in South Africa, who was monitoring applications for immigration to Katanga and press reaction to labor unrest there – reveal the strategy that was adopted by the UMHK and the metropolitan Government. There were two lines of argument. One was to insist that the strike was instigated by non-Belgian personnel (even though the secretary of a newly formed union was a Belgian; see Perrings 1979: 52, note 92). Tension did exist between Belgian and foreign employees, owing to differential treatment and usually better conditions for the latter. These feelings were to be made use of and fueled with nationalist rhetoric. Apparently, though, those who used that strategy had to convince themselves in various ways that the foreign threat was real. One sort of 'proof' given is of special interest to us and should be quoted here. The already-cited report to the Minister on the 1920 strike(s) begins with this passage:

> The letter which expresses their [the strikers'] demands in threatening terms constitutes a veritable ultimatum. You will notice when you read the document that it was *visibly translated from the English* and even has a stamp with

inscriptions in the English language. These suggestive details point to foreign participation in the conflict...(My emphasis.)[18]

Another issue that could be exploited for the purposes of the Company was that of guarantees demanded by the strikers that they would not be replaced by blacks. This made it possible further to discredit the South-African-led movement as racist. A telegram from the Minister of Colonies to the Vice-Governor General in Elisabethville urges the recipient to take note of agitation to prevent blacks from being employed as mechanics and fitters, and to determine whether the attempts to exclude blacks are based on 'racial prejudice and [motivated by demands] that blacks be employed at lower salaries than whites.'[19] The last part of the statement is somewhat cryptic – was giving equal pay to blacks ever seriously envisaged? Be it as it may, there can be little doubt about the pragmatic (and hypocritical) nature of this denunciation of racism. Racial discrimination was an issue to be used, not resolved.

SWAHILI AS A WORK-LANGUAGE: SOME STRUCTURAL
DETERMINANTS

We may conclude that, around 1920, vague national and specific capitalist interests in Katanga converged in policies directed at reducing dependence on 'foreign', especially South African, white employees and on black workers supplied in the main by Robert Williams and Co. and similarly oriented firms. The decision to link the ousting of Robert Williams as a recruiting and managing agency for the compounds with the issue of language had several significant implications. As a 'language spoken by Congolese workers', Swahili had by 1918 apparently acquired sufficient symbolic–ideological significance to be used as political medium. That it was used in such a manner further contributed to its 'promotion' not only as a work jargon, but as *the* African language of Katanga. Nor was it accidental that the institutional context in which Swahili was first given privileged status in southern Katanga should have been that of the management of black labor. Functions connected with that task were concentrated in the office of the compound manager/*chef de camp*.[20] Reflecting the dominant position of the mining industry, the company settlement and its administration became the model and focus of urban native policy (*politique indigène*).

The office of *chef de camp* was defined in unabashedly paternalistic terms. But all the affirmations of fatherly benevolence and philanthropic concern which make such good reading for students of a peculiarly Belgian brand of colonial discourse should not distract attention from the fact that, as paymaster, justice of the peace, and arbitrator in disciplinary matters, as chief of police, head of municipal and social services, and distributor of food and housing, and also as keeper of civil records, the *chef de camp* accumulated awesome power over workers and their dependants. All these functions grew in importance as the famed policies of stabilization, the principal means of implementing the decisions of 1917/18, began to take shape.

After 1918 the BTK began to recruit in Pweto (Tanganyika–Moero), Bukama, Kongolo, Lukonzolwa and Ankoro, and in the regions of Lomami, Kabinda and Lulua (see Perrings 1979: 55). There were setbacks in this development for technical reasons, such as a temporary oversupply of labor because not enough ore could be transported to the smelters. Coal from the Wankie mines in Rhodesia did not arrive because of strikes there. Many of the voluntary Rhodesian workers left Katanga (see Perrings 1979: 57–8). Private companies and the colonial administration began to realize that long-term planning was needed if the desired autonomy in matters of labor policy and supply was to be achieved. A broad campaign for promoting work as an obligation was started (see Perrings 1979: 59). It also became increasingly clear that stabilization had to go hand in hand with schooling and professional training.

A Commission on Native Labor was set up in 1924/5 and formulated the principles that guided the policy of stabilization until about 1930, when the economic crisis caused another break in development (see Perrings 1979: 77ff.). The details of that story are well known. For our purposes it suffices to state that stabilization succeeded in creating ultimately a self-reproductive labor force whose 'unit' was no longer the individual worker, but a nuclear family (with an emphasis on 'nuclear'; polygamy and other extensions of the nucleus of husband, wife, and their offspring were strongly discouraged). Inasmuch as stabilization meant taking control of more and more aspects of a worker's and his family's life, from sanitation to religion, the social sphere of Swahili was no longer limited to the mine or workshop.

This did not mean that the camp/compound provided a free space of communication as opposed to controlled situations at work. Once the UMHK had decided to match social stabilization with urban planning and more permanent construction (workers had for years been housed in reed shelters and wattle-and-daub huts) the workers' settlement became an incarnation of hierarchical order and discipline. Company stores, offices and social facilities (later including Catholic churches and schools constructed by the Company) provided a physical center presided over by a small number of Europeans – usually no more than three or four, none of whom resided in the camp during the period covered by this account.[21] Vertical communication – that is, communication along hierarchical channels – was in Swahili, at least after 1919. What was this Swahili like? Even before we examine guides and manuals from that period, we can answer that question partly and indirectly if we consider the major determinants of communicative situations in which this language was used. Contacts between white administrators and African workers were not ephemeral, and stabilization required that they become less and less so. The Company encouraged long-term contractual commitments from workers and valued 'long experience' among the administrators. Actual encounters between the two groups, both casual and official, were relatively frequent (even at a much later time, *chefs de camp* were reputed to know almost all the workers and many of their family members by name). Nor were these contacts restricted to a few types of mainly 'practical' interaction. A great variety of speech situations and events corresponded to the many functions accumulated in the office of the administrator. The most important of these were connected with maintaining work discipline (disciplinary measures were proposed by supervisors at work, but imposed and enforced by the *chef de camp*) and with adjudicating in cases of litigation ('palavers'). These involved a great variety of matters, from theft and adultery to witchcraft. Furthermore, the administrator would frequently converse with his clerks, guards and other informants on everything that could have even a remote bearing on workers' reliability and productivity.

All this does not resemble the conjectural situation of reduced interaction that is assumed to have been at the source of pidgins. Yet, as we shall see when we examine descriptions of the kind of Swahili company employees were expected to master – descriptions, moreover, given by Europeans with 'practical' experience – a greatly reduced pidgin variety was apparently considered sufficient to meet all the communication needs that were likely to arise on the work site and in the settlement. What explains this apparent discrepancy? On grounds of principle one might answer that there is no direct relation between the grammatical and lexical form of a language and the functions it serves or the content it may express. This is a good principle to keep in mind if one wants to avoid wrong inferences from linguistic forms to mental or social functions. But, unless one regards linguistic form, all linguistic form, as a reality outside and above history, *some* interrelationship between form and function/purpose must be admitted. It would seem that the decisive factor in the pidginization of Swahili documented in the context of industrial labor in Katanga was not so much a narrow range of functions or types of communicative interaction as the highly structured and hierarchical nature of interaction between European personnel and African workers. Some 'true pidgins' presuppose, if they exist, a relation of equality among partners of exchange (at least at a given moment of linguistic interaction) and a limited purpose. There is a lack of pressure or motivation to structure and order speech; certainly there will be no rules of correctness that must be observed for their own sake. Such ephemeral, anarchic situations may account for the 'reduction' of linguistic forms which is thought to characterize pidgins. But 'pidgin' may also be a pseudo-form (a non-spontaneous form) resulting from relations of inequality and from active restriction of purpose/function. Use of Swahili by white supervisors in Katanga was inseparably tied to enactment of power in a hierarchical organization. Communication being, in the end, always *command* (i.e. consisting of speech acts performed as one-way orders), a way of speaking once acquired or chosen would be maintained without response to those correctives which might improve linguistic competence in truly interactive situations. (Of course, there are other types of inequality and hierarchical organization besides the ones that exist between

108

administrators' supervisors and workers, and their effect on the choice of a linguistic form may be the opposite – as we shall see when we turn to missionaries and the kind of Swahili they used.)

Before we go on to discuss some further aspects of communication in the context of labor, a caveat needs to be issued. 'One-way' (i.e. highly restricted) use of Swahili in situations of command was structurally required by the organization of labor management in Katanga; it oriented white supervisory personnel, especially the *chefs de camp* and their assistants. But these constraints did not prevent individual employees or agents, some of whom had experience in colonial administration in other territories and with other African languages, from acquiring competence in Swahili beyond the call of duty. Strictures against fraternization (formulated as soon as more extended contacts were seen to pose a danger to discipline; during the pioneer times relations between individual Europeans and individual Africans were quite close)[22] put limits on the use to which increased linguistic competence could be put. Still, it is important to remember that controls on communication did not operate with total success and that separation between the races grew with time.

In order to understand why and how linguistic reduction, individual exceptions notwithstanding, could be developed and maintained, one needs to consider, in addition to the pragmatics of the situation, certain cognitive aspects of language-use. Order and organizational hierarchy found their linguistic expression in an emphasis on labeling and classification. Synthetic and often polysemic (multi-purpose) terms representing classes of objects, persons, and activities were obviously of the greatest interest to the compilers of practical vocabularies. This reflects a cognitive interest in taxonomizing – that is, in keeping a grip on semantic nodes and their lexical expressions. Differentiations and subtleties of meaning, or at any rate their lexical realizations, could largely be ignored. Similarly, limitations on interaction dictated by the need to institute and operate hierarchical order apparently found their expression in a reduced range of syntactic differentiation. As we shall see, there are examples of early language guides where infinitives and imperatives are the only verb-forms recommended for learning.

With these observations we are moving from social-historical context to linguistic forms. These will have to be discussed when we take a look at Swahili manuals of the period. Some observations have been made here in order to introduce two propositions, one of a general kind, the other specific to the labor situation in Katanga. First, if we see interrelationships between a certain labor policy and its attendant linguistic practices correctly, then it follows that at least some of the documented instances of pidginization were caused not by actual linguistic incompetence in relatively reduced communicative situations, but by a kind of over-determination due to the rigid, hierarchical and taxonomic nature of actual and possible speech events. Second, language manuals conceived for use by company personnel and other Europeans in Katanga were not just grammars for command, but embodiments of discipline – reflecting and supporting an order of command and consent, and suited to a practice of rigidly defining classes of objects, persons, and events according to their relevance for labor relations in the widest sense of the term.

For these structural reasons alone it is inconceivable that the Swahili spoken by the workers and their dependants among themselves should be adequately represented in these early language guides. The work-jargon can have been only one of the registers available to speakers in the compounds of the 1910s and 1920s. Statistics are available to show rates of mortality and desertions, average length of contract terms, and so forth, but very little is known about social life in the labor camps prior to stabilization. Were workers able to move between compound and town in their free time? In fact, how much free time was there before certain 'protective' regulations were enforced? How frequent and intense were contacts between company workers and the growing population of the *cité libre* – called *usa bulongo*?[23] Fetter's research (1973, 1974) has shown that an intense cultural life, centered on ethnic, mutual-aid, burial and dance associations, flourished in Elisabethville by the 1920s. There is hardly any information on how important Swahili was in this emerging African urban life-style. Vernacular languages were undoubtedly used in ethnic organizations. Contrary to an opinion held by Europeans at the time (and later), however, 'tribal' affinities were not the major determinant of social life in the town. Many of the activities were present- and future-oriented and found in Swahili an appropriate common medium. At any rate, it is reasonable to assume that, if and when that language was used by urban Africans, it was employed in a form appropriate to ordinary communicative situations and comparable to that of vernacular language in a multilingual context. Swahili was never a minimal code adopted to fill a gap that could not have been filled by any number of languages (*including* English and French). In the light of later developments, the most plausible hypothesis seems to be that Swahili became the common means of expression for a shared experience of an urban life-style. It was a creole without having gone through a pidgin stage.

One accepted definition of a creole, however, is 'a pidgin that has acquired native speakers' (R. J. Hall, quoted, with comments, in Bickerton 1976: 169). We have seen in Chapter 1 that Lingala had reached that state before the turn of the century. Swahili in Katanga was set on that road before 1910, and by 1925 Katanga-born children of immigrants from other regions were old enough to take up work and start families of their own. An African community at Elisabethville was recognized as such (that is, as not simply an agglomeration of squatters) by 1912 (see Elisabethville 1911–61: 122–3). Moreover, urban settlement above and beyond the requirements of the dominant enterprises was soon actively encouraged by the authorities. In 1923, Gaston Heenen, then interim Governor of Katanga, stated that

> active elements [among the Africans] who wish to cut their ties with the traditional milieu, either definitely or for an extended period, should be permitted to reorient themselves and form a new society, based on certain

principles of our civilization, a society which should develop in an original way through the evolution of everything custom has to contribute. (Elisabethville 1911–61: 123)

To be sure, this profession of a progressive native policy was already part of designs to bring the 'free city' under control and to bend spontaneous African urbanization and embourgeoisement to colonial aims. By the same token, statements such as the one just quoted attest processes in which a 'new society' was being created.

It is in such a perspective that one must see the 'imposition' of Swahili in the pursuit of control over a labor force. Work discipline was paramount but cannot be regarded as a settled fact or state of affairs; it was a changing practice that had to be established and constantly defended. Order did not come naturally, nor was it a simple consequence of an increased differentiation of tasks and skills called for by technological developments. Industrialization was erratic in Katanga. It was complicated by external factors (war, crisis, fluctuations in the world market and in currencies, policy changes in neighboring colonies) and by the precariousness of labor procurement. This created contradictory demands: having to supply sufficient numbers of cheap workers while keeping intact their rural bases in order to assure human reproduction and agricultural production. Order, also in linguistic matters, needed to be *imposed*; it was therefore essentially a reality after the fact. A variety or register of Swahili made by administrative decree and by linguistic codification, no matter how amateurish and 'incorrect', a vehicle of order and discipline still presupposed a substratum to be manipulated, selected from, and reduced. This substratum was not Swahili in some abstract, correct form (as it is often suggested by apologetic references to 'good Swahili') but a practice of speaking Swahili that had emerged *previously*. It makes little sense to place the documented mining-company pidgin at the beginning of later evolution toward a creole, because Swahili was established as part of a multilingual repertoire *before* labor policies changed from short-term contracts for unattached, unskilled males to the stabilization of workers with their families which began soon after World War I and was carried out on a large scale after 1925. Furthermore, Swahili in Katanga acquired its status *before* the UMHK took labor recruitment into its own hands and concentrated on rural areas to the north in which Swahili undoubtedly had a strong position as a medium of wider communication. This concentration happened on an appreciable scale only after 1917 (see Perrings 1979: 55–6). Finally, firm implantation and an important status in the urban context were assured for Swahili *before* the mining company, with the help of the missions, set up a system of (training) schools in which that language was used in teaching. There were some early beginnings, initiated by the CFK, but the school system was not established before the late 1920s.

5

Talking tough and bad: pidginization in Katanga

Our attempt to trace the complicated, intertwined history of labor and language in Katanga has led us to formulate some structural conditions or constraints which made pidginization of Swahili all but inevitable without, however, rendering it a necessary stage in the emergence of Katanga Swahili. Several objections can be brought against such a procedure. It may be said that it is too deductive and hence conjectural. Or, even if it is granted that our view is basically correct, it could be argued that it applies only to what might be called 'communicative pidginization' – a certain manner of reduced, overdetermined verbal interaction – and that it remains to be seen how this process is reflected in linguistic forms that are characteristic of pidgins. Admittedly, this study has been conducted with a 'bias' in favor of the priority of pragmatic–communicative factors and determinants. This does not mean that linguistic evidence is lacking (and that expert linguists would find it more important and impressive than the social-historical information that has had our attention so far). It is to such linguistic evidence that we turn now, resuming the account of colonial language description where it was left off in Chapter 3.

MISSIONARIES TEACHING COLONISTS

The Swahili guides to be examined in this chapter were published in the years between the annexation of the Independent State by Belgium (1908) and World War I. With one exception, they were sponsored by the Ministry of Colonies. In quality and purpose they differed widely. To illustrate this we begin with some texts, written by missionaries, that provide the background against which the degree of pidginization in the two main documents can be appreciated.

There is, first, the *Vocabulaire français–kiswahili et kiswahili–français, precédé d'une grammaire* by Émile Brutel of the White Fathers (Brussels: C. Marci, 1911). This was a very substantial guide, which began with a grammatical section (58 pages), followed by a French–Swahili (ca. 2700 items) and a Swahili–French dictionary (ca. 2100 items). The *Vocabulaire* was destined to become a standard work. A second edition, more or less identical and with the same title, but reset in a larger type, was also published by the Ministry of Colonies in 1921. But it is interesting to note that the same book led, as it were, another life. In a bibliography of White Fathers publications it is listed as published in Algiers by Maison-Carrée (the publishing house of the order), first in 1914 and then again in 1925 and 1928.[1] It grew in the process, so much so that its final edition in 1930 is listed as abridged. The 1925 edition which I was able to see shows the author's continued efforts to improve the dictionary; it now had ca. 6000 items in the Swahili–French and ca. 7250 in the French–Swahili part. It had thus risen above the level of the 'practical' guides that were of interest to the Ministry. Perhaps the abridged version of 1930 represented an attempt to stay in the colonial market.

The danger of breaking the genre and thereby losing the sponsorship of colonial authorities was avoided by another White Father, P. Colle. His *Abrégé de grammaire swahilie*, published by the Ministry of Colonies in Brussels, carries no date, but from other references (see below) we know that it came out before 1912. Compared to Brutel, its scope is reduced; it has a total of 53 pages. Several things are remarkable about this concise introduction. It has a French and Flemish version side by side (conforming to the spirit of Article 3 of the Colonial Charter of 1908). Although it is extremely brief it represents high grammatical standards (as witnessed by the number of noun-classes, emphasis on class-concordance, and a fairly complete treatment of verb-forms). We know that the *Abrégé* goes back to courses taught by Fr Colle to future colonial agents in Belgium.[2] It was accompanied or followed by a *Guide de conversation en langue swahilie: À l'usage des émigrants se rendant au Katanga et au Haut-Congo belge* (Brussels: Librairie Coloniale, R. Wever-bergh, n.d.). It is one of the earliest Swahili guides in which Katanga is mentioned explicitly. I have been unable to determine the exact date of the first edition. An early reference (see below) establishes that it appeared before 1912. A second, revised edition, co-authored by Colle's confrère Fr Thiele-mans (who by then taught at the Université Coloniale), appeared in 1928.[3] The copy I have seen has no publication date; its sub-title reflects the expansion of Belgian colonial possessions in Africa after 1918: the guide is now destined 'A l'usage des émigrants se rendant au Katanga, au Haut-Congo Belge, Kivu, Urundi, Ruanda, Etc.' There is, incidentally, no indication that different varieties of Swahili may have been spoken in these widely separated regions.

During the period before World War I there appeared one other Swahili vocabulary written by a missionary (it has, to my knowledge, so far escaped the attention of bibliographers). Fr R. Buttaye, a Jesuit, published a *Dictionnaire kikongo–français, français–kikongo* (Roulers: Jules de Meester). The publication date is not mentioned but was probably 1909 or 1910. Neither listed in the table of contents nor otherwise explained, an appendix 'kiswahili–français' is included, with three pages of 'Notions grammaticales' and a French–Swahili vocabulary with more than 1400 entries. The best explanation for such interest in Swahili in a region where that language was not used as a vehicular medium (the Jesuits had their mission in the lower Congo–Kwango area) would seem to be that it was connected with the *fermes-chapelles* scheme.[4] The Jesuits 'collected' young people who were bought free from slavery or were abandoned by their families. They were brought to rural centers, where they received some education and worked in agriculture and the crafts. The system was centered around Kisantu and counted in 1902 more than 5000 'children' in numerous settlements; and we may assume that a substantial number of the freed slaves came from the upper Congo and were Swahili-speakers. Buttaye, who notes in his dictionary that a handwritten 'edition' was available in 1901, may have aimed the Swahili appendix at this group and the missionaries who worked with them. But this remains guesswork until documentation can be found of the circumstances under which his work was conceived.

Frs. Brutel and Colle described (and taught) Swahili in a quasi-academic setting. Their Swahili guides cannot really count as scholarly contributions, but the condensed introductions they provided were up to the linguistic standards of their time. At the Ministry of Colonies there must have been a feeling that these manuals made too many demands to be really useful to agricultural settlers – a type of colonist which, for a relatively brief period, became the center of attention. In Katanga, the growth of the labor force that was employed in the mines began to result in increased demands for agricultural products. As we saw in the preceding chapter, African producers initially began to seize on that opportunity as an alternative to earning cash through wage labor. This was immediately perceived as a danger to the labor supply for the mines. Schemes of agricultural colonization were conceived as a way of counteracting undesirable African initiatives as well as the danger of dependence from Rhodesian and South African producers.

COLONISTS TEACHING COLONISTS: A GUIDE FOR FARMERS IN KATANGA

In his book *Le Katanga*, A. de Bauw (whom we encountered in Chapter 2 as Director of the BTK, and later of the CSK) mentions that the Government conducted a first experiment with agricultural colonization in 1911–12. Although it was not much of a success, the experience gained was put to use when, in 1918, a Commission d'Immigration was set up in Elisabethville in order to formulate policies regarding agricultural settlers.[5]

In the same book, under the heading 'The problem of native labor', De Bauw says that the European employer must know the native:

> The better the European understands the language of the natives the better he will be able to direct them (*manier*) and the higher will be the yield he is going to get from his personnel. Study of the native language appears, therefore, to be a prime necessity. Kiswahili, which is the most widespread dialect among the

black population of Katanga, can be learnt easily. The colonist will greatly facilitate his start if, before his arrival in Africa, he learns the most frequently employed terms. That can be done easily with the aid of small manuals obtainable in Belgium. (1920: 108)

Two examples for the kind of manual[6] that De Bauw must have had in mind have come to my attention. Both will be studied more closely because they seem to be the earliest printed vocabularies pretending to describe Swahili specifically as it was spoken in Katanga.[7] The first one was an 'Annexe' to a *Guide pour les émigrants agricoles belges au Katanga*, published in Brussels by the Ministry of Colonies in 1912. The *Guide* appeared in French and Flemish, and the text, but not the annexe, was signed by E(dmond) Leplae (Director of Agricultural Services at the Ministry).[8] In the form of questions and answers, Leplae's guide provides advice to future colonists. It recommends preparations to be made before departure and gives instructions for travel and information about tools, equipment, crops, and agricultural techniques suited to conditions in Katanga. An important theme is the recruitment and supervision of local labor. In that context the significance of language is touched upon (in the main text of the guide). The relevant passages are worth quoting *in extenso*:

> *What are the languages spoken by the negroes of Katanga?* Almost all of them speak Swahili or Ki-Swahili, which a European learns easily. At any rate, in the beginning some common words and gestures will be sufficient to make them understand what one wants. They are familiar with agricultural work and understand what they have to do when one shows them how they have to work. *How can the colonists learn the language of the negroes?* The Agricultural Service [of the Ministry of Colonies] will give to each family, free of charge, small books in which they find complete information on the subject of the Swahili language as well as a large number of common phrases. One can also obtain these at the Ministry of Colonies.
>
> As soon as they arrive in Katanga, the colonists will find that it is very easy to make themselves understood by the negroes and that it is sufficient for this purpose to know a very small number of words.
>
> The few words that follow are the most necessary ones in the beginning. The accent is always placed on the next-to-last syllable.

Yes	Ndio	Bring, Give	Leita
No	Apana	Do	Fania
Good, Beautiful	Mzouri	Where?	Wapi?
No good	Apana Mzouri	How much?	Ngapi?
Quick	Bio	Who?	Nani?
Very quick	Bio Bio	What?	Nini?
Here	Hapa	Why?	Kwa nini?
There	Koulè	Much	Sana
Come here	Kwisa hapa	Many	Minggi
Go away	Kwenda		

(Ministère des Colonies 1912: 38–40)

Fewer than twenty phrases, most of them consisting of one term only, are here listed as the essential core of a language: affirmation and negation, some indications of quality and quantity, two locatives, a few interrogatives relating to all of the above, and four verbal commands are what it takes to 'make oneself understood by the negroes'. *Not a single noun is part of that ration, let alone a pronoun.* With the innocence of the linguistic amateur the author of this list provides us with a precious document – the embryonic form of a colonial pidgin. His list could give much food for thought to the philosopher of language; to us it is valuable as an indication of the locutionary attitudes and fundamental communicative situations that characterized colonial relations at a particular time and place. Even though, strictly speaking, some of the phrases are questions and others affirmations, all of them express the imperative, commanding position that befits the employer of black labor. Granted, some of the entries are, after all, questions that ask for answers. That alone indicates that the user of this minimal vocabulary must have been able to comprehend more than is covered by these terms, perhaps through gestures (as pointed out by the author; see the quotation above) and by other non-linguistic means. That the colonists could supplement the listed imperatives with various ways of 'encouragement' is more than hinted at in the guide.

All of this is prefatory to the annexe that follows the main text. It bears the modest title 'Some words of the Swahili language spoken in Katanga'. Mostly it consists of wordlists in the strict sense. Items are not listed alphabetically but are grouped in the following semantic domains:

> Family, persons, the body, clothes, personal care (*toilette*)
> Greetings
> Food, cooking, meals
> House, furniture, construction, tools
> Trees, forest, road, streams, hunting
> Animals, planting, agricultural work
> Time, colors, numbers, buying, paying, money
> Caravans, porters, marching, camps.

Two grammatical categories frame these semantic domains: pronouns at the beginning (with, under the same heading, some adjectives, adverbs, prepositions, and conjunctions) and verbs at the end (followed by paradigms for the auxiliary verbs 'to have' and 'to be', the latter also in the past tense). The verbs in this section are all listed in the form we have come to expect, the imperative (a few verbs occur in other sections in the infinitive or the first person singular). For some reason, perhaps as an afterthought, the vocabulary concludes with terms for 'Illness and injuries'. The total number of items listed (excluding paradigms) is almost 600; a few appear in more than one semantic domain, as is to be expected (and as is later explained by the author).

At a few points the author inserts explanatory remarks; these are interesting enough to be quoted in full. Immediately following the title he repeats something that was said in the text of the guide:

116

> It is sufficient to know a very small number of Swahili words so as to be able, with the help of gestures, to make oneself understood by the negroes of Katanga.

But now he shows that he is aware of the limitations of his language guide and adds:

> The colonists could study Swahili from two brochures published by the Ministry of Colonies: the *Guide de conversation Swahili* by Father Colle and the *Vocabulaire Swahili* by Father E. B[rutel]. In the lists below they will find the words that are most commonly used. (Ministère des Colonies 1912: 1)

A comment follows the section on pronouns. It is characteristically sweeping but also offers a glimpse of the ethnography of labor relations:

> The negroes designate the whites by the word Bwana (master), followed by an adjective recalling a characteristic trait; Bwana mofoupi (the short master); Bwana unzouri (the good master); Bwana n'dèfou (the bearded master); Bwana talatala (the bespectacled master), etc. Every European is baptized by the blacks, usually in a very exact and sometimes ironic manner.

The author then goes on with an observation that is of special interest to us:

> In the summary language (*langue sommaire*) which is used by colonists in Katanga, certain words are applied to a whole series of analogous notions. Thus Moto can mean that which burns and is hot: fire, the sun, the temperature of water, the heat caused by fever, the searing sensation of burns, etc.
>
> The word Mti (tree) designates a tree, a stick, a beam, etc. To be precise one says: Mti mlefou (long piece of wood), Mti ngloufou (a solid or big piece of wood), Mti kiloko ngloufou (a picket), etc. (1912: 2).

We may file this for later comment and go on to another statement made under the heading 'Verbs':

> The verbs begin with Kou [the prefix marking an infinitive]; by omitting Kou one gets the imperative. Thus Koufania signifies: to make; fania signifies: make (1912: 10).

Finally it is said of the verb 'to be' that it is 'either not expressed or is expressed by Ni... The past is expressed by Alikouwa' (1912: 12).

No other grammatical instructions are given to the users of this guide. As is typical of the genre, nothing is said about the sources or manner of compilation. The vocabulary is, however, full of indirect information regarding the variety it describes.

To begin with, the mode of transcription (orthography) is predominantly of the French type, comparable to that used at an earlier period by Dutrieux and Becker (see Chapter 1). In many instances, however, the 'English' way of transcribing bantu sounds begins to interfere. Thus 'belly' is rendered as Toumbo (ECS:[9] *tumbo*), but 'I leave' is noted as Nakwenda and not Nakouenda. 'Aunt' is Changazi (ECS: *shangazi*) but 'water' appears as Maji rather than madyi or madji, and Bwana is no longer boina. This makes for much confusion but is also one of numerous indications that the compiler did collect and note the terms, or at least most of the terms, directly from informants or his own memory rather than copying them from a printed source.

Orthography attempts to render sounds consistently and 'correctly'. Inconsistent and imperfect as it may be, it reflects phonology, the system of sounds of a language or a variety. In this respect our vocabulary shows some interesting features. Congo Swahili in general, and Katanga Swahili in particular, are said to be affected by certain typical (i.e. recurrent, if not necessarily regular) changes if compared to East Coast phonology. The earliest and most extensive summaries of these features date from the 1850s or go back to research conducted at that time (Lecoste 1954 for 'Ngwana', and Polomé 1968 for 'Lubumbashi Swahili'). Polomé's list stresses the influence of Luba and Bemba and other traits that are 'typically Central Bantu'. If it is taken as a guideline, the following observations can be made on our vocabulary:[10]

1. *Palatalization before 'i' (optional but frequent), from 's' to 'sh', 'z' to 'zh', and also 't' to 'tsh'.* There is little evidence for this having been noticed as a typical trait by our author. He lists 'Eousi', black, and Kousimama, stand up, Maziba, milk, Sindanou, needle, and many others which in Katanga Swahili are likely to be pronounced as *mweushi, kushimama, mazhiba, shindano.* There is one very common and important term which does show the postulated trait (together with two others; see below) and therefore takes on a typical Katanga flavor: *Bilachi,* sweet potatoes (*ch* standing for *sh* in this French orthography). The East Coast form would be *viazi,* pl. of *kiazi.* But this is not the rule in our source. Polomé notes that palatalization is sometimes involved in *hypercorrection* producing the inverse result, i.e. a change from ECS *sh* to KS *s.* I found one example: *Soka,* 'hoe', for ECS *shoka.* Only one instance confirms *ti* to *tshi* palatalization: Djoua katji, noon (lit. 'sun in between'), corresponding to ECS *jua kati.*
2. *Devoicing from 'g' to 'k' and 'v' to 'f'.* The vocabulary confirms this in instances such as Kiloko, small, ECS *kidogo*; Ndoukou, brother, ECS *ndugu*; Ndeke, bird, ECS *ndege*; Mboka, vegetable, ECS *mboga.* On the other hand, Mgongo, back, would be *mukongo* in contemporary KS. Sougari, sugar, should be *sukari.* Again, there is at least one instance of hypercorrection (but not one that would be typical of KS): Mtou na gazi, worker, compared to ECS *kazi,* and KS *muntu wa kazi.* This gives rise to an imaginary etymology for porter(s): 'Wa pa gazi' (plural prefix + locative? + gazi). *V* to *f* change is confirmed in Ndefou, beard, compared to ECS *ndevu.*
3. *Insertion of an epenthetic η* (pronounced *ng*). It occurs in *Mangaribi* 'morning', for ECS *magaribi.*
4. *Shift from 'r' to 'l'* is amply documented in this text: Mouléfou, long, ECS *mrefu*; Balidi, cold, ECS *baridi*; Kouangalia, to watch, ECS *kuangaria,* are some examples. On the other hand, some items are listed in a form almost

never heard in KS: Barabara, highway, ECS *barabara*, should be (*m*) *balabala*, and Ngurube, pig, ECS *nguruwe*, is almost always *ngulube*.

5. *Weakening of 'd' to 'l'* appears in *Kiloko*, 'small', ECS *kidogo*, and in *Oulongo*, 'soil', ECS *udongo*, but in another place the same term is rendered as *Oudongo*.

6. *Insertion of 'l' between adjacent vowels belonging to two syllables.* On this point the vocabulary is quite confusing. It lacks this trait in instances where it consistently occurs in KS, e.g. Makaa, charcoal, ECS *makaa*, always *makala* in KS, and Foungoua, to open, ECS *fungua*, typically *fungula* in KS. Similarly Kaa, to sit, ECS *-kaa*, is *kukala* in KS; Kiatou, shoe, ECS *kiatu*, should be *kilatu*; and Mvoua, rain, ECS *mvua*, is in KS *mvula*. But then there is Lelo, today, ECS *leo*, which in KS is always *leo*. One oddity, otherwise characteristic of the resourcefulness of KS, is the listing of ECS *kofia* once as Kofia, hat, and, immediately following, as Kofila, cap, fez. Construing semantic contrast by seemingly arbitrary phonological means can be observed in other instances.

7. *Merging of palatal 'j' with 'y' except after nasals.* This is often noticed as one of the most typical features of Kingwana and KS. Our vocabulary does not contain a single instance, as far as I can see, not even in the case of Jambo, greeting, ECS (*hu*)*jambo*, KS always *yambo*.

8. The vocabulary gives too little information for us to be able to say much about changes in class prefixes. The author does not mention the existence of noun-classes (although he must have known of them if he looked into the Brutel and Colle manuals). Nevertheless, some indication can be found in the lexicon, and it is again surprising. Contrary to expectations, the syllabic *m* of the 1st and 2nd noun-classes does not change to *mu*, as is typical of KS: M'tou, human being, M'ke, woman, M'zoungou, European, Mti, tree, all correspond to the East Coast forms, while KS would have them as *muntu, muke, muzungu, mut(sh)i*. Only in a few adjectives does an *m* to *mu* change show up: Moulefu, long, Mokubwa, big, etc.; but this is not consistent, because what would be *muzuri* in KS is here listed as *Mzouri*. The form *kouamcha*, 'wake up', is also closer to ECS *kuamsha* than to KS *ku(l)amusha*. Changes from *vi-* to *bi-* and substitution of *bu-* for *u-* are documented in examples such as Bilachi (see above) Bilauri, glass(es), ECS *vilauri*, and in yet another variation on ECS *udongo*, namely Boulongo.

9. There is not enough evidence for some of the morphemic changes mentioned by Polomé. The prefix *ka-*, which has a diminutive connotation in KS, was apparently not known to the author (the one term that is identified as a diminutive, Kisoka, little hoe, has the ECS *ki-* prefix).

In sum, if checked against a list of traits considered distinctive of Kingwana and Katanga Swahili, our text scores unequivocally positive only on devoicing and intervocalic *l*; it is mixed and therefore inconclusive on *r* to *l* shift and *d* to *l* weakening. With an exception or two that may be significant, the vocabulary does not conform to expectations regarding evidence of the influence of Luba in palatalization, nor does it have an example for a *j* to *y* merger. Replacement of syllabic *m* by *mu* is documented only in a few adjectives.

What can be concluded from those changes that are documented? *If* the author collected his vocabulary from African informants in Katanga (or learned his Swahili from Africans in Katanga), and *if* he noted more or less exactly what he heard, one would have to say that in 1912 the variety spoken in this region had developed only some of the phonological traits that are characteristic of its contemporary form.[11] Not much can be done about checking on the 'ifs' preceding this conclusion (although they can be illuminated by some internal evidence from the text). What found its way into the vocabulary was filtered by the constraints which pidginization imposes on a language – or, rather, on learning and using a language. As noted already, the author ignores noun-classes and is therefore uncertain about singular–plural distinctions. For instance, Bilauri, a plural form, is translated as *verre*, glass (and accompanied by a synonym, copo, also in the singular). Tchoupa, on the other hand, is given as a singular form, while ECS *chupa* is rendered as a plural, bottles. Person in pronouns, and pronominal prefixes and possessives, are listed, but in a much reduced form. The result looks as follows:

	Person	Prenominal prefix (subject)	Personal	Possessive	Demonstrative prox.	rem.
	1st	Ni	Mimi	Angou		
Sing.	2nd	Ou	Wee	Yako		
	3rd	A	Yee	Iake	Houyou	Youle
	1st	Tou	—	Yetou		
Plur.	2nd	—	—	—		
	3rd	—	—	—	Hawa	Wale

(Ministère des Colonies 1912: 1–2).

The same omission of second and third person plural shows up when the author conjugates Kuwa na, to have (1912: 11). He notes only three examples for the past tense (all of them of the verb *kuwa*, to be) and it is in this connection that typical pidgin forms appear. Besides the correct form, Nalikouwa, 'I was', there is Ni alikouwa, for the first person, Ou alikouwa, for the second, and A likouwa for the third. It is as if the author began to compose forms in the pidgin manner (a prenominal prefix, interpreted as pronoun, plus a verb in the third person singular, interpreted as invariant) until he came to the third person singular, where this method did not work, and then abandoned his attempt; no plural forms are listed. A few more examples could be adduced for grammatical 'reduction', but the point is made and we can now turn to evidence for pidginization in the lexicon.

One of the traits one expects to find in a pidgin lexicon is pronounced polysemy, i.e. the use of one term for many referents. Because this vocabulary is arranged according to semantic domains, polysemy is easily recognized. Often the same term is listed under several headings. Another well-known trait is paraphrasing, which compensates for lexical shortcomings especially in the category of verbs. A few all-purpose verbs are combined with nouns and an occasional adverb such as in Koupiga m'bio, to run, Koupiga niama, to shoot game, or Koufania moto, set fire, and Koufania safari, set out on a trip. A similar mechanism works for nouns and adjectives, as in Maji na moto (lit. water with heat, fire), warm water; Maji na moto kiloko (lit. water with little heat), luke-warm water. All these forms one still encounters in kitchen varieties of contemporary Katanga–Shaba Swahili. Yet precisely because they are derived by means of mechanisms that are typical of many pidgins, they prove neither that the Swahili of the *Guide* represents the 'origin' of a pidgin variety in Katanga nor that there exists a continuity between this form and later vehicular Swahili as it was propagated in manuals for the use of expatriates well into the 1960s. Reasons for doubting any sort of continuous development are to be found in the lexicon.

In a number of instances (about 10% of the items listed in the *Guide*) our source shows significant deviation from current Katanga Swahili. Many of the instances are items one would expect to be part of a core of the most common terms, which are unlikely to change (except perhaps through loans from vernacular languages and French). A list of these words, compiled in the order of their occurrence in the *Guide*, is given below (Table 7). It contains information in three columns: Swahili terms and French glosses as given in the *Guide*, East Coast Swahili form and English gloss, Katanga Swahili form.[12] Terms in parentheses designate synonyms; paraphrases and current loans appear between square brackets. A question-mark marks gaps and precedes tentative glosses. These items should be checked with native speakers. Quite likely the gaps would then be filled with loans from French and local languages.

Most striking about this list is the number of East Coast terms used in the *Guide* which are not found in Katanga Swahili, either because they are obsolete or because they were never part of its lexicon.[13] One word for an important agricultural tool (no. 14) comes from Luba (Van Avermaet and Mbuya 1954: 236). In several domains the *Guide*'s vocabulary is more extensive than that of later Katanga Swahili manuals. If the pieces of evidence are put together – French orthography, little or inconclusive evidence for typical changes in phonology and morphology, too little grammar to form an idea of the syntax, East Coast influence on the lexicon – then the *Guide* begins to look more and more like a somewhat reduced example of the expeditionary genre (see Chapter 1), which we found characterized by its 'Arab' perspective, its openness,[14] its richness in certain domains, and its disregard for all but the most rudimentary observations on grammar. Incidentally, the attention given in the *Guide* to the domain 'Caravans, porters, marches, encampments' confirms 'the road' as its communicative setting. Its martial outlook (terms for

121

Table 7

No.	Guide	French gloss	ECS, English gloss	KS
1	Bibi	Grand'mère	*bibi*, 'grandmother'	*bibi*, 'wife', 'Mrs'
2	Kijagazi	Femme esclave	*kijakazi*, 'young slave girl'	(? obsolete) [*mutumwa kijana mwanamuke*]
3	Mtoumichi	Domestique	*mtumishi*, 'paid servant'	*boy*
4	Kitana	peigne	*kitana* (*kichana*), 'small comb'	*kichanuo*
5	Bourachi	Brosse	*burashi*, 'brush'	*kisugulio* (*bolosso*)
6	Marhaba	Merci	*marahaba*, 'thanks'	*aksanti*
7	Siagi (syn. manteika)	Beurre	*siagi*, 'butter'	*manteka*
8	Bira	Bière	*bira* (Sac.), 'European beer'	*pombe*
9	Kacha	Armoire	*kasha*, 'box'	*kabati*
10	Pata	Charnière	*pata*, 'hinge'	? [charnière]
11	Kitasa	Serrure	*kitasa* 'cupboard-lock'	? *kufuli*, 'padlock'
12	Mraba	Carré	*mraba*, 'square'	? [carré]
13	Choo	Cabinet (WC)	*choo*, WC	*musalani*
14	Loukesou Loukasou	Houe Houe	Kiluba: *lukasu*, 'hoe'	*yembe*
15	Kigai	Tuile	? *kigae* (dim. of *gae*), 'large potsherd'	? *malata*
16	Chokaa	Chaux	*chokaa*, 'lime'	*swakala*
17	China	Souche	*shina*, 'root-stem'	? *mzizi*
18	Dembo	Vallée	?	
19	Ilongo	Vallée	?	*bonde*
20	Gougou	Buisson	*gugu*, 'undergrowth'	?
21	Kahinda	Nord	?	*kaskazini*
22	Ziwa	Marais	*ziwa*, 'marsh'	? *potopoto*
23	Merkebou	Vaisseau	*merikebu*, 'foreign ship'	*mashua*
24	Kalamu (syn. *simba*)	Lion	?	*simba*
25	Houa	Tourterelle	*hua*, 'dove'	? *njiwa*
26	Kousaka	poursuivre le gibier	*kusaka*, 'chase, hunt'	*kulumbata*
27	Fahali	Taureau	*fahali*, 'bull'	*mume na ngombe*
28	Ngombe djike	Vache	*ngombe jike*, 'cow'	*ngombe muke*
29	Beberou	Bouc	*beberu*, 'he-goat'	*mbuzi mume*
30	Oungou	Chenilles	*ungu* (Sac.), 'caterpillar'	*tunkubyu* (plur.), (edible variety)
31	Mchwa	Termite	*nchwa*, 'termite'	*mchwa, muswa, inswa*, (edible variety)
32	Koa	Limace	*koa*, 'slug'	?
33	M'Boleo	Fumier	*mbolea*, 'manure'	?
34	Mtchanga	Pasteur	? *mchunga*, 'shepherd'	?[*mwenye*] *kuchunga kondoo*

Table 7 (*Contd.*)

No.	Guide	French gloss	ECS, English gloss	KS
35	Kouchanua	Fleurir	*kuchanua*, 'bloom'	? *kutosha maua*
36	Voandzu (syn. Njougou)		*njugu*, 'ground-nut'	*kalanga, njuku mawe, soja*
37	Mchikichi	Elais	*mchikichi*, 'oil palm'	*mungazi*
38	Oukvajou	Tamarind	*mkwaju*, 'tamarind'	?
39	Radi	Tonnere	*radi*, 'thunder'	*ngurumu (radi*, 'lightning')
40	Moja (syn. Mosi)	1	*mosi*, (obsolete), 'one'	*moya*
41	Foungou (La tatou)	1/3	*fungu*, 'portion'	? *kipande*
42	Franki	Franc	—	*franga*
43	Zariba (syn. Boma)	Enceinte	? *boma*, 'enclosure'	*lupango*
44	Kouangalia	Veiller	*kuangalia*, 'to pay attention'	*kulala zamu*
45	Adoui	Ennemi	*adui*, 'enemy'	?
46	Hasira	Colère	*hasira*, 'anger'	*kishilani*
47	Zulia	Tapis	*zulia*, 'carpet'	?
48	Seta	Écrase	*kuseta*, 'to crush'	*kuponda*
49	Teka	Puise	*kuteka*, 'to carry water to'	*kushota*
50	Anika	Sèche	*kuanika*, 'to set out to dry'	*kukausha*
51	Raroua	Dechire	*kurarua*, 'to tear'	*kukata, kupasula*
52	Fouta	Éssuie	*kufuta*, 'to wipe'	*kupangusha*

enemy, combat, anger, threat are listed in this domain) might also mean that the political situation which the agricultural colonists of 1912 were going to find in Katanga was far from being 'pacified'.

Still, we are no longer in the period of exploratory expeditions. Supervising labor has replaced earlier concerns with (military) information-gathering, and political–commercial negotiations. An emphasis on command and on the barest referential use of language is now even more pronounced. As regards grammatical categories, for instance, only nouns and verbs are listed, with very few exceptions. Almost all of the nouns serve as labels for concrete objects or physically perceptible features of a narrowly defined environment. The verbs, mostly listed in the imperative, refer to movements and activities connected with domestic and agricultural labor and with employer–employee relations. Unintentionally, one entry provides a pathetic comment on the reduced and restricted human relations to which this vocabulary corresponds:

the verb *Kupenda*, 'to love', is listed in the imperative as

Aime Penda – 'Love!'

THE MOST COMMON WORDS IN KATANGA:
A CURIOUS EARLY MANUAL

A real *trouvaille* in this search for documents has been the *Petit vocabulaire des mots ki-swahili les plus usités dans le Katanga*, published by the Belgian Ministry of Colonies in pocketsize, without indication of author, date, or place. It has a total of 45 printed pages, each facing a blank page, something for which we have seen earlier examples. Dating the *Petit vocabulaire*, as I shall call it from now on, is largely a matter of conjecture. Since it was sponsored by the Belgian Ministry of Colonies, it cannot have appeared before 1908. On the basis of internal evidence to be discussed presently (especially noting that it does not list terms relating to work in the mines), I believe that it is roughly contemporary with the *Guide* of 1912. At any rate, it belongs to a period before the Union Minière took the decision to make Swahili its official work language (1918). That the same Ministry should publish two Katanga–Swahili vocabularies at about the same time probably reflects internal bureaucratic divisions (the Agricultural Service was a special department).

The *Petit vocabulaire* is somewhat more extensive than the *Guide*, listing ca. 700 items, French–Swahili, in alphabetical order. Except for a note on orthography, it offers no explanatory comment whatsoever. It has even less grammar than the *Guide* but does contain two pages of useful phrases (with some syntactic information). Although the two vocabularies were published at about the same time with a roughly similar purpose, they could hardly be more different.

First some observations on phonology in the *Petit vocabulaire*. One gets the impression that the author was either more removed from the East Coast perspective of earlier publications or, at any rate, not yet under the influence of attempts at standardization (as exemplified in the Brutel and Colle manuals). This shows up in his transcription of terms. Some oddities can probably be discounted as idiosyncratic (e.g. *s* stands for both voiceless *s* and voiced *z*; *o* frequently stands for *u*; *j* represents *dy* but also *ny*, as in jumba, 'house', ECS *nyumba*). Otherwise, the text is more consistent in that it contains far fewer alternative spellings than the *Guide*. The problem of orthography is the only aspect that occasions an explanatory remark by the author:

> In no way do we guarantee the orthography of this little vocabulary; above all, we have tried to render, as exactly as possible, the expression and pronunciation of the most common words in the Ki-Swahili language. (p. 3)

Such stereotypical cautionary remarks can be found in many publications of this genre. Anxieties about orthography that were acquired during education may express themselves in this manner, but there is also a certain feeling of power derived from the fact that this language is being not only written but transcribed. The author transposes the words of his vocabulary from an oral to a literate existence. All this lends to 'orthography' rather more significance than a purely linguistic evaluation could admit. Most importantly, the author *did not choose the French orthography* we found in the *Guide* and earlier publications. It is no longer *Tchoupa*, 'bottle', but *tshupa*; not *kousaficha*, 'to clean', but *ku-safisha*, and so forth. Thus, the *Petit vocabulaire* becomes one of the first examples in the Belgian colonial sphere where the East Coast (i.e. English) spelling replaces the earlier French-oriented mode of transcription. The East Coast spelling was from then on used in all Katanga Swahili manuals (with few exceptions). Given the fact that the *Petit vocabulaire* seems to have been compiled without recourse to East Coast Swahili, it is likely that the author was English-speaking.

An even more striking contrast to the *Guide* appears with regard to phonetic traits characterizing Congo Swahili. Because the evidence is in this case so clear and plentiful, there is no need to document, point by point, the list of diagnostic traits established by Polomé (1968; see above, p. 118). In all of the seven relevant features the *Petit vocabulaire* shows Congo–Katanga Swahili *phonological and morphological characteristics*. This is not to say that the text is always consistent: there are a few instances where East Coast traits are maintained. Most of these, however, occur as alternatives to a Katanga Swahili form, e.g. M'boka, elsewhere Mbuga, ECS *mboga*, 'vegetable'; kuienga, elsewhere kujenga, ECS *kujenga*, 'to build'. M'bwa, ECS *mbwa*, 'dog', lacks the expected i-prosthesis (KS *imbwa*).

The variety of Swahili represented here, however defectively, has undergone phonological influences, above all from Luba (whereby it remains an open question which of the Luba languages of Katanga was decisive). This is confirmed by some peculiar entries in the lexicon. As I did for the *Guide*, I compiled a list of items in which the *Petit vocabulaire* differs from Katanga Swahili usage (checked against Verbeken, Annicq, and my own competence). The degree of 'deviation' (56 items) is roughly equal to the one found in the *Guide* (52 items) but *there is no overlap to speak of between the two lists of 'deviant' forms* (the single exception being Kiluba *lukasu*, 'hoe', for KS *yembe*). As will be remembered, most of the items in the *Guide* that differed from Katanga Swahili reflected East Coast usage. In the *Petit vocabulaire* most of the items on the list could be traced to Kiluba with the help of Van Avermaet and Mbuya (1954), although it remains unclear exactly which dialect was the source.[15]

The author is conscious of lexical borrowing; thirteen items he designates 'synonyms' for Swahili terms. At the end of the vocabulary he lists numerals and a few possessives in Swahili and 'en dialecte indigène' (39, 41), without telling us which indigenous language he refers to.

What makes the Luba loans in the *Petit vocabulaire* especially interesting is that, in contrast to phonological 'lubaization', they are not characteristic of Katanga Swahili. Only in a few instances are Luba terms that occur in the *Petit vocabulaire* also typical of current usage (e.g. *ludimi*, 'tongue'; *lupango*,

Table 8

No.	Petit vocabulaire	French gloss	Source, English gloss	KS
1	Ku-osa (syn. kupota)	Acheter	Kil. (537) -*pota*, 'to buy'	*kuuza*
2	Moganga buka	Apothicaire		
3	Ku-sikata	Asseoir (s')	Kil. (607) -*shikata*, 'to sit'	*kuikala*
4	Ku-hinga	Attacher	?	*kufunga, kutia*
5	Lelo	Aujourd'hui	Kil. (346) *lelo*, 'today'	*leo*
6	Mokwabo	Autre	Kil. (192) -*kwabo*, 'another of the same kind'	*ingine*
7	Biloko	Bagage	Lingala *biloko*, 'things, 'belongings'	*bintu, mizigo*
8	Ku-kupia	Brûler	Kil. (526), -*pya*, 'caught by fire'	*kuchoma, ku-ungaza*
9	Kapia	Chaud		*ya moto*
10	Mbwe	Caillou	Kil. (86) -*bwe*, 'pebble, stone'	*ibwe*
11	Pemba	Chaux	Kil. (510) *mpemba*, 'caolin'	*swakala*
12	Mongo	Ciel	? = *Mungu*, 'god'	*mbingu (ni)*
13	Mulopwe	Chef	Kil. (368) *mu-lopwe*, 'chief'	*sultani*
14	Maongo	Corps	?	*mwili*
15	Ku-shinda	Demeurer	ECS. -*shinda*, 'to pass time'	*kukala, kubakia, kushinda*
16	Mai (syn. mema)	Eau	Kil. (400) *mema*, 'water'	*mayi*
17	Kalabu	Epingle		*pengele* (Verb.)
18	Dilungu	Etang		*ziwa*
19	Tamba-tamba	Etoile		*nyota*
20	Mukaira	Faché	?Kil. (215) -*kaila*, to mock make fun of'	*kukasilika*
21	Moto (syn. modjilo)	Feu	Kil. (115) *mudilo*, 'fire'	*moto*
22	Buluba	Fleur		*(ma) ua*
23	M'toni (syn. mukola)	Fleuve	Kil. (271) *mu-kola*, 'ditch, canal'	*mutoni*
24	N'docho	Foie	? ECS *nso*, 'liver'	*maini*
25	Ku-piuka	Franchir	? ECS -*vuka*, 'to cross (a river)'	*kupita*
26	Tepe	Galon	ECS *debe*, 'tin can'	?
27	Tshofwe-kiboko	Hippotame		*kiboko*
28	Lukasu	Houe	Kil. (236) *lukasu*, 'hoe'	*yembe*
29	Manioko-pumbafu	Imbecile		*pumbafu*
30	Masafari	Ivre		*mulevi*
31	Oku	Là	Kil. (9) *aku*, (adj. dem. proxim.)	*huku*
32	Mulume	Male	Kil. (383) *mu-lume*, 'male'	*mwanaume*
33	Buki	Miel	Kil. (251) *buki*, 'honey'	*asali*
34	Sarkani	Militaire	? ECS *serikali*, 'government'	*askari*
35	Katwa	Mille (1000)		*elfu*
36	Gondo	Mois		*mwezi*
37	Kufwa	Mort	Kil. (151) -*fwa*, 'to die'	*kufa*

126

Table 8 (*Contd.*)

No.	Petit vocabulaire	French gloss	Source, English gloss	KS
38	Apana-yô	Non	Kil. (199) *yo*, 'expression of response'	(*h*)*apana*
39	Meso	Oeil	Kil. (620), *meso* (plur.) 'eyes'	*mecho*
40	Kafi	Pagaie	Kil. (141) *ka-fi* 'bad luck'	*kafi*
41	Mukati, Mampa	Pain		*mukate*
42	Tata	Pere	Kil. (679) *tata*, 'father'	*baba*
43	Wembe	Pigeon		*njiwa*
44	Bwato ou mutombwe	Pirogue	Lingala *bwato* Kil. (35) *bwato*, 'dugout canoe'	*mitumbwe*
45	N'zolo, kuku	Poule	Kil. (832) *nzolo*, 'hen'	*kuku*
46	Pepi-karibu	Près	Kil. (513) *pepi*, 'nearby'	*karibu*
47	Kushika	Prêt (c'est)	Kil. (606), *-shika* 'to finish'	*tayari, inaisha*
48	Moganga zambi	Prêtre	*munganga*, 'diviner, healer' + *Zambi*, (Bantu), 'God'	*mupadri, mupele*
49	Mosebo	Route		(*m*) *bala* (*m*) *bala njia*
50	Moio	Salut (action de saluer)		*yambo*
51	Fwanka	Tabac	Kil. (157) *mfanka*, 'tobacco'	*tumbako*
52	ku-koka	Tirer (sur une corde)	Kil. (266) *-koka*, 'to pull'	*kukokota*
53	Issatu	Trois	Kil. (584) *isatu*, 'three'	*tatu*
54	Moya, kimo	Un	Kil. (405) *-mo*, 'one'	*moya*
55	Kweri, kine	Vérité	?	(*u*) *kweli*
56	M'bio, bukidi	Vite	Kil. (252) *bukidi*, 'haste'	*mbio*

'enclosure'; *kudya* instead of ECS *-la*, 'to eat'; these are not on the list, which only records divergence between our source and Katanga Swahili usage).

What is the significance of the remarkable differences between *Guide* and *Petit vocabulaire*, assuming, as we do, that they are roughly contemporary? Do they represent varieties of Katanga Swahili? Or do they simply reflect the different linguistic backgrounds from which the authors approached Swahili: the author of the *Guide* through French and perhaps 'Kingwana', the author of the *Petit vocabulaire* through English and Luba? Both writers have put a personal stamp on their products by odd or fanciful transcriptions, by showing their peculiar idea (or ignorance) of Swahili morphology, and by their selection of items included in the lists. Both give rudimentary but sufficient evidence of pidgin usage. The *Petit vocabulaire* especially demonstrates a connection which deserves further inquiry: precisely the 'practical', action-oriented attitude to a vehicular language that presumably encourages pidginization also results in highly personal description. To dismiss these idiosyncrasies as signs of linguistic amateurism is, in my view, to oversimplify a rather more complex linkage between power, inequality, and 'reduced' ways of speaking. We shall return to this topic later on; first it will be instructive to look more closely at those features that give to the *Petit vocabulaire* its distinctive flavor.

To begin with, a number of items in the *Petit vocabulaire* appear in forms that differ from Katanga and East Coast Swahili, although they remain recognizable. Most of them can be taken as examples of the idiosyncratic liberties the author took with the language; some may be typographic errors. This is illustrated in the following short list:

Table 9

Petit vocabulaire		ECS/KS	English
Chercher	Ku-futafuta	*kutafuta*	to search
Compter	Ku-barika	*kubadilika*	to count
Demander	Ku-lisa	*kuuliza*	to ask
Jour	Yuba	*yua, jua*	sun(light)
Lit	Kitenda	*kitanda*	bed
Mauvais	Mobeia	*mubaya*	bad
Partie	Kipende	*Kipande*	part
Poursuivre	Ku-fuita	*kufwata*	to follow
tête	Kitswe	*kichwa*	head

Then there are instances where the author shows that he learned a rule of Swahili morphology – in this case that the prefix *ku-* marks an infinitive and is retained in monosyllabic verbs after the *-na, -li*, and *-ta-* affixes marking tense. He has heard these verbs in forms other than the infinitive and then reconstructs the latter, schematically and wrongly, in such a way that another *ku-* is added to the prefix, which he interprets as part of the stem:

Table 10

Petit vocabulaire		ECS/KS	English
Boire	Ku-kunwa	*kunywa*	to drink
Dérober	Ku-kwiba	*kuiba*	to rob
Donner	Ku-kupa	*kupa*	to give
Manger	Ku-kudia	*kul (y) a*	to eat
Mourir	Ku-kufwa	*kuf (w) a*	to die
Partir	Ku-kwenda	*kwenda*	to go, leave

As in the *Guide*, the existence of noun-classes and corresponding prefixes is not mentioned. As a rule, noun prefixes appear as integral parts of the lexeme

128

(unlike the infinitive marker *ku-* they are not separated by a hyphen from the stem). Again, some have erroneously a plural prefix where the French gloss suggests a singular form (e.g. Arbre, Miti, KS *muti*, tree; Oeil, Meso, KS *licho*, eye; Verre, *Bi-lori,* KS *kilauri*, glass). As far as I can see, singular–plural contrast is noted only in two instances: Homme, Muntu; Hommes (des), Bantu (both are typical KS forms) and Brique, Tufari (plural = Mutufari), KS *matafari*, bricks. Distinctive Katanga Swahili usage is reflected, phonetically as well as semantically, in terms such as the following:

Table 11

Petit vocabulaire		KS	English
Camisole	Mopila	*mupila*	sweater
Cause (à)	Maneno	*maneno*	because
Enceinte	Lupango	*lupango*	lot, enclosure
Farine	Bonga	*bunga*	flour
Fleuve	M'toni	*motoni*	river
Immédiatement	Sasa-evi	*sasa hivi*	immediately
Langue	Ludimi	*ludimi*	tongue
Retourner (un objet)	Ku-pindula	*kupindula*	to turn over
Serviteur	Boy	*boy*	servant
Sommeil	Busingizi	*busingizi*	sleep
Village	Mokini	*mukini*	village

Para- or peri-phrasing, to make up for lexical poverty, can be a pidgin trait, although it would be hard to draw a line between 'normal' circumlocutions and others that are actually necessary because of gaps in the vocabulary. Much paraphrasing occurs in current Katanga Swahili, and most of it is due to stylistic rather than strictly lexical reasons. At any rate, our author documents this form of creativity, albeit sparsely and in a manner one suspects as being idiosyncratic. The following five examples from the *Petit vocabulaire* are comprehensible but definitely not usual in Katanga Swahili:

Table 12

Petit vocabulaire		KS	English
Ecrire	Ku-fania mukanda	*kuandika*	to write
Encre	Mai na mukanda	*wino*	ink
Est	Wapi yuba anatoka	*mashariki, asubui*	East
Pantalon	Koti na mukulu	*sarwali, patalo*	trousers
Prêtre	Moganga zambi	*padri, monpère*	priest

Another example, Levure, Lawa na mukati, for 'yeast', I found neither in Verbeken nor in Annicq, but it does have the authentic flavor of Katanga Swahili, which continues to use *lawa/dawa*, 'medicine, ingredient, additive', etc., as an all-purpose word. In one last instance, enchainer, *Ku-funga maio-lolo*, 'to put in chains', the omission of a preposition between verb and noun (*na* or *kwa*) is idiomatic in East Coast and Katanga Swahili (ECS *kufunga mnyororo*). It is the sort of expression which traveled unchanged with the practice it designates; it is a phrase, not a paraphrase.

At the end of the wordlist, following the numerals, the *Petit vocabulaire* contains the only notes that provide some 'grammar'. A weak attempt is made to list possessive pronouns in Swahili and 'En dialecte indigène' (p. 41). The resulting paradigm looks like this (notice the merger of third person singular and plural; all plural forms are lacking in the 'native language'):

	Person	Swahili	En dialecte indigène
	1st	Yango	Ya me
Sing.	2nd	Yako	Kiobe
	3rd	Yake	Yendi
	1st	Yetu	
Plur.	2nd	Yenu	
	3rd	Yake	

This is followed by another sort of paradigm which appears as a list:

Ici	Awa
Un homme	Muntu
En avant	Ku-meso
Là	Aku
Des hommes	Bantu
En arrière	Ku-niuma.[16]

Singular and plural, proximity–remoteness, relative position, are here put together in what looks like a pathetic attempt to designate interpersonal relations without the use of pronouns (and hence without having to mark the speaker's position; this set of relations is, as it were, described from a point outside).

While there is almost nothing that can qualify as explicit grammatical description, we do get a glimpse of the author's 'Swahili in action' in two pages of text that are appended to the wordlist. What we are given resembles the section 'useful phrases' in many language manuals, except that no attempt is made to cover a number of typical situations. Instead we are offered a string of statements, imperatives, and questions addressed by a traveler to his guides and servants. Because these fragments are to my knowledge the first printed instance of a text pretending to be in Katanga Swahili they deserve to be quoted in full (English translation added in parantheses):

Quel est le chemin pour arriver au village de . . . (Which is the road to get to the village of. . .)?
N'dzila a kufika na mokini . . . wapi?
Passez devant pour me montrer le chemin (Go ahead to show me the way).
Pita ku-meso bwalo a kutandika n'dzila.
Je désire que vous placiez mes malles là (I want you to put my trunks there).
Mi anataka wei anatula sanduku yango aku.
Je m'en vais, mais faites attention à mes affaires (I go but you watch my belongings).
Mi anakwenda–Fungula meso na biloko yango.
Nous nous arrêterons au village de . . . Vous dresserez la tente, ferez de suite à manager, et mettrez en-suite de l'eau chaude pour mon bain. Je désire un peu d'eau chaude pour mon bain (We shall stop at the village of . . . You are going to put up the tent, then you prepare the meal, and then you warm up water for my bath. I want a little warm water for my bath).
Shie anashinda kwa . . . wei anatandika hema, sasa evi wei anafanya tsakula, tena wei anatia mai na sanduku. Mi anataka mai na motto kwanza bwalo na kunawa.
Je suis fatigué; faites mon lit; je vais coucher; puis vous éteindrez la lumière (I am tired; prepared my bed; I am going to bed; then you extinguish the light). Mi anatshoka; fania kitenda yango; mi analala; tena kuzima tala.
Demain vous m'appelerez au lever du soleil (ou quand les coqs chantent); fermerez la tente et mes malles; puis vous chercherez au village un guide pour arriver chez le chef . . . (Tomorrow you call me at sunset/or when the cocks crow/; then you pack the tent and my trunks; then you look in the village for a guide to get to the chief. . .)
Kesho wei anamwita mi kana Yuba anatoka (kana kuku anadila); anafunga hema na sanduku yango; tena wei anafuta futa kwa mokini, muntu na n'dzila bwalo a kufika pa mulopwe . . .
(Ministère des Colonies n.d.: 43, 45).

Just on the basis of cursory inspection a number of observations regarding morphology and syntax can be made on this text. There is, first, the omission of a copula in the opening phrase. *Petit vocabulaire* and *Guide* agree that the auxiliary verb 'to be' is 'not expressed in Swahili', although the *Guide* mentions the use of *ni* and acknowledges the existence of *kuwa*. Verb-forms are employed only in the present, or rather in a non-specified 'tense' derived from ECS/KS -*na*-. Conjugation of verbs, what there is of it, is done by combining an invariant third person singular with a varying pronoun. In the text just quoted the expression of person in verb-forms is thus limited to three: *mi* (first person singular), *shie* (a typical KS form for ECS *sisi*, first person plural) and *wei* (second person singular). Adjectives do not occur; *na* is used as the only preposition, except in one instance where *kwa* appears (in conformity with ECS/KS usage). The connective *a* occurs without modification (the most frequent form in Katanga Swahili is *ya*, with a tendency to observe class concordance with forms such as *wa*, *la*, and *za*). I have been unable to identify *bwalo na/a*, 'so that, in order to'.[17] It is unknown in current Katanga Swahili. In the kitchen variety it may have a corresponding form in *maneno ya*, 'because, in order to'.

131

The texts in our two sources are too fragmentary for the drawing of far-reaching conclusions. Nevertheless, absence of copula, reduction of verb-forms in every respect from person to tense, and the particular manner of combining a pronoun with an invariant third person singular, are all symptoms of pidginization. Lexical poverty is another trait postulated of pidgins and it may be the one of which speakers of such varieties are most conscious. It is, however, impossible to define 'poverty' exactly, and our sources offer little help in this respect. That their lexicon is 'limited' in quantitative terms is obvious. This is illustrated by Table 13, which provides a check of the two manuals against the first 29 items (terms beginning with letters a–d) in the Swadesh list of the basic vocabulary.[18]

Table 13

No.	English	Guide	*Petit vocabulaire*	Standard Swahili
1	all	Yote	Yote	-ote
2	and	na	na	na
3	animal	niama	Niama	manyama, nyama
4	ashes	Jifou	—	majivu
5	back	Mgongo	—	mgongo
6	bad	Baya	Mobeia	-baya
7	bark	—	—	mguno
8	because	—	Maneno	kwa sababu
9	belly	Toumbo	Tumbu	tumbo
10	big	Mokoubwa	—	-kubwa
11	bird	Ndeke	N'deke	ndege
12	black	Eousi	Niusi	-eusi
13	blood	Damou	Lamu	damu
14	blow	—	—	-toa pumzi
15	bone	—	Mufupa	mfupa
16	breathe	—	—	pumzika
17	burn	—	Ku-kupia	-choma
18	child	M'toto	Mutoto	mtoto
19	cold	Balidi	—	baridi
20	come	Kwisa	Ku-kuya	-ja
21	count	Koubadilicha	Ku-barika	-hesabu
22	cut	Koukata	—	-kata
23	day	Sikou	Yuba	siku
24	die	Koukoufa	Ku-Kufwa	-fa
25	dig	Kouchimba	—	-chimba
26	dirty	Chafou	Patshafu	-chafu
27	dog	Bwa	M'bwa	mbwa
28	drink	—	Ku-kunwa	-nywa
29	dry, be	—	—	-kavu

Both texts show considerable gaps (eight in the *Guide*, ten in the *Petit vocabulaire*; in other words, about one-third of the basic terms is lacking), without, however, agreeing in where they occur. It is doubtful that comparison with the complete Swadesh list of 200 terms would reveal 'systematic' omissions, and hence similarities between the two Katanga Swahili vocabularies. Qualitatively *Petit vocabulaire* and *Guide* differ so widely that mere quantitative evaluation becomes meaningless. Compared to the *Guide*, for instance, the *Petit vocabulaire* lacks specificity. As might be expected, a manual for use by agricultural colonists covers domains that are important to its users. The *Petit vocabulaire* does not list items by domain. Even though it contains more entries (ca. 700 compared to the *Guide*'s 600) it turns out on closer inspection that it lists fewer verbs (ca. 80 vs. ca. 120 in the *Guide*). Perhaps this 'nominal' bias should also be counted as a pidgin trait (corresponding to an overriding interest in labeling objects). Being both more general and more reduced, it is difficult to place the *Petit vocabulaire* in a concrete pragmatic context. Perhaps the text at the end is a clue to the author's 'generalized' perspective. He uses Swahili less as an employer or supervisor of labor, than as a roaming prospector or administrative agent.

CONCLUSION: NO MISSING LINK

Correspondences and differences between *Guide* and *Petit vocabulaire* could be worked out in more detail. It is doubtful, though, that much could be added to the pattern that is already visible. More than incidental divergence can be observed in five aspects: (1) orthography (French vs. English), (2) phonetic characteristics (weak vs. strong Lubaization), (3) lexical traits (East Coast Swahili vs. Luba origin of items not shared with current Katanga Swahili), (4) evidence for pidginization (considerable vs. extreme reduction), (5) semantic scope and perspective (specific, oriented to rural life and labor, and to *activities* vs. generalized, oriented to *objects*).

Sponsor, region and an orientation to 'the road', i.e. to the mobile form of incipient colonization, are areas of agreement between *Guide* and *Petit vocabulaire* that justify comparison; they make the lack of agreement in other respects even more conspicuous. That colonial authorities considered Swahili (rather than Luba or Bemba) to be *the* language of Katanga around 1910 is now sufficiently documented. However, the texts we have examined in this chapter do not give us a clear picture as to the *kind* of Swahili that was to be promoted among colonists and agents of government and private enterprise. The Brutel and Colle–Thielemans manuals were used mainly in Belgium for teaching future colonials. They are limited to essentials but do not propagate a 'reduced' pidgin variety; nor do they stress deviation from some standard (they are not advertised as 'Congo Swahili' or 'Kingwana'). *Guide* and *Petit vocabulaire* claim to describe what is 'most common' in Swahili as it is *actually spoken* by Europeans in Katanga (the *Guide* especially stresses this by referring to Brutel and Colle for the benefit of those who want to go beyond that level). This would seem to indicate that a generalized vehicular idiom or jargon had established itself in that area. Yet, certain traits which are considered symptomatic of a pidgin notwithstanding, the two descriptions disagree in so many important respects that they cannot be said to document a single pidgin variety commonly spoken to Africans by Europeans, let alone one that might have been used by Africans among themselves. Idiosyncrasies and circumstantial differences are conspicuous in the two vocabularies, and this may have to be taken as their really significant common characteristic. As descriptions, both texts are very *personal* statements. Their authors assert competences they acquired not from studying Swahili, but from learning and using it in communicative situations of an extremely limited sort. As far as one can tell from these vocabularies, human relations were restricted to contact during travel and the supervision of labor; questions (or rather requests) and imperatives, requiring a specialized repertory of nouns, a small number of verbs, and the most rudimentary syntax, appeared as dominant forms because they reflected domination. Inasmuch as these texts document pidginization, this should, perhaps, be considered the result of a certain kind of pragmatics – a style of 'talking tough and bad' – rather than (primarily) as the 'output' of quasi-universal grammatical and lexical mechanisms at a certain stage of language acquisition.

To say that the vocabularies are personal statements is not to deny their historical value altogether. Both are anchored, however slightly, in linguistic contexts that point beyond the vocabularies' immediate practical concerns. The *Guide* evokes East Coast influence, perhaps a survival of earlier commercial and political relations with 'Arabs' in the north of Katanga; the *Petit vocabulaire* shows influence from local languages and maybe even some interference from another vehicular idiom, Lingala. It also shows more than just incidental similarities to Katanga Swahili. Although contemporaneous, the two sources may differ historically in that the first looks back to the Free State era and the second adumbrates industrial, urban Katanga. But neither one nor the other can be taken as documentary proof for a pidgin stage of Katanga Swahili.

6

The end: illusions of colonial power

According to the canons of linguistic relativism pidgins are languages like others. This approach is prudent and formally correct; but, like other sorts of relativism, it must not be allowed to resorb through anemic generalizations all that is historically, psychologically, and perhaps esthetically specific. Pidgin Swahili *is* ridiculous and sometimes funny. That pidgins can embarrass or entertain, often the users as much as the observers, must have reasons analogous to those that make jokes work. Exaggerations, unexpected combinations, discrepancies between form and content, and violations of something deeper than linguistic rules seem to require relief through laughter. Be that as it may, speaking a pidgin and listening to it, keeps the participants in such exchanges reminded of a ridiculous precariousness even when the dominant relation is one of ruthless abuse and exploitation. I have argued that documented Swahili pidgins in Katanga are best understood, not as languages reduced to their most general patterns, but as personalized ways of selecting linguistic means for limited purposes. If that view is correct, then it follows that 'development' of pidgin speech should be triggered and determined by changes in the communicative situations it serves. This also applies to the history of *descriptions* of Swahili, which we take to be attempts at defining and controling linguistic means according to perceived or desired goals for communication.

By the mid-twenties, and at the latest when the economy of Katanga picked up speed after the great crisis around 1930, the swashbuckling times of conquest, pioneering heroics, and boom-town life were over. *Mumbunda na mampala*, the filth-spouting chimney and the growing slag heap of the Lubumbashi smelter, had become a symbol of European rule, personified as '*bwana* Union Minière'. As we know from later testimony, it was to the population of Elisabethville at once a looming, threatening presence and a comforting daily sight.[1] In relations between Europeans and Africans, open violence, which had its elements of unpredictability and farce, gave way to routine – a drab if protected existence under a paternalist regime. As some observers have noted, the gap between those who were employed by the mining company and lived in its compounds and the population of the *cité indigène* widened with the years,[2] and so did the one between European and African employees. Swahili remained the one means of verbal communication that, somehow, bridged these gaps. However, while it fulfilled that unifying function on the symbolic and (minimally at least) on the practical level, it did not become unified as a language. The creolized form to which we reserve the designation 'Katanga Swahili' became the carrier of a new urban culture and continued to thrive and develop – and to be ignored by Europeans for generations to come. Their problem, I shall argue, became a rather difficult one.

Swahili was expected to serve three purposes, two of them more or less explicitly, one tacitly. There was, first, the need for a work jargon to replace Kitchen-Kaffir. It had to remain as little as possible above the level of individualized pidgins and kitchen-varieties, so as to be easily learned by expatriates. Second, in religious teaching and certain branches of secular education a 'pure' Swahili was thought to be the only vehicle (apart from French, but that option was ruled out) capable of transmitting Christianity and Western civilization. Both kinds were to be used, in such a manner that they remained one-way conduits for command and persuasion, and that a third function of Swahili in Katanga – namely, to serve as an effective, protective barrier against free communication – was not endangered. The longer one ponders over the forms of what I have called 'descriptive appropriation', whose products were the vocabularies, guides, grammars, and manuals that make up the main body of documentary evidence for this study, the more impressed one becomes with the essentially defensive nature of codifications and formulations in the fields of language study and language policy. By carefully rationing French for Africans and presenting Swahili to Europeans either as forbiddingly difficult or as ridiculously easy, any free flow of exchanges that could have gone beyond the necessities of formalized relations was effectively discouraged. Professional routines and ideological stereotypes, it seems, always needed to be protected against the subversive effects of close human interaction.

As we approach the last decades of the period to be covered in this account, matters get more and more complicated. To keep our story as simple as it can be made without distorting history, I proceed in two steps. First, I shall describe the terms that were laid down for the use of Swahili in Katanga at, or shortly after, the end of World War I. 'Terms' are here understood as legal prescriptions, institutional settings, defined functions, and social–political constraints. In this frame of conditions, which remained relatively constant, I shall then place developments and processes that found their external form in a genre of Swahili guides which was typically 'Katanga' (and which stayed virtually unchanged until the end of direct colonial rule and beyond).

SWAHILI AND SYMBOLIC POWER

In Chapter 3 I explained at some length what is meant by 'symbolic power'. The term is *not* used to designate power that is 'only' symbolic (and therefore vague and weak); on the contrary, it was introduced to help understand colonial rule that relies on force and coercion but is ridden with internal contradictions and therefore needs reinforcement through cultural symbols. This implies a more narrow and more negative notion of 'symbol' than is current in anthropological and sociological writings.[3] The stress is on instrumentality and manipulability, both made possible by a capacity to ignore or repress spontaneous symbolic creations and to impose from above and outside what is thought to serve the aims of colonization.

Maintaining such power was the foremost concern in policies regarding Swahili in Katanga. In part, I have shown this in Chapter 4, where we found Swahili being used as a symbol of political 'reorientation'. What this implied for the codification of Swahili in Katanga should now be spelled out in more detail. From the point of view of the colonial administration and of industrial–commercial interests in Katanga, Swahili was above all a means to implement certain labor policies. As methods of procurement changed from short-term recruitment to stabilization, it became expedient to stress the symbolic value of Swahili as a vehicle of a Katangese regional and social identity. It is perhaps pointless to try and decide whether that reason for promoting Swahili was stronger than the more 'practical' idea that it would solve problems caused by multi-lingualism, help to unify government bureaucracy and labor management, and facilitate professional training and elementary education. But it is important to see that the promotion of Swahili was prompted by ideological, political concerns; that the primacy of ideology prevented authors of language manuals from appreciating the actual linguistic situation that existed when they began their work (around 1920); and that self-imposed limitations to describe only what was of 'practical use' further widened the gap between linguistic reality and descriptive codification. Paradoxically, or perversely, 'practical' qualifies these texts as symbolic in the sense defined above.

Besides demonstrating unity where there was little or none, Swahili served multiple purposes that were indeed practical, albeit in different ways to different speakers. Only some of these were directly controled by the colonial powers. Foremost among them was everything that pertained to administration and supervision – that is, to identifying, instructing, and directing workers. The institutions concerned included, apart from labor management, the territorial administration, recruitment agencies such as the Bourse du Travail, the courts, the police, and the army. Already before the War, an inventory and minimal description of vernacular languages in Katanga had been ordered so as to facilitate territorial and ethnic administrative divisions.[4] This served the *divide* of colonial rule; Swahili was to take care of the *impera* wherever command and instruction required linguistic means.

Narrowly linked to administration and labor management were elementary schooling and vocational training. In Katanga, even more than in other parts of the colony, education was to transform rural agricultural producers into wage-earners. Missionary orders and societies had agreed to perform that task in return for land grants, cash subsidies, or simply permission to operate in the area. In Katanga as elsewhere, Protestants were the first to arrive and to concentrate on rural regions. Catholic missions also had rural bases, but they were privileged in the emerging urban centers. In Elisabethville, the Benedictines were the first to arrive (in 1910), but the Salesians, who came a year later, and whose official recognition in Katanga dates from 1912, were by their specific orientation toward work among the youth destined to take the lead in setting up a system of schools and training shops.[5] Unlike the White Fathers in the north, neither of these two orders had vested interests in Swahili; both used it strictly as a vehicle. The Benedictines whose rural bases were in the region west of Elisabethville even took a rather negative attitude toward Swahili. They reserved all education not directly catering to the needs of industry and commerce to the vernacular language of their choice, Sanga.[6] The Salesians missionized the territory along the railroad to the south (with Sakania as their headquarters) and consequently relied heavily on Bemba in their elementary rural schools. As we saw from their responses to the 1917 survey (see above, p. 59), they had a less defensive attitude toward Swahili and were prepared fully to cooperate when the Government and the UMHK decided that it should be the language of urban Katanga.[7]

In the contexts mentioned so far, colonial agencies which in one way or another promoted the use of Swahili were also able to prescribe the form and manner in which it was to be employed. When we now indicate some situations where Swahili was still important to colonial aims but could no longer be directly controled, we are, as it were, moving down the scale of symbolic valuation. At the same time, we are moving up toward a higher degree of integration of ways of speaking with the popular use of Swahili by the urban masses. Given the scanty information we have about the period, it would be ill advised to construct an elaborate typology of speech situations. A few distinctions can give an idea of the degree of differentiation and complexity that existed.[8] This will at the same time highlight the extent to which 'symbolic' use of Swahili corresponded to colonial wishes and delusions rather than to realities.

In each of the contexts of controled usage enumerated so far formal speech had its informal counterparts. A few symbols will simplify the discussion of some of the most frequent situations, and combinations, that result from this distinction. We shall assume that Europeans (E) and Africans (A) were the partners in verbal exchange (leaving possible subdistinctions aside) and that, furthermore, their exchanges were characteristically (uni-)directional. It is safe to say that all E to A communication tended to be formal, permitting little other than task-specific, restricted exchanges of the sort to which a pidgin variety would be most adapted. Communicative restrictions of this kind not only operated within the verbal mode; they also necessitated habitual and frequent recourse to non-verbal means. What counted in the end was not mutual comprehension but *se faire comprendre du travailleur noir.*[9] A few observant Europeans gave an occasional thought to differences that might exist between E to A and A to E communication. They knew that Africans as a rule adopted the restricted jargon of their immediate European masters. This was a matter of expediency and – seldom noticed as such by the European – a widely enjoyed form of parody.

These situations do not cover all formal settings (see below), but it will be useful first to consider the contrast to informal communication that had the A to A form. Government clerks, policemen, school children and workers vitally depended on exchanges among themselves and with the wider population. From all available evidence these exchanges were conducted in Katanga Swahili, except when participants could easily resort to a common vernacular language or to a variety of Swahili other than Katanga Swahili (in the case of recruits from the north). These situations are here designated as 'informal' because they were not subject to direct colonial control. This neither precludes further internal differentiations (A to A communication permitted degrees of informality) nor should it be taken to suggest that these exchanges were somehow less important. Explaining (perhaps defending) and implementing orders down the hierarchical line of command, making inquiries amongst the population, exchanging information about, or discussing, lessons in school, all this was done in popular Swahili. Apprenticeship in the trades and even in the mines vitally depended on communication in Katanga Swahili. In official colonial documents and publications there is always much talk of the importance of professional training; and that may create the impression that skills in the crafts, and especially the less defined qualifications of workers operating equipment and handling materials in the mines, were mainly taught in schools and training shops. In reality, the UMHK found it always profitable to have most of the training done on the job. Older, more experienced workers initiated new arrivals against payment, a practice which continued to exist in the sixties and seventies, according to my own observations. It is safe to assume that this system was even more developed among employees in some of the smaller industries and services. If we furthermore consider the many situations where women depended on, and exchanged, information in Katanga Swahili, we see how vital command of that language in its uncontroled form was for a *savoir populaire*, the knowledge and skills required to survive in the towns.

Of course, it was not possible hermetically to seal off formal E to A from informal A to A situations. Some degree of 'seepage' occurred in areas such as the public courts, litigation in the labor compounds, certain informal contacts between missionaries and their converts, the sports, and other leisure activities. Europeans who worked in these settings were likely to acquire some competence in popular Swahili, but even they were most of the time 'protected' from direct exchanges by court interpreters, clerks and catechists. And if this was not sufficient to make them, as it were, immune to Katanga Swahili, their inclination to civilize and improve the language they heard certainly was.[10]

To complete the picture a further distinction is needed. It may at first seem to overlap with the formal–informal opposition, but it does add some

139

important aspects. This is the contrast between public and private settings for the use of Swahili. To start with the latter, private language-use (within the family, among friends, in casual encounters) allows us to state differentiation within the uncontrolled A to A type of informal communication. Presumably, in this private sphere a higher degree of linguistic interference from other languages could be tolerated, especially in exchanges between men and women, and between parents and children.[11] Most important for the development of a common language, however, was the experience of using Swahili for personal, intimate purposes. It must have been crucial for those speakers to whom Swahili became the principal linguistic medium of personal and social identity. A handy sociological term for this function is 'internalization'. This concept can take on additional historical significance if it is recognized that the implied stress on personal, individual acquisition corresponds to processes of incipient *embourgeoisement* in an urban population with rural roots. In this respect, too, Swahili fulfilled not only private but 'privatizing' functions. For instance, a private literacy emerged – i.e. the use, especially in personal correspondence, diaries, and similar documents, of a variety of Swahili which otherwise existed only in an oral form.[12]

If our distinction is to be productive, there should be, opposed to private use of Swahili in A to A situations, public settings which are not identical with those that were earlier characterized as formal. Decisive is the difference between predominantly symbolic, hence controled, functions and others which escaped control by the colonial powers. If one takes a look at public settings and events, as reported, for instance, in Fetter's studies of the growth of Elisabethville (1968, 1976), two interesting qualifications can be made. First, while the colonial agencies may have had an interest in imposing their rule on the public use of Swahili, they managed to do so only for relatively narrow purposes and areas. The UMHK certainly was most successful in this respect because it had a captive population, virtually interned near the sites of work and production. There was hardly an aspect of a worker's and his family's life that was not public in the sense of being open to inspection and intervention – marital arrangements, health, leisure, the state of living quarters, clothing and demeanor, movements (including vacations in the rural areas) and religious affiliation were all matters of concern to the employer. But, as we have seen, on precisely those occasions when the Company found it necessary to meddle with the workers' lives and to communicate with them about matters other than work, the *chefs de camp* and the European supervisors in the mines and shops would resort to a highly personalized pidgin variety of Swahili (with some qualification the same was true of other colonial agents). Symbolic use of Swahili for the purpose of control, therefore, neither created nor presupposed a sphere of public exchanges such as would have encouraged the development of a public register or form of discourse in Katanga Swahili. Yet it is difficult to imagine how this language could have developed the way it did if it totally lacked public settings. As it turns out, such an assumption need not be made if within the public sector we further distinguish between overt and covert situations and settings. Overt, 'official' public life was of course conducted in English and French; few Africans had access to either. Yet many activities within the African population went beyond private interaction. To the outside they remained covert in varying degrees, from going unnoticed to being clandestine. There was, for instance, the life of clubs, 'cercles', and associations. It lies in the nature of these activities that very little is *documented* about the role that Swahili might have played in maintaining a public life. We do know that it served as a vehicle for certain religious movements that were politically most threatening and therefore most closely watched by colonial authorities. During the period that interests us here the Watchtower or Kitawala Movement infiltrated Katanga from the south. By 1924 it was firmly implanted and continued to preoccupy administration and missions for decades after.[13] Research on religious movements that emerged in the 1950s has indicated continuities not only through persons who had been members of the Kitawala but also through certain tenets of doctrine and their formulation in Swahili. Popular religious discourse in today's Shaba has roots in movements of religious–political independence. At least one of the elements that made it possible to formulate complex religious doctrines and to transmit them, albeit in changed form, through several generations was Katanga Swahili.

We may now summarize what was to be accomplished by the distinctions we introduced. Even if much of the historical evidence remains to be filled in, as it were, the determinants of verbal communication in Katanga which we have been able to identify were far too many to be met by a single unified variety of Swahili. Furthermore, these determinants were internally connected. They characterized the colonial situation as a whole, because economic, political, and social complexity were, so to speak, an overnight phenomenon in Katanga. That means that the conditions under which Katanga Swahili emerged did not 'evolve' slowly and progressively and that the rise of that language is best conceived in terms of the image of a crystallization of a system of varieties whose linguistic status ranged from pidgins to a creole.

When we applied distinctions such as formal vs. informal, private vs. public, we had to employ numerous auxiliary concepts. Setting, occasion, participants, purpose/function, variety, register, and others indicate that by determinants we mean roughly what sociolinguists have called the 'components of speech events'. These have been described as rules governing verbal communication in given speech communities. In that sense, what we have done so far has been to construct a sociolinguistic frame in which to place and interpret the use of Swahili at a given period. Inasmuch as it helps to form a more differentiated picture of communicative situations this approach is quite useful. It presents problems when, as in other attempts to formulate 'rules' of interaction, the stress is laid on order and predictability.[14] The account I try to give here is not so much concerned with predictable social integration as it is with conflict and contradictions. What sociolinguists must treat as given – the speech community or the code, for instance – are the problems we try to understand. It is therefore crucial to the notion of determinants as it has been used here that it should not be reduced to 'rules'. Determinants are interrelated in such a way that it may make sense to treat them as a 'system'. But that must never obscure the fact that conflict and contradiction are among the ways in which they interrelate. For such a system to remain operative more is needed than rules; *rule* is needed – that is, the exercise of political power and coercion. It is this 'super-added value' of domination that makes a self-contained sociolinguistic approach not only awkward but in principle inappropriate.

'Symbolic' use of Swahili was to signal that political dimension. It points to a terrain in which the colonial society built a kind of bridgehead, from which Swahili was to be controled. Maybe this is too concrete an image, but it does evoke the aggressive defensiveness of colonial ideology and discourse, and it describes the function of the documents to be examined now. These descriptions of Swahili from the years between the World Wars took their generic form from those determinants of speech and communication that were the target for symbolic control. This made them, in the precise meaning of the term, symbolic language guides. That their authors should affect linguistic humility, limitation to practical purposes, and awareness of the tentative character of their works belongs to the generic traits of this kind of fiction; for fiction it was, measured against what a disinterested description of Katanga Swahili in the twenties and thirties might have looked like.

CODIFIED SWAHILI IN THE EASTERN CONGO: AN INVENTORY 1918–38

When we introduced the notion of *genre* into our analysis of language manuals we immediately had to add the idea of differentiation. Generic interpretation makes sense only if, at any given time, more than one genre is represented in a body of literature. The situation was relatively simple when we dealt with polyglot, military *vocabulaires* or even with manuals used in Belgium to prepare candidates for colonial service. The two early guides written in a pidgin variety of Swahili which we discovered were an occasion to narrow down our search and to focus on Katanga. But evidence for pidginization by no means simplifies our story. As will be seen presently, the Swahili manuals which appeared between 1918 and 1938 moved in the opposite direction toward diversification and 'improvement', and those that were addressed to Katanga were not the only ones to be published. An attempt has been made to present this wider context in Tables 14 and 15. For the sake of convenience, and also in order to make certain developments visible, the texts are listed chronologically. For a number of reasons, which will become clear as we discuss the material, manuals authored by the White Fathers have been treated separately (in Table 15).

The first overall impression one gets from this synopsis is of a much greater degree of variation than was found in genres described earlier. Still, it is a

Table 14 *Swahili guides for eastern Congo 1918–38 (except White Fathers)*

Author	Year	Sponsorship	Destination	Dialect	Region	Type
Salesians	1918/21	mission	trade school	improved Congo Swahili	Katanga/urban	reader, grammar, vocabulary
Quinot	1925	commerce, industry	expatriate employees	'Kingwana'	Eastern Province	vocabulary, grammar
Quinot	1926	commerce, industry	expatriate employees	'Kingwana'	Eastern Province	grammar, conversation
Soors	1927	administration	junior administrators	Northern	Eastern Province, Kivu, rural	conversation
Labeye	1928	UCB – colonial preparation	expatriates	'Kingwana'	Eastern Province, Katanga,	grammar, vocabulary
Whitehead	1928	mission	missionary personnel, schools	Kingwana	R.-Urundi Eastern Province, Kivu	grammar, conversation, vocabulary
Van de Weyer and Quets	1929	industry/UMHK	UMHK personnel	pidgin Swahili, Bemba, Kitchen-Kaffir	Katanga/urban	vocabulary, conversation, special conversation
Soors	1933	administration	judicial agents	Northern	Eastern Province, Kivu	special vocabulary
Verbeken	1934–6	private	educated Africans, expatriates	improved Congo Swahili	Katanga/urban	instalments in newspaper, grammar, conversation
Marists	1936	mission	school	improved Congo Swahili	Eastern Province	grammar, exercises, vocabulary, conversation
Verbeken	1938	?private	expatriates	improved Congo Swahili	Katanga/urban	grammar, vocabulary
UMHK	1938	industry	UMHK personnel	pidgin Swahili	Katanga/urban	grammar, vocabulary, conversation

143

patterned variation, one that is not due to accidental circumstances or to an author's idiosyncratic approach, as was often the case in earlier periods. The differences that are visible now express conditions under a colonial regime that has settled in. To begin with *sponsorship*, a division of labor (and of targets) shows up among the institutions of the colonial triad: government/administration, private enterprise, and the missions each have their own practical reasons for promoting a certain kind of knowledge of Swahili. This is expressed in the *destination*, explicitly stated or not, of these guides for different categories of users: agents of the territorial administration, the expatriate personnel in industry and commerce, African school children, students, and apprentices in the trades. Among the publications listed in Table 14 destination is stated in the title or preface or can be easily inferred. For instance, the Whitehead and Whitehead manual of Kingwana (which, incidentally, is the only one apart from White Fathers' publications to have acquired some scholarly reputation) contains not only Swahili–French but also Swahili–English vocabularies. This can only mean that it addressed itself to missionary personnel. That, too, made it exceptional. All the other manuals listed in Table 14 have a downward destination; not the writer's own reference group, but some lower, junior, or less educated readership is envisaged. Almost all the authors, therefore, take pains to stress that there exists a 'higher' form of Swahili, to which users who have higher linguistic aspirations are referred. These manuals, in other words, aim to describe Swahili for the lower strata of colonial society. As one of them puts it, the texts were conceived in such a way as to be within the reach of 'subaltern personnel' of European companies (Quinot 1926: 2). The formula *à l'usage de . . .*, which already occurred in the Free State period, now takes on a social connotation. Class differentiation within colonial society becomes one of the factors determining the generic form of language guides.

Under the heading *dialect*, Table 14 gives some indication of awareness in these texts that there was more than one kind of Swahili. The terms given in this column should be taken only as approximate labels, expressing the opinion of authors (sometimes stated explicitly, sometimes implied). Their claims would have to be checked by close, independent analysis. For our purposes, the following meanings can be assigned to the terms listed: 'Kingwana' (with quotation marks) is used by authors who want to indicate that the variety described is a derived or 'bastardized' form of some pure Swahili. Kingwana (without quotation marks) is used only for Whitehead's normative text. Improved Congo Swahili designates efforts to apply rules of East Coast Swahili, especially in the grammar and conversation parts. Northern (Swahili) is our own label for the manner in which only one of the authors (Soors) renders actual usage outside southeastern Katanga. Pidgin Swahili refers to a codification typical of manuals pretending to describe Katanga Swahili and will be justified in some detail below. In most of the White Fathers' publications *region* was listed as 'not specified'; this expresses their normative, standardizing intent, which implied disregard regional for variation.

The very least one can say is that 'dialect', read in conjunction with 'region' (i.e. regional destination), indicates certain broad distinctions that were absent or less pronounced in the earlier literature. It shows, first of all, awareness of geographical differences between the ways Swahili was spoken in the northeast (Stanleyville, Kivu, northern Katanga) and in southeastern Katanga. Notice that Verbeken, however, insists on calling Swahili spoken anywhere in the Belgian Congo 'Kingwana', anticipating a nomenclature which was eventually adopted by scholarly linguists. As might be expected, regional variation was taken to reflect historical developments. Most observers, and some of the authors on our list, noted relatively higher standards in proximity to the major routes and centers where Swahili entered the Congo with the Arab traders. One only needs to take a glance at the conversation sections in, say, Soors and Van de Weyer and Quets to realize that the difference between these texts could easily be described in terms of 'degeneration' from center to periphery. The problem with this view is that, after the ruthless anti-Arab campaigns in the last decade of the nineteenth century, Swahili centers existed, if at all, only in the form of a few *chefferies* (i.e. colonial administrative units) which in any case had lost contact with the East Coast. What looked like variation according to proximity to a postulated East Coast standard corresponded or overlapped, in the 1920s, with differentiation between a rural–agricultural and an urban–industrial environment. In the north, the remnants of Swahili presence were ethnicized as Wangwana or *arabisés*. The influence of the Swahili-speaking Arabs (and of their religion, Islam) was severely curtailed, and it was the non-Swahili, rural political elite that, with a conservatism characteristic of such groups, upheld the 'higher' standards of Swahili. Developments that were perceived as bastardization (pidgins and creoles) occurred above all in the rapidly changing world of Katanga, and the forms of 'pure' Swahili that were oriented to the past and preserved by a conservative traditional elite did not function as a standard for the speakers of 'progressive' varieties. It is true that Swahili-speakers from northern Shaba or Kivu continue today to perceive the differences between their dialect and Lubumbashi Swahili in terms of good and bad. But the point is that, in practice, they switch or change dialects when they settle in Shaba and make little or no effort to 'improve' the local variety.

To resume our comments on Table 14, although there is agreement in these texts about the limited, instrumental function of the language they describe, they differ widely as to the *type* of instrument they offer for learning. Most of these publications combine several of the types we encountered in earlier periods: vocabularies, grammar, useful phrases/conversation, readings, and even exercises. Exceptions are the manual by Soors and texts published by the White Fathers (1929, 1931). The days of the simple, 'open' vocabulary as a modest aid for travelers are definitely over. Manuals now present the language

145

Table 15 *Swahili guides for eastern Congo published by the White Fathers 1921–31*

Year	Destination	Dialect	Region	Type
1921	mission/seminary	'standard'	not specified	vocabulary Swahili – Latin
1925	mission/seminary	'standard'	not specified	grammar Swahili – Latin
1925	mission/seminary	'standard'	not specified	vocabulary Latin – Swahili, reader
1928	(Colle–Thielemans) colonial preparation	improved Congo Swahili	Eastern Province, Katanga, R. -Urundi	conversation, grammar grammar
1929	mission, schools	'standard'	not specified	grammar
1931	mission, schools	'standard'	not specified	exercises

as a complete, rule-governed entity, even if they do this in an 'abridged', fragmentary form.

By 1929, the White Fathers had produced their famous *Sarufi*, a scholarly grammar of Swahili in Swahili, this codification being the high-standard counterpart to the pidgin guides promoted by the UMHK (the first of which appeared in print in the same year, see below). This missionary organization had its headquarters at Albertville/Kalemie – that is, in a region where a conservative, high-standard Swahili was spoken. This enrivonment, combined with the traditional orientation of the White Fathers to the Swahili–Arabic sphere, influenced their policy of using Swahili as the vehicle of evangelization and (higher) education. The most conspicuous trait of the manuals in Table 15 (with the exception of the Colle–Thielemans guide, intended for colonial preparation) is the virtual absence of French, the official language of the colony. Up to the mid-twenties, the White Fathers in the Congo (and elsewhere in eastern Africa) tried to conduct training for the clergy, the highest form of learning then available to Africans, in a kind of Swahili capable of translating Christian doctrine directly from a Latin tradition without a detour through a European language. Religious idealism was certainly one of the motives for this (short-lived) practice. Implantation of Christianity and spreading of Western civilization were to be carried out separately, even at a risk that was often pointed out by missionary and lay critics – namely, that promoting Swahili was tantamount to promoting a vehicle for Islam.[15] The White Fathers (or at least the proponents among them of that policy; there were inside critics who disagreed),[16] with their tradition of attempts to confront Islam directly and of adopting for that purpose its language(s) and certain external elements of Arab culture (in dress, architecture), saw things differently. Nevertheless, from all we know about colonial policies in the Belgian Congo (see Chapter 3) it was to be expected that their scheme of direct transfer should conflict with the aims of the administration. Education and its vehicles, including Swahili, had to serve the principal purpose of transforming rural Africans into wage-earners with professional skills and various degrees of functional literacy. Because it needed their cooperation, the colonial regime would tolerate the strictly religious work of the missions. Any educational endeavor that threatened to short-circuit official purposes had, however, little chance of survival in the Belgian Congo.

As Table 15 shows, the Latin–Swahili texts were eventually discontinued and followed by what may have been a 'flight forward', the *Sarufi* of 1929 and 1931. The strategy was successful in that this text became the canonical high-standard Swahili grammar in the Congo and maintained that position for decades to come. It was intended primarily for educating Africans, and the 'dialect' it propagated was a purely literate one. Even in that respect it was programmatic rather than descriptive of an existing literary practice. It had little or no connection with any variety that was actually spoken; *Sarufi* remained an instrument of normative teaching and a point of reference for writers with literary ambitions.

147

It would seem that the White Fathers, by opting for the highest standards, lost touch with the specific practical aims to which the colonial regime had reserved the use of Swahili in administration, commerce, and industry (something that we noted earlier in connection with the Brutel dictionary; see above, p. 13). That this was not so can be understood if we go back to our earlier remarks about the symbolic nature of colonial appropriations of Swahili. One could even argue that if the White Fathers had not produced *Sarufi* an equivalent would have been sought elsewhere, because one way to maintain symbolic control *and* to pursue practical aims with Swahili was to adopt in this field, as elsewhere in 'native policies', a dualist approach. By branching either in the direction of an unattainable high standard or in that of an irremediably low level just above pidgin usage, passages between the two, in fact the entire spectrum of variation of Swahili as it was actually spoken by Africans among themselves, could be ignored and contained at the same time.

In what sense can Katanga Swahili be said to have been 'contained' by a dualist frame? It is more than probable that the standard dictated by *Sarufi* blocked spontaneous, grassroots movements toward literacy in Katanga Swahili beyond the 'private' type on which we commented earlier. Put slightly differently, literate Katangese wishing to write, and be read, in high-standard form had to switch dialects. The path to developing their own characteristic literacy was blocked by a quasi-mythical *Swahili bora* (pure Swahili) which was no longer equivalent to the refined way in which the Swahili of historical memory had used the language, but an artificial standard, in turn oriented on a normative standardization undertaken by another colonial power in eastern Africa.[17]

Toward the other end of the spectrum, the codification of a more or less 'improved' pidgin variety – less 'improved' before 1938, more thereafter – for use by expatriate, non-missionary personnel also required speakers of Katanga Swahili to switch dialects when communicating with Europeans. Maintaining this second language frontier was especially important to colonial society. While the high-standard 'ceiling' put a break on spontaneous developments toward literacy, the pidgin barrier protected colonial rule against the potentially subversive effect of normal communication in situations and about topics other than those required by supervision, instruction, and information-gathering.

'IMPROVED SWAHILI': UNION MINIERE AND A. VERBEKEN

What started as an inventory of Swahili manuals in the inter-War period soon turned into a sketch on dialect differentiation. Geographical, historical and sociopolitical factors were involved, first in the emergence, and then in the description and codification, of varieties of Swahili. Not only because it is sketchy, but also because it suggests changes from earlier to later states, our account invites further questioning. Are we talking about chronological succession, contingent on all sorts of events and conditions, or is there an idea of logical sequence, of necessary stages in an evolution? Can causal relations be inferred from evidence for succession? Everything that has been worked out so far in this study leads us to expect that no matching of causes and effects, however sophisticated and well-documented, could produce a historically convincing account. A first step toward a different kind of interpretation, and an *ostinato* theme of this book, has been to insist that we seek historical–political understanding, not neutral systematic explanation. Language-spread, and changes in linguistic form on all levels from phonetics to style, must be seen together with changes in the perception, utilization, and description of Swahili (a series of questions that comes on our methodological agenda in reverse order). Some or all of these interrelated aspects can furthermore be linked to historical events such as wars, crises, and epidemics, and to less obvious but specifiable conditions such as demographic factors, changes in technology, constraints on the economics of mining, urbanization, and so forth. The influence of each of these conditions is variable (and must be so in order to be distinguishable, even if we do not employ the concept of variables in an operational sense). In this historical inquiry variable conditions are linked not by statistical correlations but by an interpretation that attempts to read changing characteristics in a corpus of documents – language manuals mainly – as indicative of historical process. We seek to establish the *conditions of production* of language guides and related texts.

It may seem that such strenuous focusing on documentary material that is obscure and of doubtful descriptive value unduly magnifies the problems of a project that is itself complicated enough. Yet the twenty or so publications, from Dutrieux to Verbeken, which form the core of our material are so rich in direct and indirect information that I have constantly had to limit myself to generalized observations. Only now and then, in Chapter 5 for instance, did we take a closer look at details. Any single text on our list could, with some imagination and much painstaking research on background and context, be the subject of book-length treatment. In a word, selectiveness is inevitable, and one can only hope to cast a good bet when certain documents are given more attention than others.

This is also the case with the texts to which we turn now. All I wish to give is convincing illustrations of the ways in which one of the fences that were to contain Katanga Swahili was defined and erected. Setting high standards was not limited to a region; giving shape to a desired low-standard vehicle was; and, as might be expected, it was initiated by the Union Minière du Haut Katanga. The first language guide sponsored by that company was the *Vocabulaire français–kiswahili (et bemba) et éléments de conversation* by P. Van de Weyer and J. Quets (Brussels: Imprimerie Industrielle et Financière, 1929).[18] It consists of three parts: a vocabulary, in the strict sense, with Swahili glosses for ca. 770 French words listed alphabetically; useful phrases – that is, the typical imperatives and requests we encountered in earlier texts, ordered according to situations (travel, workers' camp, home); a list of special terms employed at work. Van de Weyer, a *chef de camp* at the UMHK, was the author of the first two parts. Absence of a grammatical section, many orthographic idiosyncrasies, and pidgin traits in the phrase section give this part of the text a close resemblance to the vocabularies examined in Chapter 5.[19] Especially in the 'elements of conversation' one gets the feeling that the author worked from his own repertoire and competence and that he faithfully reproduced the language he used in his daily work as *chef de camp*. It is obvious that he never studied the basics of Swahili morphology from a book. He segments and separates items and phrases in ways that betray his ignorance, even though his method has some consistency. Of the traits we observed in the *Petit vocabulaire* (Chapter 5, p. 125) several are even more pronounced in this text. Pigdinization, especially in verb-forms, appears somewhat mitigated. As regards the semantic scope and perspective of the lexicon (generalized, object-oriented), Van de Weyer and Quets is comparable to earlier pidgin texts. All in all, it can be stated that this codification of Swahili in a pidgin form was the point of departure of the series of descriptions that led up to Verbeken's canonical text.

That the choice of such a variety of Swahili was an option, not a necessity, is in my view demonstrated by the third part of this manual, whose author was J. Quets. His approach was radically different. For ca. 340 French entries (single terms or short phrases) glosses are given, with up to four synonyms each. The terms and phrases on the list are identified as being in Swahili, Bemba, Luba, Lala, Lamba, Nyanja, or Kitchen-Kaffir. Quets concentrated on actual usage of these expressions at work in the mines, the smelter, and workshops. Items are grouped according to these domains, and there is no reason to doubt the claim made in the preface: namely that this vocabulary represents terms actually 'heard in the factory [i.e. the Lubumbashi smelter] and verified by questioning workers'. In fact, this was, to my knowledge, the first attempt, and the only ever to be published, of an *empirical* lexical study of Katanga Swahili conducted under Belgian rule. It is a rich source, not only in the extent to which its lexicon covers various domains, but also because it reveals in many instances the semantic mechanisms by which a technical vocabulary was formed from elements in languages that had never before served the communicative needs of industrial work.

There are, first, the classic sources of lexical innovation such as loanwords (mainly from English) and ingenious paraphrases.[20] Metaphors, incidentally, are hardly used at all, while some of the most striking lexical inventions are based on metonymy (in the form of synecdoche and, perhaps, irony). In a metonymic relationship it is contiguity rather than similarity that determines the semantic function of a word. In this vocabulary, the most interesting instances are those where contiguity was established not so much by physical as by 'historical' association. When Quets informs us about the derivation of these terms he provides historical vignettes on Lubumbashi and the smelter. Some examples will illustrate this. A 'normal' case of metonymy (which is also a paraphrase) would be 'centrale' rendered as 'kumashini', lit. where the machines are (p. 53). Here a building/section in the factory takes its name from the implements it houses. *Courroie*, a drive-belt, is called 'nkanda (B.) (litt. peau, cuir)', i.e. animal skin, leather, the material it is made from (p. 55). *Tuyau, conduite*, a pipe or tube becomes 'pompi (K.) (altération de pump)', i.e. a term for an ensemble is restricted to one of the parts (p. 55). All these are, as it were, routine formations that can be analyzed without much local historical information. This is not the case with the following items: That 'kwa Mandefu (litt. chez le barbu)' refers to Steinberg's store makes sense only to those who knew the bearded Mr Steinberg (p. 52). Similarly, it would be difficult to trace the etymology of *chitumbo*, the term for coke-furnace, without knowing that the literal meaning, 'the one with the belly', does not (or not only) refer to the shape of the furnace but to a certain Jack Luke who was the (obese) foreman of that section in 1916 (p. 53). In UMHK terminology the smelter was divided in Usine A and Usine B. The African workers called A *mandona*, after MacDonald, formerly a recruiter for Robert Williams and Co., and B *ndjermani* ('German') after a Mr Zimmermann who constructed the test smelter in 1914 (p. 53). Similar principles are operative in terms such as *Kasumbalesa* for iron ore (p. 57); Kasumbalesa is the place where the iron was mined.

Because Quets only collected terms and phrases, little can be said about the variety of Swahili in which these items were used. In his transcriptions of the words he heard he is insecure about morphology, and hence segmentation, but much less so than Van de Weyer, and there are a few instances, for example of prefix concordance when using the connective *-a*, that are not likely to occur in a pidgin form (where the stereotypical connective is (*n*)*a*). Quets writes 'chapu *cha* mbau', carpenter's shop, 'ofici *ya* ndarama'; laboratory, 'mukini (muchini B.) *wa* sasa', new furnace. He also notes 'kutupa nkuni mu moto', throw wood on the fire, with the locative *mu* characteristic of Katanga Swahili (*na* would have been used in pidgin) and the correct lexical item for firewood (*mbao* would most likely have been the term in pidgin). In several cases, *ka-* (sg.) and *tu-* (pl.) class prefixes show a Katanga Swahili trait adopted from a vernacular language (although it may at the time still have been perceived as Bemba). These examples, of which more could be cited, suffice to underscore the degree to which an empirically established vocabulary reflected actual usage among the workers and, in this particular case, also the continued predominance of English together with Bemba and Kitchen-Kaffir. In 1929, more than ten years after measures against that influence had been decided upon, the results of Quets' approach must have been embarrassing to the authorities.

In spite of these linguistic and political shortcomings, the Van de Weyer and Quets manual seems to have served for another decade before it was replaced in 1938 by another UMHK publication, *Langage kiswahili: Vocabulaires et éléments de conversation à l'usage des agents de la Société* (Brussels: Imprimerie Industrielle et Fincancière, marked 'Première Edition'). The latter showed that this was to be a long-term project, but as far as is known it never came to another edition. The role that was destined for this manual was, it appears, simply taken over by the second and many subsequent editions of Verbeken's *Petit cours* (see below), not, however, without some changes in outlook and function.

Before we get to that we should at least briefly note that from the missions in urban Katanga no major efforts came in the years prior to World War II – with one exception, the Salesians' textbook for use in their trade schools.[21] Other *ad hoc* teaching aids probably existed and may be preserved in the local archives of the Salesians and Benedictines. Any major plans for an authoritative Swahili textbook that might have existed were probably preempted by the work of the White Fathers at Albertville.

This would leave the colonial administration, the third major agency, as a likely proponent of an 'improved' and therefore domesticated Swahili. The most that can be said is that government circles were interested in the idea; but in Elisabethville the initiatives that were eventually taken (at least, one should perhaps prudently add, those that resulted in printed publications) came from one person, Auguste Verbeken (1887–1965).[22] By the time he started his career as the most successful codifier of 'practical Swahili' in Katanga he had left colonial service. If he represented anyone but himself it was not the government bureaucracy but an expatriate bourgeoisie that grew in numbers and self-confidence and began to play an independent role in Elisabethville politics. In culture, class, and ideological allegiance it was by no means a united group, and conflict between assimilationists led by Msgr de Hemptinne, the Benedictine ecclesiastical leader, and his free-thinking opponents began to characterize local politics in the 1930s. Fights and machinations reached impressive levels of intensity and complexity after the great crisis, and, initially at least, organizations of educated Africans such as the mission-sponsored Cercle Saint-Benoît took an active part.[23]

Verbeken's creed was: 'The black man must be civilized in his language and through his language, because the principles of our civilization must be adapted to his concepts.'[24] He defended this anti-assimilationist position with energy and at great personal risk. By 1930 he had risen through the ranks of the territorial administration to become District Commissioner of Haut-Luapula, that is, of the region around Elisabethville. Then, in 1933, after 22 years of service, he resigned in protest against the new centralist policies introduced by Governor General A. Tilkens. After a brief stay in Europe he returned to Elisabethville and immediately took part again in local politics. He was a sponsor of the Cercle Saint-Benoît and tried in other ways to promote the cause of the *evolués*, the educated Africans. He was back in town in April 1934, and a few months later he started the first independent weekly newspaper for Africans, *Ngonga – Journal des indigènes du Congo Belge*. The paper had to cease publication after only 46 numbers. Verbeken, who had financed the venture from his own savings, blames, in his farewell message to the readers, the economic crisis. Other observers, such as Fetter and Jewsiewicki, noted his failure to get outside financial support in the form of advertising (by European business) and at least indirect pressure from ecclesiastic circles, who were not ready to tolerate a serious threat to their monopoly on information for natives.[25] Verbeken moved on to become editor of *L'Essor du Congo*, the city's leading expatriate newspaper (was this a consolatory measure on the part of the local powers?). In 1938 he left Elisabethville for Bukavu in Kivu Province and a series of high positions in several government and private organizations. After the War, it seems, Verbeken returned to his earlier projects. He organized an 'Information and Propaganda Service for Natives' – something whose intentions were probably better than its name – and even founded another newspaper for Africans, *L'Étoile-Nyota* which survived into post-colonial times.

Verbeken was a man of many talents and apparently had imagination, a quality which helped him in his work as a writer and ethnographer. As a linguist he was an autodidact and in that respect no different from other authors of language manuals which were eventually eclipsed by his *Petit cours*. His diary of 1911–12, the year when he started colonial service, already had some notes on Swahili, but then his career directed him to other languages. By the time he seriously turned to Katanga Swahili he had published, apart from a treatise on drum-language, one manual of Tshiluba and compiled another one in Kishila.[26] To his projects of improving communication among and with Africans by improving Swahili he came with a background in Tshiluba (or Kituba), and he shared this perspective with much of the new black elite, which was the first target of his efforts. Many of the *evolués* came from regions in Kasai Province, where he had served as administrator. One of the after-effects of the great crisis and of the subsequent mass dismissal of workers was an increase in ethnic–tribal associations and ideology, centered on the principal vernacular languages rather than actual places of origin. In all probability this was less of a return to pre-urban traditions than an urban strategy to cope with the economic and social vicissitudes of life in the cities. Little is known about whether and how the development of Katanga Swahili was affected by the revaluation of vernaculars during that period of growing 'tribalism'.[27] At any rate, when Verbeken conceived *Ngonga* it first appeared in four languages: French, Swahili, Bemba and Tshiluba. However, multi-lingual equality was maintained only on the editorial first page and there only until No. 17 (September 22, 1934), after which the Bemba column disappeared altogether. Even Tshiluba was eventually dropped from the editorial page (in January 1935). From the first to the last issue practically all non-editorial matter – city news, sports, court notices, advertisements – was in Swahili. That Verbeken and his Congolese collaborators reserved a key role to that language was expressed in a weekly instalment of a language course 'Pour apprendre le Kingwana'. This was in fact the first published version of Verbeken's Swahili manual and it may or may not have been accidental that the course, including elements of grammar and conversation, was completed when *Ngonga* folded on April 13, 1935.

In its editorial contents, *Ngonga* was frankly paternalistic; its general tone was pedagogical, sometimes indoctrinating. The 'Kingwana' course it offered was clearly to serve the same general purpose of 'civilizing' literate Africans. Swahili material other than Verbeken's course was of three kinds. On the first page one finds translations, most probably by one of his African assistants, of Verbeken's editorial. The variety of Swahili used here combines high grammatical ambitions with strong lubaization, especially in its orthography. A detailed analysis of this material would be needed to locate exactly the various ingredients that gave its special flavor to the Swahili used by *Ngonga*. It is my own impression that, because the writer(s) worked without accepted standards of literacy, the written Swahili tended to differ from the commonly spoken language both through grammatical 'refinement' and through strong interference from the writer's vernacular phonetics (most likely stronger than would have been noticeable in oral communication). Side-by-side with this 'original' material, *Ngonga* regularly published educative excerpts or adaptations from '*Elimu ya intshi*, Procure des Pères Blancs. Albertville', an elementary reader written in the Swahili promoted by the White Fathers. Finally there was some material (in the news section, folk tales, etc.) contributed by readers, sometimes with a less pronounced background in Tshiluba, or none at all. Many of these texts, as a comparison with recordings from recent years would show, are characteristic examples of Katanga Swahili and may have been the only ones in *Ngonga* to reflect popular usage.[28]

If Verbeken was the sensitive observer we have reason to believe he was, he must have realized how precarious his campaign for 'Kingwana' was in the face of so much variation in the Swahili used by contributors to his paper. It is safe to assume that this confirmed his belief in the need for 'improvement' (i.e. standardization), but it also caused a major change in perspective. A year and a half after the *Ngonga* adventure he resumed his efforts with another instalment course, now called 'Petit cours de Swahili' (no longer 'Kingwana') and published in *L'Essor du Congo* – that is, addressed explicitly to an expatriate audience. In 26 instalments, ending with No. 3275 of April 13, 1937, Verbeken again gave a sketch of Swahili grammar followed by *phrases usuelles* and elements of conversation. By February 1937 his plans for publishing a *Petit cours de Kiswahili pratique* as a book had been finalized (he announces its publication in *L'Essor du Congo* No. 3217 of February 2, 1937). It appeared in the following year at IMBELCO, the printing firm which also published *L'Essor*.

In the absence of explicit statements by Verbeken it is hazardous to guess what brought about this remarkable change of direction and purpose. Did he realize the futility of trying to 'improve' a language full of vitality by imposing on it his own limited grasp of 'Kingwana'? In favor of this interpretation are statements he made in an article, written for *L'Essor du Congo*, which appeared on May 1, 1936, in the period between his *Ngonga* venture and the instalment course for the readers of *L'Essor*. Verbeken advocates Swahili as part of a colony-wide solution to the problem of vehicular languages. Remarkable for the time is that he rejects too rigid a distinction between vernacular and mere vehicular languages. The latter arise 'spontaneously' and have already proved their vitality. 'This is the case with the Kingwana of the Belgian Congo', he continues 'which was born, lives, and develops according to the norms of local bantu dialects. It is neither a stranger nor an intruder. Its evolution, which started many years ago, proceeds. At this moment it would only need to be given uniformity.' He recommends the Whitehead manual as exemplary (and not the White Fathers' *Sarufi*!) and ends by expressing his conviction that 'Kingwana' will gain ground among the natives as well as among those Europeans who are in constant contact with them.

Greater linguistic wisdom, then, may be one explanation for Verbeken's changed orientation. But other questions can be asked. Did he react to resistance among his *evolué* collaborators, who perceived his linguistic work as part of a larger scheme to limit access to, and expression in, French for educated Africans, and who came to resent his efforts to promote African languages however well-intentioned they may have been? On two or three occasions when *Ngonga* published letters by readers touching on political and racial issues these were written in French.[29] To be sure, French was indicated by the addressees of these complaints; but this was just the point – educated Africans knew that their voice would have more chance to be heard in that language and found little satisfaction in expressing themselves in Swahili, except as a means of reaching the masses from which they were eager to distinguish themselves.

To continue our questions, was Verbeken after all coopted by the policy-makers in missionary and industrial circles and therefore obliged to resign himself to codifying a somewhat improved pidgin variety for use by expatriates? In fact, what was his role in preparing the UMHK manual that appeared in the same year as his *Petit cours*? Internal textual evidence (e.g. the composition of the grammatical section, including specific examples and formulations) makes it almost certain either that Verbeken collaborated directly or that the sketches he had published in *Ngonga* and *L'Essor* were adapted by the author(s) of the UMHK publication. Careful philological analysis and detective work, for which this is not the place, might very well establish that he was in fact the one who reworked the Van de Weyer and Quets text of 1929 into the anonymous *Langage kiswahili* of 1938.[30] Be this as it may, there is no doubt whatsoever that Verbeken's *Petit cours* – which stayed in print at least until 1965 (the year when its author died), and reached with that (its eleventh) edition a print-run of somewhere between forty and fifty thousand copies – became the quasi-official standard introduction for expatriates to Swahili in Katanga.[31]

A more thorough comparison of the grammatical and lexical qualities of the Swahili manuals that appeared between 1929 and 1938 explicitly for use in Katanga would require detailed technical analyses of interest only to a few specialists. It would not much change the general outlines that are now visible. Related to our main argument, these can be summarized as follows. Between Van de Weyer and Quets (VQ) and Verbeken's *Petit cours* (V) we see, above all, a change from a modest, thoroughly practical vocabulary, destined for

155

specific use at work in the mines, to a full-blown, if amateurish, linguistic description. VQ has only the barest traces of grammar; the UMHK text (UM) contains a brief sketch; V attempts to give a complete grammar (it even has a somewhat cryptic section called 'syntaxe'). In the vocabulary parts, VQ only has a French–Swahili wordlist with ca. 770 items; UM enlarges this list to 1200 entries and adds a Swahili–French list with ca. 1050 entries; in V the French–Swahili part has more than doubled (ca. 3000 entries), while the Swahili–French list remains constant at ca. 1050. If this is indicative of improvement, the conversation and special-terms sections show an inverse trend. Domains as well as number of entries are reduced between VQ and UM, and further reductions, as well as generalization of content, takes place between UM and V. These patterns correspond to expressions of intent in the prefaces or introductory notes to the three texts. VQ insist that they want to offer but a modest help for those who want to get familiar with Swahili 'as it is spoken in the various centers of the Union Minière du Haut Katanga' (1929: 3). UM has a more ambitious statement of the linguistic situation in Katanga. Numerous vernaculars are recognized and so is variation within Swahili, for instance 'the Swahili of Whites' (1938: 10). The latter, it is said, has been subject to many influences, depending on where the majority of African workers came from. Interference from English, and here, for the first time in our documents, from French, are noted. One paragraph in the UM introduction, in all likelihood written by Verbeken, differs from the work's otherwise factual tone. Here a guess is offered on the history of Katanga Swahili, with an insistence that this language is 'often called KINGWANA' (1938: 10). Both VQ and UM contain a reference, for readers who want to learn 'literary Swahili', to the work or works of 'Messieurs E. Bruttel [*sic*] & P. Delaunay, Pères Blancs' (thus in VQ 1929). UM repeats this with slight alterations but without correcting the spelling mistake in Fr Brutel's name, an indication that one was copied from the other and that neither VQ nor the UM authors were on intimate terms with the scholarly work of the two White Fathers. But perhaps this stereotypical reference is most significant as a topos characteristic of manuals in the pidgin variety (see the texts discussed in Chapter 5, where Brutel and Colle are recommended in a similar fashion).

The paragraph on the origins of Katanga Swahili is elaborated in the preface to Verbeken's second edition (1944), i.e. the one that replaced or continued the UM manual of 1938. It reiterates the claim that this language 'is called Kingwana' and speaks, more pointedly than in the other texts, of differences between 'classical Swahili' and this *lingua franca*. But even more important is a change as regards the user; not the foreman, junior engineer, or compound manager, but 'the European' *tout court* is now the target.

A development which we postulated as being generally characteristic of language appropriation by Europeans (see above, Chapter 3) here ran its course within a decade. From task-specific, modest description, based on actual experience and some research, however defective, these manuals moved to generalized, normative prescription. The symbolic once again outran the pragmatic. The 'improvements' which Verbeken's undoubtedly sincere efforts made on earlier descriptions were so many steps in the direction of codifying an illusion, a 'Kingwana' spoken by no one – not by the population in the northeast that could have had historical connections with Wangwana, not by the urban population of Katanga, and certainly not by expatriates, who, even if they studied his *Petit cours* assiduously (and in the 1960s I still met a few who did), quickly settled for an individualized pidgin politely referred to by amused Africans as *kizungu*, the way white people talk.

A VOICE NOT HEARD: A. MÉLIGNON AND THE 'REHABILITATION' OF SWAHILI IN KATANGA

This could be the end of our story, were it not for the chance discovery of an extraordinary document, made at a moment when research for this study was almost completed. In December 1939, a certain A. Mélignon submitted, probably to the directors of the UMHK at Elisabethville, a typed memorandum entitled *Réhabilitation du Swahili au Katanga*.[32] The carbon copy, which I found among the Verbeken papers preserved at the Royal Museum of Central Africa at Tervuren, runs (with an appendix and an extensive summary) to about 175 tightly typed pages. With a critical vigor and on a level of competence unexpected from a linguistic autodidact (who found the time to write this book-length treatise within one year while serving in the management of Sogefor, a UMHK subsidiary, at Jadotville/Likasi), Mélignon undertakes three major tasks. First, he places the language question in Katanga in the context of contemporary linguistic and, *avant la lettre*, sociolinguistic knowledge. He was familiar with basic issues regarding the nature and development of language, having read, or read about, de Saussure, Meillet, and others. He has followed Belgian colonial debates on the 'linguistic question', especially on the choice and unification of official vehicular languages (he comments on De Jonghe 1933, De Clercq 1934, and Verbeken 1936, among others) and is aware of similar debates in neighboring colonies (citing, for instance, Steere and H. Johnston, and referring to the International Institute for African Languages and Cultures and the Inter-University Committee of African Studies). He presents his own position on the matter of language choice with arguments that could easily have held their own in the company of experts then writing in scholarly journals.

Second, and this was the immediate occasion for his memorandum, he formulates the most detailed (and, if one accepts his clearly defined criteria, the most devastating) critique of what I have called 'improved Swahili' in the Van de Weyer and Quets manual, in Verbeken's instalment courses in *Ngonga* and *L'Essor du Congo*, and in the UMHK manual of 1938. More than 80 pages are filled with detailed comment and corrections, with counter-examples and alternative forms.

The third part of the study is devoted to an alternative proposal to teach a 'literary Swahili' to Africans as well as to expatriates in Katanga, and completes what must count as the best critical treatment of Swahili in this region and period. Even though it is, in the spirit of its time, predominantly normative and policy-oriented (as we would call it now), it contains a wealth of concrete observations on communicative practice and actual language-use in Katanga on the eve of World War II.

Because it is uncertain whether this document will be publicly available in the near future, I decided, with some trepidation, to conclude this study with a summary review of Mélignon's insights and proposals; not without some self-serving motives, I should add, because I believe that the positions taken by this active participant and astute observer strongly confirm many of the arguments advanced in this last chapter.

Although he wrote on a surprisingly high level of theoretical and methodological sophistication, Mélignon was above all driven by practical goals. Not just scholarly analysis, but 'practical comprehension' in the concrete situation of an industrializing colonial society, dictated his effort. With other colonials he shared a sense of the precariousness of the colonial enterprise. 'Mutual incomprehension of the language' (p. 6) was to him the principal cause of mutual incomprehension among Europeans and Africans in general.[33] What caused him to put so much energy and time into his memorandum was the realization that the attempts to 'promote' Swahili through the texts I have discussed in the preceding sections could only have the contrary effect – namely to codify a 'caricature of the Swahili [used] in the industrial circles of Katanga' (p. 16). He saw that, far from being an aid to better mutual comprehension, this sort of work would become an obstacle to normal, effective communication in Swahili. While others talked loosely, and often hypocritically, about promotion but meant control, Mélignon prefaces his critique with an expression of his belief in the independent life of languages:

> To become and remain the master of the evolution of a language is a pretension which neither individuals nor governments should be permitted to realize. Whichever language is adopted as a common language, its further evolution will be beyond our reach; that evolution occurs irrespective of conscious human efforts. (35)

Admiration for Mélignon's intelligence and lucidity should, of course, not preclude a critical appraisal, and it is perhaps best that such a remark be inserted now before we proceed with the summary. It must be said that his approach to the language question is, compared to that of the authors he criticizes, both more sophisticated and, at least potentially, more efficient as regards the aims of colonization, which, after all, he shares with his contemporaries. For instance, advocating non-intervention on the grounds of evolutionary laws of language development can, with historical hindsight, be recognized as advocating a more astute form of control. To preach respect for 'evolution' has been the strategy of those enlightened colonials who have felt assured that evolution would work for their aims. As we shall see later on, Mélignon was an unabashed elitist, a technocrat (if this is not too anachronistic a term) who was irritated by amateurism and sought more thorough and effective methods of colonization. As a man of integrity, he was aware of many contradictions in the colonial enterprise and of many dishonest ways to cover up these contradictions. His own response was not to doubt the entire endeavor, but to advocate a more 'modern' (his term), rational colonization based on his faith in a 'single and unique human foundation' (*plan humain*, p. 10) to be put into practice under Governor Ryckman's famous motto *dominer pour servir* (dominate in order to serve, p. 11).

But let us now return to his project for the 'rehabilitation' of Swahili in Katanga. That this language should be the principal vehicle of communication in this region he does not doubt for a moment. Historical reasons for that position do not concern him much. Although he explicitly states that his views apply to *industrial* Katanga, and thereby indirectly acknowledges historical–political aspects of the problem, he reasons in a way that anticipates later sociolinguistic arguments of the hierarchical, pyramid-type (see above p. 81). His model is based on logical, taxonomic, and ultimately evolutionary criteria. He distinguishes three levels. A multitude of 'dialects' and local languages serve on the lowest level of administrative divisions, that of *chefferies*. Some of these (he cites Sanga and Bemba) have assumed vehicular functions on the next level up, that of 'territories' and 'tribes'. Swahili occupies the apex, being the language of administration and of the missions in the urban centers (cf. pp. 38–9).

It is implied in the logic of such a description that Swahili no longer needed to be 'chosen'. It had demonstrably imposed itself as a matter of sociopolitical necessity. Because to him the role of Swahili was a *fait accompli*, Mélignon has no use for a special term to designate the Katanga variety. With a few well-put observations he therefore dismisses Verbeken's infatuation with 'Kingwana'. To him the term has only one justifiable use, which is to designate the way East Coast 'nobles' (his translation of *wangwana*) spoke (cf. pp. 40–3).

Next he takes up an assumption which is expressed in attempts to codify Swahili as *langage indigène* (a term used in the title of Labeye's guide), and which projects a faulty supposition of unity. With visible contempt for the naïveté of would-be codifiers he states: 'Not *one* type of this jargon exists; there are a thousand, as many as there are Europeans; there are no two persons who speak Swahili with the same degree of incorrectness' (p. 43). This observation, based on long local experience, directly confirms what we said earlier about 'personalization' in pidgins. Mélignon himself does not speculate about pidginization as a process. In a more static and normative manner he blames incorrectness on the absence of a standard (*étalon correct*), which should be literary Swahili. Nevertheless he does not permit his wishes to obscure realities. When he identifies pidgin usage in Van de Weyer and Quets and adds examples from his own experience he does admit that the language taught in this and other manuals 'is in fact – hélas! – more or less the one that is spoken by Europeans who have the reputation of speaking Swahili fluently' (p. 45).

The major reproach he has for those who support the teaching of Swahili in a defective, incorrect form is that they perpetuate a *chimère* (p. 48) and, in addition, fail to agree on their illusion. 'Tous ont raison, et tous ont tort' – they all are somehow right, and they all are wrong (p. 47) – is his final verdict on Van de Weyer and Quets, Verbeken, and the authors of the UMHK manual. Later, in Part II of his study, where he gives a detailed critique of these texts, he again, if reluctantly, admits that some of their pidgin traits are typical of Katanga usage, even of the way Africans sometimes speak. However, he immediately suggests that this is a spurious typicality and then advances an explanation that adumbrates the Bloomfield/Hall 'baby-talk' hypothesis of the origin of pidgins:[34]

> By adopting the barbarisms used by the natives we turn in the same vicious circle as those parents who, by imitating the puerile talk of their children, ridiculously prolong the use of childlike words among their brood. Incidentally, we should note that the Blacks don't practice this at all; children directly learn the language of adults. (p. 78)

In fact, Mélignon, by offering the baby-talk hypothesis *together* with a refutation on ethnographic grounds, can be said to have been, in this matter, a more astute observer than Bloomfield and other experts.

Among the traits in Verbeken's writings, and in the UMHK manual, that he selects for critique is their liberal admittance of loans, especially from English. This is an occasion for Mélignon to set up a battery of political arguments. He does not object to English loanwords that have entered Swahili long ago in 'Zanzibar, its home country'. But 'in Katanga, we, the Belgians, must deplore a veritable invasion of English words into our vehicular Swahili' (p. 88). He considers leniency toward this process as devoid of 'a shadow of linguistic reason or any other legitimate motive' (p. 88), even though its historical causes (economic dependence on the south, large numbers of Anglophone expatriate employees and of Rhodesian African workers) are clear enough to him. Belgians never were fanatic nationalists, he says, and he does not want to be taken for a chauvinist when he vows to continue his 'solitary campaign' against this tendency, especially – and here he reaches for some heavy political ammunition – 'in these troubled times where the future of Colonies appears so somber and uncertain' (p. 88).[35]

Mélignon opts for 'literary Swahili' as the only viable alternative. Several reasons underlie his choice; some undoubtedly must be sought in his biography. As a graduate of the Université Libre of Brussels he belonged to the liberal faction of the intellectual elite. Nevertheless, he seems to have been respected by missionaries,[36] and had himself especial respect for the linguistic work of the White Fathers – the Salesian reader of 1921 (see above) gets a grade of 'très honorable' (p. 143). As proof of his own credentials he cites his 'professor of Swahili written in Arabic, Bagari bin Aman, of Ujiji' (p. 74), with whom he must have taken a regular course together with other students. There certainly were very few colonials in Katanga, apart from some missionaries, who had comparable competences on which to base their pronouncements about Swahili.

His elitist outlook also shows in the proposals he makes in Part III for a program of teaching Swahili. He assumes class, and hence educational, differences among expatriates and therefore suggests different levels of introduction (without, however, compromising on the 'correct' form of the language, cf. pp. 142ff.). Taking up ideas that go back to the Independent State era, he also demands that proven knowledge of Swahili be made a condition for renewal of contracts and hence of professional advancement in a colonial career (p. 140). In other words, Mélignon positively values social hierarchy, and he extends this view to language acquisition and use. Still, this does not mean that he is blind to the many ways in which differences he disapproves of, those that are motivated by racism and bigotry, inform colonial attitudes toward Swahili. Now and then he draws some acerbic vignettes of the expatriate society of Katanga. Mélignon speaks of Jérôme Becker and his female African teachers, as a model that could only scandalize his fellow-Belgians. There are other examples such as his comments on the typically Katangese semantics of *boy* (p. 9) or on the term used for African women, *manamouk*. Having pointed out that the correct plural form for women is *wanawake*, he adds:

> Our European jargon-speakers will probably have difficulties in recognizing (in this form) the word which they employ, even in French. Saying 'the women' in Swahili they believe to be saying 'the black women' and when they say 'les manamouk' they wrongly employ the singular 'mwana muke' to form a plural. They attach a pejorative meaning to this expression which it does not have at all in Swahili. This went so far that the author of these lines profoundly scandalized a beautiful lady in Katanga when he, having overheard her once speaking of 'the manamouk' with that deep contempt that always masks an obscure and non-admitted feminine rivalry, tried to explain to her that, in the true sense of the word, she herself was a 'manamouk'. (p. 110)

It is in asides such as these that Mélignon shows a quality that was rare, and undesirable, among colonials. He had a degree of competence in Swahili, as well as practical experience and personal finesse, which enabled him to see through an enterprise that was fundamentally hypocritical – i.e. the enterprise to 'promote' Swahili in a pidgin form designed to serve strictly limited, one-way exchanges. He reacted as strongly as he did because he was intellectually offended by the sloppiness of the manuals he criticized. His political motives are another matter. His proposals, after all, shared with the initiatives he rejected a certain disregard for the language as spoken by the people; he too wants to 'improve' on popular practice. If realized, his ideas would have barred Africans even more effectively from using French and thus gaining direct access to their rulers' knowledge and politics. They would have helped to project elitism inside the community of Katanga Swahili speakers and to undermine the solidarity that was badly needed to resist at least the more atrocious effects of colonization.

We do not know how Mélignon's treatise was received. Evidently it came into the hands of A. Verbeken and made a strong impression on him.[37] It did not stop him from promoting his vision, or illusion, of Swahili. The authorities that could have listened to Mélignon were probably too busy with the 'war-effort' and that may in part explain why his manuscript disappeared in the archives. It is also safe to assume that they preferred to his rationalist, if elitist, project a *status quo* supported by a dualistic symbolic control of Swahili which was more in style with their principles of 'native policy'.

Notes

Introduction

1 In a letter to Johann Georg Zimmermann, dated May 9, 1785 (quoted in Fodor 1975: 18–19). The translation is my own, as are all translations in this study, unless otherwise stated.

2 See Fabian 1979 on rules and ethnography, 1982 on non-instrumental, 'poetic' borrowing from French in Shaba Swahili, and 1983 on notions of time in anthropological discourse.

3 See Polomé 1968 and 1972, Rossé 1977, and Schicho 1980, 1981, 1982. Other writings by these and other authors will be quoted in the text.

4 Foremost among them is Perrings 1979, which will be used extensively in Chapter 4.

5 'Valungwana,' i.e. Wangwana, are first mentioned in C. A. Swan's diary of July 17, 1889 (*Echoes of Service* (*EOS*) No. 223, July 1890: 212). Tipo-Tip first appears in a letter from F. S. Arnot of June 9, 1889 (*EOS* No. 226, October 1890: 312). Letters in Arabic (script) to Msiri from a Wangwana or Ruga Ruga raiding party are reported by Swan in the following year (*EOS* No. 229, January (Part I) 1891: 11). Swan also speaks of Msiri addressing 'Arabs' in a speech but does not specify the language (*ibid.* 12). 'Va-Swahili' as an ethnic term and synonym for Valungwana does not appear before 1890 (in Swan's diary of July 27, 1890, *EOS* No. 239, June (Part I) 1891: 140).

6 *Echoes of Service* No. 273, November (Part I) 1892: 258. (This is also the first instance where Crawford reports that he actually started learning Swahili.)

7 *ibid.*

8 A recent collection of papers on language spread (edited by R. L. Cooper 1982) contains a wealth of information and conceptual discussion (Swahili being treated or touched on by several contributors).

9 This document will have our attention later; see Chapter 6, note 12 for a fuller reference.

1 Prelude: expeditions and campaigns

1 A connection between American coastal trade (which left its trace wherever Swahili is spoken in the term (*a*)*merikani* for calico cloth) and increased Swahili expansion inland were noticed by Whiteley (1969: 45). His study remains the best treatment of the 'rise of Swahili', although it is sketchy for areas outside East Africa. An older essay by Struck (1921) and a recent history of Swahili in Swahili (Shihabuddin and Mnyampala 1977) are useful but suffer from similar limitations, as do Calvet (1981: 42–50) and Philippson (1982). See also Mazrui and Zirimu 1978.

2 The autobiography of Hamed ben Hamed el-Murjebi, known as Tipo-Tip, was first published and translated into German by H. Brode in 1902–3. This text served for an English translation by H. Havelock in 1907. A new edition and a translation into English were then published by

W. H. Whiteley in 1958–9. The most recent translation, into French, was prepared by F. Bontinck with help from K. Janssen (1974, which see for references to earlier editions/translations cited above). Bontinck's text is richly annotated, a mine of historical information on the times and contemporaries of Tipo-Tip. Language and communication problems are not prominent in Tipo-Tip's reminiscences. Perhaps this is to be expected because the reporting is mostly quite summary. The reason may also be that language was not experienced as a problem. Only in a few instances do we get a hint of the limits of Swahili when in a given situation it is mentioned that 'Kirua' (Luba) was used (which Tipo-Tip says he spoke; reported for 1870–72: see Bontinck 1974: 87, 88, 91). European travelers seem to contradict Tipo-Tip's own account (Bontinck 1974: 283, note 488; 175–6). Notice also that Cameron, who took the 'southern route' in his journey across Africa, included a Kirua, not a Swahili, vocabulary in his account (1877: II 347–56).

3 Henri Delaunay was among the first group of White Fathers who traveled from the East Coast to the Great Lakes. There is no indication in the journal of these early caravans (*À l'assaut des pays nègres*, see below) that he distinguished himself as a linguist. Fr Delaunay died in Africa in 1885, at the age of 36.

4 On the early missions of the White Fathers in the Congo, see Boyd 1978, Heremans 1966, 1978, and the monumental study by Renault (1971). Msgr Roelens published his reminiscences in 1949. The system of *fermes-chapelles* (settlements of freed slave 'children' around mission posts) was developed most successfully, from the point of view of the missions, by the Jesuits in the lower Congo (beginning in 1893 at Kimuenza, near Léopoldville). It was also experimented with in the east by the White Fathers, among others. As a method of missionizing and colonizing it was criticized almost as soon as it appeared, and the discussions continued many years later: see Thibaut 1911; *Les Jésuites belges et les missions* 1921, and 'De la légalité des villages chrétiens' 1922. Further research would have to establish to what extent these concentrations of presumably Swahili-speaking former slaves (and, one might add, the villages of runaway slaves one finds occasionally mentioned) gave shape to 'Congo Swahili'.

5 It is not clear from this brief statement whether Stapleton is enthusiastic or defensive about the spread of Swahili. The last section of this chapter will show that it was the latter. I owe this quotation and the one that concludes this chapter to W. J. Samarin.

6 This well-produced book was destined 'for use in the *fermes-chapelles*' (see above, note 4) and printed in Belgium for the Dominican missions near Stanley Falls. The preface concludes with a remarkable statement: 'Note also, that the teaching of *Kingwana* (*Swahili*), the only *classical language* in the Congo, is the best means to teach French to the natives' (Vicariat de Buta 1909: 7). This view of Swahili as a stepping-stone to (French) civilization one encounters occasionally before Belgian colonial language policies took their definitive shape after World War I. As we shall see in the following chapter, it was opposed by those who saw in Swahili a protection against Africans mastering the language of their colonizers. Although Belgian attitudes always remained somewhat confused, their development resembled that of German colonial policy. Here, too, initial enthusiasm for Germanization made place for the promotion of Swahili as a kind of screen between colonizers and colonized: see Wright 1965: 45, and Mehnert 1973: 388.

7 Although it would have to be substantiated with more documentation than can be given here, the thesis can be advanced that political resistance in the Luba–Lunda area to both Swahili and European expansion provided checks against the free spread of Swahili southward, at least for some time prior to World War I. Even Nyamwezi conquerors under Msiri, although they knew Swahili and used it in contacts with Arabs and Europeans, could not impose it (let alone their own language) on the populations of Katanga. On Msiri, see Verbeken 1956, and Munongo 1967.

8 In a recent bibliography of African lexicons (Hendrix 1982) 'polyglot' publications are listed as a separate genre (others are monolingual, bilingual, special and classified, conversation and

phrase books). The list includes much heterogeneous material, not only polyglot wordlists, such as Koelle's, but also vocabularies in manuscript, as part of travelogues and inserted in articles. Nevertheless it is interesting to note that of the 109 items that are not doubtful two-thirds were published before 1920 and, if certain titles that appeared after the period considered here are discounted, almost half before 1900.

9 The best-known among these, Lemaire 1894 and Stapleton 1903, will be examined more closely in the following section. Bibliographically, a polyglot orientation is sometimes not easily detected. Only by actually leafing through R. Buttaye's Kikongo dictionary (1909, first circulated in manuscript in 1901) does one discover that it contains also an extensive Swahili–French wordlist (and a Dutch–Kikongo part).

10 See Raddatz 1892; but notice that it dates from a time before German administration had settled in and adopted its Swahili-only policy (for references, see above, note 6).

11 This is Father Van der Burgt's remarkable French–Kirundi dictionary of 1903, which also gives German and Swahili glosses intended for use by colonial administrators.

12 On vocabularies in West Africa before Koelle's *Polyglotta*, see Hair 1966, and especially the very thorough study on vocabularies before the nineteenth century by Fodor (1975).

13 Heinrich Barth first published his *Collection of Vocabularies of Central-African Languages* in 1862 (it was reprinted in 1971).

14 On the background to Koelle's work, see Hair's introduction to the re-edition of *Polyglotta* (1963) and further references in his 1966 article (p. 209, note 1).

15 The language guides to be commented on in the following date from a period between 1880 and 1903. The role of language(s), first in making contact with, and then in administering, African populations was recognized before the Independent State officially existed, and repeatedly stressed by its officials in later years: see the informative recent study by Yates (1980). Foremost in the minds of planners and administrators was a common and official language which had to be an effective means in situations of command in the military and among workers. In the field, actual language skills, to be acquired and disseminated through 'vocabularies', were necessary, especially to assure the flow of information and to deal directly with populations not yet 'pacified.' This is not the place to treat EIC language policies systematically, but a few references and quotations will help to provide a minimum of background to this section. In a letter dated June, 1885, John B. Latrobe, President of the US Colonization Society and supporter of King Leopold's Congolese plans, wrote to the American intermediary in matters of the EIC, H. S. Sanford: 'What, *en passant*, is to be the language of the Free State? Has this been thought of? It seems to me worthy of a good deal of thought... Of course, my preference would be English, not because I speak English, but for reasons connected with commerce alone. What are the natives to be taught? I mean what language or is there to be a "pidgin English" or "pidgin French"? In the history of the world there have never been such opportunities as are now presented to mould the people of future ages in a vast continent' (Bontinck 1966: 332–3). Latrobe's dreams did not come true, but English continued to be a serious competitor for the status of official language. This could not be permitted for political reasons. Certain administrative documents indicate that the Government first decided to prescribe French for all communications with African personnel (as early as 1887: see circular letter or 1895, to be quoted below, note 20). Only when this proved ineffective in counteracting the continued influence of English were 'native languages' seriously considered as a vehicle for administration: see the circular letters of March 11, 1896, signed by Governor General Wahis, and of August 7, 1903, signed by Governor General Fuchs, respectively in EIC *Recueil mensuel*, March 1896: 46, and August 1903: 118). This link-up of the promotion of African languages with the defense of French is of special significance. We will encounter it again, this time applied to Swahili and French in Katanga (see the following chapter).

16 The length of a wordlist is in any event a very rough measure (it is not at all certain, for

instance, that French lists of a certain length will have a comparable number of different Swahili glosses). Therefore exact counts in this and other texts were not deemed necessary. An approximate total was calculated by multiplying the (average) number of items per page with the number of pages of a vocabulary. If this involves inaccuracy the error is minor and about the same for the vocabularies that are compared.

17 One thoroughly used copy of Dutrieux was discovered in the historical archive at the Royal Museum of Central Africa in Tervuren. It was part of a collection containing extensive notes including additional wordlists and phrases, some Swahili stories with translation, and the manuscript copy of a Swahili grammar in English. Additions to the Dutrieux vocabulary (not counting phrases) numbered about 500 (in French, English, and Swahili). The user who took his study of Swahili very seriously was Ch. Callewaert (see *Biographie coloniale belge*, Vol. V, 1958: 115–17). According to an inscription on one of the documents, he worked on Swahili when he was stationed at the AIA post of Vivi (on the lower Congo) in 1882. These documents are rich enough to deserve separate treatment, but two things of interest should be noted now: one is the obvious importance of English (see also above, note 15), the other is the fact that so much attention should have been given to Swahili in a place on the lower Congo. Both point to communication with the foreign (military) personnel as the major motive of Callewaert's exercises. In 1882, a majority of the soldiers and other auxiliaries were still recruited outside the Congo, mainly in Zanzibar or in West Africa (see Flament *et al.* 1952, especially 'Annexe 5', p. 510, on the origin of recruits).

18 Struck (1909: 76) simply has 'Dutrieux' without initials or title; Whiteley and Gutkind (1954: 48) write 'Dutrieux, P.'; Van Bulck (1948: 693) seems to have been the first to assign Dutrieux to the clergy, followed by Van Spaandonck (1965: 22) and most recently by Hendrix (1982: 168), who has 'Dutrieux, D. (Père)'. In fact there is nothing mysterious about our author, who was a well-known figure in the earliest phase of Belgian explorations starting on the East Coast. Pierre Dutrieux (1848–89) was a physician in the Belgian army when he joined the First Expedition of the International African Association (which departed from Zanzibar in October 1877). On his life, see *Biographie coloniale belge*, Vol. I, 1948: 352–3, and a longer article by Jadot (1950).

19 I only saw the second edition. Van Spaandonck (1965: 23) describes the first edition as 'LEMAIRE, CH., 1894, *Vocabulaire français–kisouahili*', but this is obviously the second edition of Dutrieux. Struck lists the first edition (with the seven languages in the title) and notes '2nd edition 1897': see 1909: 72. On Charles Lemaire (1863–1925), see *Biographie coloniale belge*, Vol. II, 1952: 603–8. The article fails to list the vocabulary among his writings but does mention his linguistic interests (he published on Esperanto, *ibid.*, p. 606).

20 On Émile Storms (1846–1918), also a member of an expedition of the International African Association (the Third, which left Zanzibar in September 1882), see *Biographie coloniale belge*, Vol. I, 1948: 899–904, and Heremans 1966. Lemaire was one of about twenty authors (almost all military men) of a traveler's and resident's guide for the Congo (Société d'Études Coloniales 1896). From a list of recommended underwear to a list of missionary establishments, this remarkable document contains detailed advice on all aspects of life in the Congo. It also touches several times on language and vocabularies. Already on the boat from Europe to Matadi, 'the study of an African idiom' is recommended as a way to pass the time (*ibid.*, p. 42). After arriving at Boma, seat of the Government and point of departure to assignments throughout the colony, the *Manual* recommends 'that everyone ... should seek to be shown the vocabulary of the language commonly used (*l'idiome usité*) in the region where he is going; one can make that request to the Secretary General. It is important to take along a copy of this vocabulary. We are planning to put out vocabularies of this sort among the publications of the Société d'Études Coloniales' (*ibid.*, p. 47). In a later section on 'relations between the resident and the populations that surround him' the necessity to know native languages is spelled out in more detail. The European should learn them through frequent conversations with his personnel, whom, at the same time, he teaches French. Especially officers of the colonial army

must know the native language for military reasons (leading troops, reconnaissance, negotiations with natives). Interpreters should be used only if absolutely necessary and with the greatest diffidence, or when the native style of negotiating requires that a person of authority should talk through an intermediary (see *ibid.*, pp. 131–2). The *Manuel*'s recommendations rest on government instructions. In a circular dated Boma, July 1, 1895, the then acting Governor General F. Fuchs repeats and spells out earlier orders relating to 'the necessity to draw up vocabularies of different indigenous dialects'. He then lists vocabularies that already exist at Boma: 1. 'for the route of caravans from Matadi to Léopoldville' (see below, p. 22); 2. 'of the language Wa or Dendi (Ubangi)'; 3. 'of Mombuto (zone of the Makua)'; 4. 'Français–Kiswahili' (this must be the Dutrieux text); and 5. 'of Kiswahili, Fiote, Kibangi–Irebou, Mongo and Bangala, by Lieutenant Lemaire' (EIC *Recueil officiel*, July 1895: 15–16). Collecting vocabularies, again linked to instructions regarding French as the official language, is the subject of article 18 in the *Recueil administratif* of 1904 (i.e. the official administrator's handbook: see EIC Département de l'Intérieur 1904: 91). By 1910 the same Governor General, Fuchs, found it necessary to attach certain sanctions to his orders regarding knowledge of native languages: the degree of proven competence will determine advancement in the colonial service. This is repeated in stronger terms in 1912, by which time colonial administrators were increasingly employed as judges in litigations among African workers and their employers – giving us a first hint of a shift of context from military–administrative to labor relations (see Chapter 2). These instructions appeared in Congo Belge *Recueil mensuel*, June 1910: 172, and June 1912: 248–9, respectively).

21 See Mazrui 1975 (title of Chapter 7).

22 On Wtterwulghe (1871–1904), see *Biographie coloniale belge*, Vol. I, 1948: 1003–6.

23 Grammars and vocabularies of a codified and 'improved' Lingala appeared a few years later (De Boeck 1904; Courboin 1908). On the different forms of Ngala (Ba-, Ma-, Li-,), see Heine 1973: 35, 56–7, and Yanga 1980: 112ff.

24 See, for instance, the wordlists in Stanley's *Through the Dark Continent* (1878: II 485–501) and in V. L. Cameron's *Across Africa* (1877: II 347–56). An earlier example was the 'Vocabulary of MALEMBA and EMBOMA Languages' established by Captain J. K. Tuckey with the help of a list of English terms furnished by the sponsors of his expedition (1818: 385, 391–9). At the end of this list the author makes a note which provides an interesting comment on the epistemology of collecting native terms: '"This vocabulary I do not consider to be free from mistakes, which I cannot find time to discover: all the objects of the senses are, however, correct.–J. Tuckey."' (1818: 399).

25 A slightly different version of this section was previously published as part of a study examining the use of Swahili in two travelogs, Becker's *La Vie en Afrique* and the already-cited journal of the White Fathers, *À l'assaut des pays nègres* (Fabian 1985). That essay should be consulted on background and for further references on the International African Association and these early expeditions (both go back to King Leopold II's Brussels Geographic Conference of 1876, on which see its centennial appraisal *La Conférence de Géographie de 1876: Recueil d'études* 1976). On J. Becker (1850–1912), see *Biographie coloniale belge*, Vol. I, 1948: 93–8.

26 These were his *Handbook of the Swahili Language, as Spoken at Zanzibar* (published in several editions after 1870) and his *Swahili Exercises* (1878–). Becker does not mention the latter but has a reference to 'Hadithi za Kiungoudia (contes de Zanzibar)' (1887: II 50) which must be the Steere's *Swahili Tales, as Told by the Natives of Zanzibar* (1870–). The form of Becker's reference (its 'French' orthography) makes it likely that he cites that book from memory.

27 This apical view of Swahili was shared, as a kind of topos, by many other writers. Becker's colleague E. Storms held it (see his memorandum in Fonds Storms, historical archive, Royal Museum Tervuren) and recommended Daull (1879) as an introduction. In 1885, Last stated in his *Polyglotta Africana Orientalis*: 'Swahili . . . This is the most important and widely known

language of all East Africa... It is so generally well known inland west of Zanzibar, that a traveller who could speak Swahili well would be able by it, without much difficulty, to find his way across Africa' (1972: 4). A generation later Sir Harry Johnston speaks of the 'SWAHILI tongue, which bids fair to become the dominant language of trade and intercourse throughout Central Africa from ocean to ocean... It is undoubtedly the easiest to acquire of all African languages.' He adds: 'Swahili [is] in some ways... as a language the best induction to the Bantu system' (1922: 38)

28   That this should be so had occurred to the men who pulled the strings, as it were. H. S. Sanford of the International African Association (see above, note 15) reports on a conversation with Stanley in which they discussed the idea of a 'permanent expedition' (see Bontinck 1966: 41). The role of women, which Becker describes in humane terms, was widely recognized as contributing to (military) intelligence. Already in 1851, Francis Galton, traveling through southwest Africa, noted: 'One great use of women in my party was to find out any plan or secret that the natives I was encamped amongst were desirous of hiding' (1891[4]: 120; see also p. 102). A similar observation is made by the Independent State *Manuel* (see Société d'Études Coloniales 1900: 76). On organizational problems involved in expeditions of the period, see an essay by Luwel (1976) on V. L. Cameron's journey from Zanzibar to Benguela, and Bennett's introduction to A. W. Dodgshun's journal of his travels from Zanzibar to Ujiji (Dodgshun 1969).

29   On Mirambo, see Bennett 1971 (where his dealings with AIA representatives are repeatedly mentioned).

30   See my study of the vocabulary in *La Vie en Afrique*, which includes an alphabetical compilation of lexical items and phrases, a semantic analysis of the scope and depth of this wordlist, and more detailed observations than can be made here on the kind of Swahili Becker learned and used (Fabian 1985). After completing the study on Becker, I found confirmation for my view on the use of exotic terms in several works. F. Hartog looked at 'translating, naming, and classifying' in Herodotus' *Histories* (1980, esp. pp. 249–59). He was in part inspired by Michel de Certeau, who focused on a sixteenth-century work by Jean de Léry (Certeau 1984 [1975]). Recently a French translation of an essay by the famous linguist, N. Troubetzkoy, became available (Troubetzkoy 1982). In this commentary on a fifteenth-century account by a Russian traveler to India, Troubetzkoy offers many suggestions that could guide further work on language use in travelogs. I am grateful to M. Harbsmeier, an anthropologist and specialist on early travel literature at the University of Copenhagen, for having directed my attention to these and other works.

31   The most convenient date for this change would be the recognition at the Congo Independent State at the Berlin Conference of 1884–5. Westward 'exploration' was curtailed immediately and Becker, who had become commander of the Fifth AIA Expedition, never left Zanzibar for the interior and returned to Europe sick and embittered. Like his colleague, Storms, he felt that he had simply been dropped by the Government of the Independent State, not realizing then that their activities in the east had been essential in securing the colony's eastern borders: see on this Heremans 1966.

32   On Stapleton (1864–1906), see *Biographie coloniale belge*, Vol. I, 1948: 894–5. Dating the *Handbook* poses difficulties. I have seen a second edition with a preface by Millman, dated Yakusu, July 18, 1910, although the publication date on the cover-page is given as 1903. Apparently, Millman published a French–English–Swahili vocabulary, probably his contribution to the *Handbook* (Millman 1917, cited in Van Spaandock 1965: 23).

33   Both assertions – that the Government had 'decided' on Lingala and that no halfway decent Lingala manual was available – are somewhat surprising. As can be seen from documents quoted earlier, the Government continues to insist on French as sole official language and speaks of 'native idioms' in the plural, without dwelling on differences between vehicular and vernacular varieties (see above note 15). Stapleton also must have been aware of Catholic missionary work on Lingala that was about to appear (see above note 23). On the other hand,

he was as a Protestant certainly aware of the suspicion that lay on him and his colleagues as promoters of 'English' influence. Proposing Lingala as a 'common language' may have been a kind of political compromise. See also below, note 35.

34 See Heine 1977. His model is convincing as a description of the 'logic' of hierarchical thought applied to language situations. I suspect that it is less useful as a description of actual situations, because a given language may serve both horizontal and vertical communication (e.g. French or Lingala in post-colonial Zaire).

35 1903, the year of the *Handbook*'s publication, marks a change in attitudes of the Baptist Missionary Society to the Independent State. Until then the BMS had maintained good relations with Leopold II's regime. The King had an interest in cultivating these relations (and expressed this in land grants and tax privileges) because they were proof of his willingness to cooperate with British subjects. As more and more evidence regarding the atrocities committed by rubber and ivory collectors became public, and the British-led international campaign against Leopold gained momentum, the BMS joined the opposition: see Lagergren 1970: 282ff., and Markowitz 1973: 6.

36 The document on which we are concentrating here is not an isolated case. Similar patterns of ideological distortion can be discerned in other areas of colonial 'concern', such as that of African religious movements. There is an analogy between labeling new linguistic media 'jargons' and 'vehicular languages' and new religious phenomena 'syncretism': see, on this point, Fabian 1983.

37 As a matter of expediency I used part of the Swadesh list as adapted by Heine (1973: 46–7). Standard Swahili terms were checked with Madan–Johnson's *Oxford Standard Dictionary of Swahili*.

38 The issue of diagnostic phonological traits of Congo Swahili will be taken up and discussed in more detail in a later chapter (see below, p. 118)

2 Questions and queries

1 Connections between language policies, a colonial system of education, and the creation of a working class will be discussed in more detail in the chapters that follow. Supporting evidence from documents and secondary literature will be cited at the appropriate places.

2 Ceulemans 1959 is the richest source on Arabs in the Congo up to the 1890s. On the persistence of Swahili–Moslem influence, see Abel 1960, Abemba 1971, Mulohwe 1969, and especially the annotated bibliography on the subject by Rossie (1975).

3 The term 'Kingwana' gained currency in spite of (or because of?) a lack of systematic description of the variety of Swahili it was supposed to cover. The manual published by J. and L. Whitehead in 1928 was the only work of any pretensions to appear before World War II (there were primers and other teaching aids, e.g. Mwalimu Yoani [-J. B. Hautefeld] 1912). In 1938, O. Liesenborghs still asked 'What is Kingwana?' (the title of his article). His answer, not unlike that of later writers, consists of a global judgment (Kingwana is inferior to Swahili) and a laundry list of deviant traits, most of them phonetic. Phonology also preoccupied Harris and Lukoff in their 1942 paper. After the War, B. Lecoste published a series of short articles culminating in his 1954 essay presenting Kingwana as a dialect of Swahili. Apart from an isolated more recent vocabulary (Spinette 1960), this is about all the first-hand description of Kingwana that exists. (Harries 1955 relies on secondary sources, and later writers such as Polomé, e.g. 1968, Gilman 1970, 1976, Hamiss-Kitumboy 1973, prefer to speak of 'Swahili' with a regional qualifier.)

4 E. Polomé, in some remarks on the history of Swahili in the Congo, takes an ambiguous position. On the one hand he points out a discontinuity (and therefore dialectal differentiation) between the northeast and Katanga. But then he affirms the hypothesis of a single, continuous diffusion through Arab traders and Msiri and his empire (1967: 1, 7–8). Later he realizes that if one were to accept the Msiri hypothesis at all one would have to postulate that

Swahili arrived in the Congo along two routes (and at different times) – through a northern Arab connection and a southern Nyamwezi link (see 1972: 68).

5 See Vansina 1966 and 1976, who gives an impressive account of the vastness and historical depth of an interaction sphere in this ecological zone reaching across the continent.

6 See also Tournay–Detillieux 1909: 111–14, for summaries of discussions in the Chamber, where it is even more apparent than in Halewyck that the status of the Flemish language was the 'hidden agenda'. The genesis and political background of the Charter are analyzed by Stengers (1963), who, unfortunately, does not comment on Article 3.

7 This is the original text of Article 3:

> L' emploi des langues est facultatif. II sera réglé par des décrets de manière à grantir les droits des Belges et des Congolais, et seulement pour les actes de 1' autorité publique et pour less affaires judiciaires.
>
> Les Belges jouiront au Congo, en ces matières, de garanties semblables à celles qui leur sont assurées en Belge. Des décrets seront promulgés à cet effet au plus tard dans les cinq ans qui suivront la promulgation de la présente loi. Tous les décrets et règlements ayant un caractère ġeńeral sont rédigés et publiés en langue française et en langue flamande. Les deux textes sont officiels. (Halewyck 1910: 109)

8 Notice the lack of precision in the note, where Kongo–Fiote is called the *language* of the lower Congo, Bangala the *trade language* of the upper Congo. Swahili is identified neither as a language nor as a trade language and merely said to be 'very widespread' in the eastern part of the colony. Kiluba again is qualified as a *language* of the Baluba in the Kasai, but it is not yet distinguished as Tshiluba.

9 Almost all the material to be treated in this section is preserved in File M 645 in the archives of the Ministry of Colonies in Brussels: The file contains correspondence, drafts for a questionnaire and most of the responses from the Congo to a survey on education conducted (between 1916 and 1918, counting preparation and evaluation) by the Governor General at Boma for the Belgian Government, which was then operating from exile in London. These documents are put together somewhat haphazardly in several folders; many of them are copies, and they are obviously not complete. Nevertheless, the broad outlines of the project and its results are well documented.

10 Return on the questionnaire was slow. File M 645 contains the draft of a telegram from London to the Governor General, 'Speed up survey education', dated May 11, 1917. It is a sign of the importance attached to the subject that the survey should have been conducted at all in these troubled years.

11 Because return on the questionnaire was patchy (or is incompletely preserved in File M 645) it would not be very useful to tabulate the results and evaluate them quantitatively. I have instead chosen to illustrate salient issues with characteristic statements quoted directly from the documents. Information on return may be summarized as follows:

1. As far as administrators are concerned, the questionnaire was presumably sent to all the district commissioners and their *premier adjoints*. According to the official Annual Report for 1916 (Congo Belge 1918: 2–5), the Congo then counted 22 districts, which would result, ideally, in 44 responses. Information on the holders of these offices in 1917–18 is not easily available (the official *Annuaire*, the standard source for such information, was not published during the war years) and many signatures on the responses are illegible. Altogether File M 645 contains 20 completed questionnaires returned by administrators (and one covering letter without the response). In other words, fewer than half of the government agents are represented.

2. File M 645 contains a printed and annotated list of Belgian commercial and industrial establishments operating in the Congo (outside Katanga) and in Katanga – the division is

significant for the spirit of the times. With it is preserved the draft of the covering letter (dated London, June 28, 1917) that was sent out together with the questionnaire. About 50 companies are listed (the figure is approximate because of some overlap among the two sections Congo/Katanga). 28 are specially marked, presumably to suggest the sample to be chosen by the Ministry. 19 responses (in some cases from companies not specially marked on the list) are preserved. Return from businessmen was higher than from administrators. It must be said, however, that their return was mostly quite short and uninformative.

12 They are referring to a variety of Tshiluba that went by this name, not to the pidgin and creole varieties, based on Kikongo, also known as Kituba: see Heine 1973: 54–5, and elsewhere, with further references.

13 File M 645 contains sixteen reactions, eight from superiors of Catholic missions, five from representatives of Protestant missions, and three from directors of government schools at Boma, Stanleyville, and Kabinda. In addition, there is a longer memorandum, *à titre privé*, from an administrative officer who had earlier been involved in education. Five responses come from Katanga, the region where 'education' as intended in the survey (i.e. above all trade schools) was a pressing problem. Among the respondents from Katanga we find some prominent names, such as Father (later Msgr) Sak of the Salesians, Bishop Springer of the Methodist Episcopal Mission, and the pioneer Luba ethnographer W.F. Burton of the Pentecostal Mission. However, as from the other groups, return was incomplete: Jesuits, White Fathers, Benedictines and several Protestant organizations (such as the Baptist Missionary Society) are conspicuously absent (at least from the file).

14 'As far as I am concerned, I don't even want to teach a European language. I also think that it is not polite to teach any [European] language but French in the Belgian Congo.'

15 Even though the CSK here figures as a private organization it was in fact a 'parastatal', as was the Bourse du Travail, for which de Bauw also signed. There is more about both in Chapter 4.

16 The importance of de Bauw's opinion is recognized in a covering letter by Vice-Governor General Tombeur, dated Boma, February 1, 1918, with an entry stamp from the Ministry of Colonies of March 5, 1918. Apart from the copy of the de Bauw memorandum transmitted by Tombeur, File M 645 has a copy of the covering letter from de Bauw to the 'Vice-Governor General of the Province of Katanga at Elisabethville', dated Elisabethville, September 15, 1917, and signed 'Directeur Général Delegué'. De Bauw insists in this letter on the 'personal' character of his remarks on professional training for blacks. They do not pretend, he says, to express the views of the CSK. Together with this letter goes a carbon copy of de Bauw's response to the education questionnaire, dated (erroneously) September 15, 1915. In it, the section 'LANGUES'. Réponse aux Questions 12, 13, 14 et 15' is heavily underlined, presumably by a reader at the Ministry. The file also contains another version of this document, distinguished only by slight editorial changes. It is dated September 15, 1917, and has de Bauw's own signature in his capacity as director of the Bourse du Travail. Finally there is a third, typewritten, memorandun, with the same date but unsigned. It differs from the other two in that it does not refer to the questionnaire and is generally in a more personal, anecdotal tone. I think it is likely that one or both of these last two documents reached the Ministry directly, without first going through official channels in the colony. This would point to the importance attached to them, either by the author or by some third person.

17 De Bauw was not the only, and certainly not the first, one to express such a policy goal. In a study carried out for the Institute Solvay (whose primary interests were in economics and industrial sociology, such as it was at the time), G. De Leeuw sums up his findings in a lapidary statement: 'The goal to reach is to weld Katanga to the regions of the North' (1911: 141).

18 The already-cited Annual Report for 1916 is informative on that point. While revenue increased from both exports and head taxes, shortage of (military) personnel tied up in the War had brought effective occupation of the Congo to a halt. With characteristic duplicity, the

report maintains that 'the internal political situation was not troubled' (Congo Belge 1918: 1). The brief summaries for each district that follow show the contrary to have been the case. Only two of them, Moyen Congo (around Léopoldville) and Haut Luapula (around Elisabethville) report no trouble. Two seem to have been relatively calm and one, Tanganyika–Moero, on the border to German East Africa, was obviously under a news blackout. The remaining seventeen districts all experienced major difficulties, ranging from insubordinate chiefs, 'fetish-movements', open rebellion and passive resistance to conflict between Protestant and Catholic missions (Congo Belge 1918: 2–5). In many of these brief reports a common theme returns: nothing can be done until the War is over. It is easy to imagine that the troubled administrators regarded the government survey on education as just another untimely bureaucratic nuisance.

19 On early literacy and its importance in Congo religious nationalism, see the study by Janzen and McGaffey (1974).

20 Answers to Question 8 by the UMHK and BCK/CFK – the two largest employers in Katanga – give us a glimpse of the situation around 1917 (see also below, Chapter 4). At the UMHK all work demanding some schooling is still reserved for Whites; the BCK/CFK has begun to hire workers trained at the trade school of the Salesians and pays them twice the wage of workers with no schooling. A similar policy is reported by another railway company, CFGL, and others claim to pay trained workers up to six times more. One respondent (Comptoir des Exportateurs Belges) says that he knows of a black laboratory assistant in Kinshasa 'who almost takes the role of a European'; but his pay is low, and, he adds, this is no exception. The implications of this statement are quite daring for the time. More typical for colonial attitudes, perhaps, is a remark by the superior of the Scheutist mission at Nouvelle Anvers: 'Work and wages should be better proportioned. Often they abandon their work because they earn too much in a short time while they really need so little to lead a lazy life.'

3 Settling in: colonization and language

1 The first three sections of this chapter contain, in a revised form, parts of an article previously published (Fabian 1983).

2 See Missions Catholiques du Congo Belge 1920. Note that this paragraph is absent in the 1910 edition (Antwerp: De Vlijt), published prior to the 1917 government survey on education; it is retained in the 1930 version (Louvain: J. Kuyl-Otto). In what must be the first document of this series (Missions Catholiques du Congo 1907) it is stated: 'Teaching the Belgian national languages will be an essential part of the program' (p. 3). Native languages are not mentioned at all.

3 See Congo Belge–Service de l'Enseignement 1948. On the debates about language choice, and for further references, see the still valuable paper by E. Polomé (1968).

4 See papers by C. E. Stipe 1980, and N. Etherington 1983, for further references. *Comparative Studies in Society and History* 23 (1981) devoted a special section to 'Missionary Messages' with contributions by T. O. Beidelman, P. Rigby, J. Shapiro and E. L. Schieffelin. See also Beidelman 1982, a work which provides much concrete illustration for the generalizations attempted here.

5 To simplify matters without, it is hoped, distorting history, this chapter concentrates on the role of the Roman Catholic missions. Given their privileged status in the Belgian Congo, this has some justification. Generally speaking, the Protestant missions were in their dealings with secular authorities forced to emulate patterns set by Catholics. See also the influential Phelps-Stokes Commissions report (T. J. Jones n.d. [?1924]) and the account of the 1926 conference at Le Zoute (Smith 1926). In both publications Belgian colonial administration receives praise, but Belgian officials often perceived Protestants as a foreign threat, and increasingly so during times when the precariousness of Belgian rule was felt. Braekman's history of Protestant

missions in the Congo (1961) is helpful as an inventory of persons, organizations, and places. For a brief statement, with references to her other writings on the subject, see Slade Reardon 1968. The paper by Yates (1980) cited above and especially her study on 'Shifting goals of industrial education' (1978), are important and well documented. On missions in the Congo in general, see also Markowitz 1973.

6 This notion was developed by B. Jewsiewicki (1979). Much of the following is inspired by this essay.

7 I have argued elsewhere that these conditions included the 'commodification of religion' (Fabian 1981). Françoise Raison-Jourde, in one of the best papers on the subject, applies similar notions to missionary linguistic work in her 'Unequal exchange of language: the penetration of linguistic techniques into an oral civilization'. There she states that lexical, classificatory description 'makes possible the reduction of all the words of the language to the same status...and by virtue of that reduction...the passage of the language of Madagascar [her case] into English. By operating such a treatment, the missionaries open the language to the laws of an exchange that could be described in terms of capitalist economy... The treatment of words makes of them products which can be exchanged among the most diverse agents without any reference to the social situation of those who operate the exchange. Thus, a common market of speech is created...permitting a 'neutral' exchange of linguistic values' (1977: 653).

8 See, for instance, Vertongen 1912. This militant anticlerical pamphlet resumes accusations made by a member of Parliament, E. Vandervelde, and is mainly directed against the Jesuits and their system of *fermes-chapelles* (charging that the young Africans who were educated in these establishments were brought there 'against the wish of relatives', p. 19). It also criticizes the Government for the high budget allocated to the trade school opened by the Salesians in Elisabethville (pp. 29–30).

9 Documents on the religious policies of the Congo Independent State were published by Roeykens (1965).

10 Missionaries had a leading role in the ambitious project of an 'encyclopedia of the black races of Africa' promoted by C. Van Overbergh, a high government official in the field of education. In 1913 he summarized what had been accomplished so far and reprinted his introduction to the work on the Baluba by P. Colle. Ten monographs, each between 400 and 600 pages, had been produced. Van Overbergh describes the project in detail and leaves no doubt that the contribution by missionaries was decisive (1913: 165–231).

11 Linguistic work by missionaries – in this case the White Fathers – received early praise in an essay by G. Monchamp (1904). Its bibliographic value is slight, but it is a most interesting document for the spirit in which such work was undertaken and received. Generally speaking, bibliographic sources documenting missionary linguistics (including translations) are plentiful if not always easily accessible. To stay with the White Fathers most important in terms of description and utilization of Swahili in the Congo as well as in East Africa, three bibliographies can be cited: Société des Pères Blancs 1932, Diemer 1961, and lists on 'linguistica anonyma' and writings (without exact indication of title) from the archives of that order, containing no fewer than 366 entries (Streit and Dindinger 1954: XX 432–75). Another bibliography is now available on publications that came out at the trade school of the Salesians in Elisabethville–Kafubu (Verbeek 1982: 112–21). Missionary contributions are of course also prominent in any overall linguistic bibliography of the Congo, such as Van Bulck 1948.

12 See Société des Missionnaires d'Afrique 1914, and Roelens 1938: 34–9. Background to the period when the educational policies of the White Fathers took shape (before 1914) is provided in a detailed study by Heremans (1978).

13 See Becker 1943: 264–5. Later he is even more explicit when he rejects foggy notions of civilization and states (in Weberian terms): 'Up to this day, native schools... are a purpose-

oriented (*zweckrational*) instrument which the Europeans use for their political and economic and, as far as the missions are concerned, for their ecclesiastic–religious goals' (1943: 267). On the issue of language choice, Becker advocates a 'unified trade language' such as Swahili and counters pedagogical arguments for vernaculars with the remark that no one complains in Germany about High German being used in education, although it, too, used to be a vehicular language (see 1943: 299ff.). The sections in this book devoted to the Belgian Congo are concise and valuable (pp. 96–104; see also the summary pp. 281–2).

14 This and other reasons against the use of 'vehicular languages' in the sense of *linguae francae* were given by a missionary in a critical comment on government instructions about education (succeeding the *Projet* of 1925): see Maus 1938: 490–525, and 1939: 1–20. Hulstaert, a most active participant in these debates, provides further arguments in support of Maus' position; see Hulstaert 1939: 85–9. There he writes: 'Pedagogical authorities are unanimous in proclaiming that the mother tongue must be the vehicular language in teaching and in rejecting any other solution as vitiating the true goal of education' (1939: 88). For an earlier programmatic statement of this view, see Schmidt 1930. Meanwhile, the Government had risen above the crude view of native languages as poor and degenerate. But the new position was such that it required no revision as regards the superiority of European languages: 'The native speaks his mother tongue quite correctly and his vocabulary is all the more extensive because it almost totally lacks general and abstract words' (Inspection Générale de l'Enseignement 1931: 7).

15 See, for instance, the already-cited Introduction by Van Overbergh to Colle's *Les Baluba* (Van Overbergh 1913: 172ff.).

16 Foucault 1973. Perhaps I should make it clear that I am using 'discourse' as an interpretative, historical concept. I do not want to pass off the observations that follow as results of 'discourse analysis' in a technical, statistical sense of the term. In this context a few studies should be mentioned (all of them dissertations not easily accessible and not equally valuable: Lanteri-Sem 1981; Ntamunoza 1980; Pirotte 1973).

17 Missionary writings, Catholic as well as Protestant, are full of such images and figures of speech. One illustration which is perhaps an extreme but by no means unique example is a document we encountered earlier (see Chapter 1, notes 3 and 25). The title alone speaks volumes: *À l'assaut des pays nègres. Journal des Missionnaires d'Alger dans l'Afrique Equatoriale* (1884). In his preface, C. Lavigerie recalls the Geographic Conference of Brussels (1876) at which Léopold II started the Association Internationale Africaine, predecessor of the Congo Independent State. He praises this association and states quite openly that the Church, in order not to be left behind by developments, should take the activities of the AIA as a model and the territory claimed by it as the space in which to spread Christianity: 'One cannot deny it, this is a great enterprise, even greater than those that try to pierce the continents just to cut down the distances, because here entire peoples, buried and dead (*ensevelies dans la mort*) shall be called to light and life' (1884: 9; see also pp. 7–8). Lavigerie, of course, did not only think in military images; he dreamed of Christian soldiers and Christian empires in the literal sense (see Roeykens 1965: 209ff., and Fabian 1985).

18 This is how the official handbook for colonial administrators treats of 'Blacks from a Linguistic Point of View.' A brief section devoted to that topic begins with these definitions: 'The word *race* which we have employed so far designates a biological group (*groupe*), based on physical characteristics which are transmitted by heredity. We reserve the term *peoples* to groups (*groupements*) characterized by their languages' (Royaume de Belgique–Ministère des Colonies 1930: 363; this is the fifth edition of the handbook). Then two lists of ethnic labels are given, grouped under 'bantu' and 'Sudanese languages' respectively. To what extent language and communication problems had been relegated to the missions may be taken from the fact that, apart from this crude classificatory statement, the handbook only contains four other passages relating to language: a quotation of Article 3 from the Colonial Charter (p. 15),

two exhortations to colonial agents to learn local languages for the purpose of exercising indirect rule, obtaining accurate information, and giving exact orders (pp. 8, 60), and, at the very end of the book, rules for the transcription and orthography of Congolese geographic names (pp. 507–8).

19 For an analysis of temporal notions in a broader context, see Fabian 1983.

20 Originally in *Recueil mensuel*, 1922: 139. See also comments on this remark by Perrings (1979: 59). For a period that falls outside the scope of this study but clearly reflects a history of religiously sanctioned work ideology, I have tried to show 'passages' between secular and religious discourse in the semantics of work in the doctrine of a religious movement: see Fabian 1973: 293–325.

21 On the Protection Committee, see Guebels 1949. This work has become a standard source but should be used with caution. Guebels was not a disinterested outsider, and he had to make selections from the committee's minutes.

22 This tree or pyramid view of relations between local and supra-local languages (or between 'dialects' and 'languages') is still widely accepted: see, for instance, W. Labov's schema, which has found its way into many recent introductory texts. Calvet (1974: 58) points to the role of naming and classifying in a more general fashion: 'colonial division begins with taxonomic segmentation'. This is certainly confirmed in many ways by the history of Belgian colonization. On the other hand, his typology of successive stages of linguistic colonization could not be used to describe developments in the Congo (see 1974: 60–79).

23 The myth was still very much alive in the 1970s – the 200 had even become 600 languages – when certain Zairean linguists used it to argue for the urgent necessity to install Lingala as the official, unifying language.

24 For complete references, see Bibliography. I have seen most of the titles on this and the following list. Question-marks indicate that the information is not given in the text or, in a few cases, in the bibliographic source.

25 *Bibliothèque-Congo* was a publication series founded by E. de Jonghe in 1921.

26 The purpose of these guides is expressed in the title of an early precursor published by the White Fathers, *Grammaire en Kiswahili à l'usage des nègres du Haut Congo* (Algiers: Maison-Carrée 1902). How numerous these publications were is documented in Mioni's additions to Van Spaandonck's bibliography (Mioni 1967) and in the lists of writings by White Fathers cited above, note 11.

27 In the collection of A. Van Iseghem (former Governor of Katanga) preserved at the library of the Benedictine Abbey of St Andries, near Bruges. Unfortunately these pamphlets contain little information apart from course announcements. An exception is the 1927 program of the Union Coloniale Belge. Here it is stated that the training is offered to 'commercial and industrial agents' and that the only requirement is to have completed primary education (this expresses the division of labor between the two major institutions that eventually emerged: the Union Coloniale in Brussels and the Université Coloniale in Antwerp). The program also summarizes results obtained since 1912 when the course in 'colonial preparation' was first given (figures in brackets are handwritten corrections on the copy I saw): 648 (743) students, 139 (194) auditing students, making a total of 787 (937). The elective nature of this sort of training is expressed in the low number of students who passed the final examinations: 206 (235). It should be added that this collection of programs does not cover a third important institution, the University of Louvain, where much of the training of future missionaries took place (especially of those who were selected for studies beyond their seminary education).

28 De Permentier is also identified as 'professor of Congolese languages at the Institut Supérieur de Commerce d'Anvers', yet another institution involved in colonial training but not mentioned in Table 14.

29 Burssens' text was destined for use by students of what by then was called the École Coloniale

du Ministère des Colonies at Brussels. Although the author was not a missionary, his principal sources and authorities still were.

4 Labor and language in Katanga

1 As will be manifest from many references in this chapter, the work of two scholars should be especially acknowledged: Bruce Fetter's studies on the history of Elisabethville–Lubumbashi (first his doctoral thesis, 1968, then a revised, shorter book, 1976; see especially Chapter 6) and Charles Perrings' work on relations between economics, technology, and labor policy in Katanga (1979). Both should be consulted by the interested reader, also for further references. Among earlier appraisals of the period with which we are concerned, R. L. Buell's *The Native Problem in Africa* (1928) remains important; to a lesser extent also J. Merle Davis' *Modern Industry and the African* (1933; reprinted, with an informative Introduction by R. I. Rotberg, 1967). The study of Grévisse (1951) on the African township at Elisabethville covers a somewhat later period but contains valuable material and profits from the author's firsthand experience with 'native policy'. Also consulted were monographs published to commemorate the foundation of the Comité Special du Katanga (Cornet 1950), of Elisabethville (*Elisabethville 1911–61*), and of the Union Minière du Haut Katanga (Union Minière du Haut Katanga n.d. [1943], 1956). On the whole, communication problems, language policies, and especially the role of Swahili, do not receive much attention in these writings (although both Fetter and Perrings note essentials and comment on events crucial in this respect). Fetter points out repeatedly that Swahili became an issue dividing Belgians and foreigners, and Catholic and Protestant missions. Of course, much material, usually in the form of short statements and asides, is scattered in travel accounts and memoirs. An exceptional example is perhaps Dugald Campbell's *In the Heart of Bantuland* (1922), Chapters 19 and 20. Campbell (who came to Africa for the Garenganze Evangelical Mission) knew the 'old Katanga' and was, as *inspecteur de travail*, familiar with conditions among recruited workers, although he held some rather curious opinions as a linguist.

2 This is not the place to address that issue in any detail. Several observations will be made when we turn to language manuals, especially in the following chapter. A standard reference is Hymes 1971, followed by Valdman 1977. Different, conflicting theories regarding the origin, nature, and later development of pidgins in Africa are summarized and discussed by Heine (1973). For later developments see an essay by Bickerton (1976). A convenient summary in French was given by Valdman (1981); see also Calvet 1981.

3 Contemporary publications give some indication of the linguistic situation at Elisabethville when it was incorporated as a town. It is not always certain, though, whether a statement expresses facts or expectations. Thus, a guide published for 'colonists and businessmen desiring to establish themselves in Katanga' probably reflects the official position rather than the actual situation. It states under 'languages employed': 'The official languages are French and Flemish. Knowledge of English is useful, many immigrants of that nationality being at this moment employed at the mines and the railway. Study of the basics (*notions*) of the Ki-Swahili language (native language) is also to be recommended' (Ministère des Colonies– Office Colonial 1911: 38). The first newspaper to appear in Elisabethville (weekly) was the *Étoile du Congo* (first issue on May 26, 1911) and it was trilingual: English, Flemish, and French. It was soon followed by the weekly *Journal du Katanga* (first issue on August 5, 1911), which had an 'English page' and published government notices in the three languages. But two years later English had virtually disappeared from its pages, a sign that measures against that language were taken quite early. Also, given the present currency of English, one easily forgets that at the beginning of this century it did not yet have a truly vehicular character. It is worth quoting Campbell on this point. He notes: 'It seems incredible, but one

can see at any time in Elisabethville a native employed as interpreter between a Belgian and a Britisher, neither of whom knows the other's language, the medium used being either Kitchen Kaffir or Kitchen Swahili' (1922: 203).

4 Source: *Journal du Katanga,* February 4, 1913.

5 Source: Report, Colonial Archives, Brussels, File AE/II 1512 (3250).

6 The 1912 estimate is given in *Journal du Katanga,* February 13, 1912. The consequences of the economic crash are visible in the following figures: in 1929, Elisabethville counted 18,700 African and 2370 European inhabitants; in 1932, the respective figures were 6670 and 548; in 1931, of 1340 houses for Europeans 350 were not occupied; in 1932 that figure rose to 470 (see *Elisabethville 1911–61*: 159–60).

7 See Grévisse 1951: 5–6. Note that the Belgian measures to take control of urban African settlements went through two stages: first the creation of (separate) native quarters in 1912 (although by that time some Europeans apparently chose to live in that section: see Grévisse 1951: 5), and then the organization of the *centre extra-coutumier,* an urban section with some measure of internal self-government but generally modeled on the *cité* of the mining company. The CEC, as it came to be called, was officially set up in 1931.

8 In 1966–7, while doing research on another subject, I spoke to several veteran missionaries who recalled caravans of 'recruits' in chains passing by (in the Kolwezi area) as late as the mid-twenties. More recently I was able to interview Fr Boniface Poulens, a Benedictine who arrived in Katanga in 1923 (interview recorded on November 28, 1982 at St Andries near Bruges). Several things of interest emerged from his vivid recollections about his work at and near Bunkeya (Msiri's former capital). At that time, the greatest 'plague', as he put it, for the missions as well as for the people was *kiwalo,* forced 'recruitment' for porterage or work in and around the mines. Perrings uses the Bemba equivalent term *icibalo* and rather euphemistically translates it as 'recruited labor': see 1979: xvi, 151ff. According to Fr Boniface, people did everything to escape recruitment. He recalls at least one case of suicide by a man who could not face the prospect of serving a 'contract' in town. Many freelance recruiters operated apart from the larger organizations, such as the BTK and Robert Williams and Co. One of their 'techniques' was to wait at church doors after Sunday service and to pick out suitable men. Fr Boniface, like other missionaries, was also offered a bonus of F 1000 for every person he could get to accept a contract. All this led to serious conflict between the mission and companies and also explains the enthusiasm of the former when the policy of 'stabilization' was conceived as an alternative. Regarding the linguistic situation in rural Katanga around 1923, Fr Boniface did not recall Bunkeya as a center of Swahili diffusion. He was emphatic about Swahili being strictly an urban (i.e. Elisabethville) vehicular language (which is not surprising given the linguistic policies of the Benedictines who favored Sanga). But he also volunteered the interesting remark that he himself got along in English during the first months of his stay, even with many Africans.

9 Much is usually made in colonial literature of the collapse of native political structures as a result of colonial administrative reorganization. Buell exemplifies this view when he states: 'As a result of this system, the whole population of the Congo has been drifting until recently toward semi-anarchy' (1928: II 482). In Katanga, as in many other regions of the colony, 'anarchy' meant the continuation of resistance with other means. Campbell (1922: 63) uses a surprisingly modern term when be observes '*Guerilla warfare* used to be much indulged throughout the Katanga by the Aborigines'. Although this probably applies to a somewhat earlier period, it remains true that continued resistance required extraordinary measures of control (see the following note).

10 Police in Katanga had a special status. According to one of the first commanders, the later General F.V. Olsen, the build-up of an important force, organized on the model of the Belgian army, was made necessary by the uncontroled influx of white 'trekkers' from the south. Many of these were armed adventurers who acted with the assurance of being protected by British

consular authorities (Great Britain had been slow to recognize the annexation of the Congo Independent State by Belgium). Olsen reports the following figures for 1910: a total of 1900 men was made up of three contingents, 650 from the former Katanga Police Corps, 250 from a 'Compagnie Mauser', and 1000 from a military unit with battle experience in the Kivu region. The total was soon brought up to about 2500 by troops from Lulua (Kasai). These troops, especially the 1000 Kivu veterans and their families, may very well have been an important 'carrier' of Swahili. At any rate, before Swahili became the official work language of the mining company, it was used by the armed forces and was the medium of instruction in a school for non-commissioned officers founded at that time (i.e. before 1914) in Elisabethville. Its first commander was Lt Labeye, whom we encountered earlier as a teacher and author of a Swahili manual (Labeye 1928; see above, p. 87), and who later became director at the Ministry of Colonies in charge of the Force Publique: see Olsen 1950: 1–5, and additional comments by Sohier 1938: 8–9.

11 In addition to measures such as the police build-up described in the preceding note, Belgians envisaged stronger economic links with the rest of the colony as a way of counteracting the constant threat of a British 'take-over' in Katanga. Already in 1911, in a report on a mission to Katanga prepared for the Solvay Institute of Sociology in Brussels, the author concluded: 'The goal to be reached is to weld Katanga to the northern regions' (De Leeuw 1911: 141; this book is also remarkable for many photographs illustrating the origins of Elisabethville).

12 On the BTK, see Buell 1928: II 535ff., and Perrings 1979: 20–1 and index.

13 A standard source is the report by one of the architects of stabilization, Mottoulle 1946.

14 See the correspondence quoted above, Chapter 2, p. 165.

15 Robert (later Sir Robert) Williams was by no means just a labor contractor. As a confidant and associate of Cecil Rhodes he represented British–South African interests. He served as an Administrator of both the Tanganyika Concessions Ltd and the Union Minière and was above all a prime mover behind much of the railway construction that was vital to the exploitation of Katanga's mineral wealth: see Katzenellenbogen 1973.

16 'Karanga' must be an error for Kabanga or Chikabanga, one of the many terms for a Nguni-type (i.e. related to Zulu) vehicular language which developed as a work jargon in South Africa. In Katanga it was known as Kitchen-Kaffir; linguists now refer to it as Fanagalo (see, for example, Heine 1973 *passim*). More of an enigma is the 'Chimoyo' language which, according to Campbell, was eventually replaced as a vehicular idiom by Swahili. In his list of 'Linguae Francae' he mentions '7. Chimoyo – Central Congo' (1922: 202). Later he reminisces: 'Meanwhile the old lingo of Chimoyo we all spoke died, and Swahili as a lingua franca took its place. White men learned it [? Swahili], natives in faraway districts picked it up, and it became the Esperanto of the Congo State' (1922: 260).

17 The form of the prefix (*tshi* rather than *ki*) and the lexeme *moyo*, a frequent Luba greeting, point to a vehicular Tshiluba (= Kituba). Source: Colonial Archives, Brussels, File EA/II 1512/3250, letter and report from Province du Katanga, Service Economique.

18 Source: Colonial Archives, Brussels, File EA/II 1512/3250, copy of a report from Province du Katanga, Service des Affaires Economiques, dated Elisabethville October 28, 1920; my emphasis.

19 From a letter by Vice-Governor Tombeur to the Minister of Colonies, dated June 11, 1920; source as above, note 18.

20 The administrator of company settlements and his office were called (and are called today) *changa changa*, a term derived from *kuchanga*, to collect, recruit. This reflects the period when recruiting agencies such as Robert Williams and Co. also administered the workers' camps. There is another meaning which prevails nowadays: *kuchanga* may also be translated as 'to mix, shuffle', defining the camp administration as an agency which holds together people from diverse ethnic and linguistic backgrounds.

21 Observations on workers' settlements are in part based on my own experience. In 1966–7,

while doing research on a religious movement, I lived for about one year in the *cité* of Musonoi, near Kolwezi. Obviously things must have changed (and some have improved) in the fifty years since UMHK had taken these camps over from Robert Williams and Co. But the continuity of basic principles of administration – and, as far as I could gather from long-term residents, of a style of life – was impressive (see Fabian 1971: 51–64 also for further literature). On another occasion, a research project on language and work carried out in 1972–4, I had the opportunity to assist (and record) a *chef de camp* in his daily sessions of adjudicating, imposing fines, and handing down administrative decisions. By that time the office was held by an African, and the Swahili used was certainly different from the *Ki-Union Minière* his European predecessors had used. But little had changed as to the function and accumulation of power that characterized the *changa changa* for generations.

22 Whether it was decisive or not, the virtual absence of European wives during the early years made expatriate men dependent on African women, and this in ways that were not restricted to occasional sexual relations. Household and marriage-like arrangements daily created necessities and opportunities of communicating about matters other than those restricted to a work/command situation. As to figures, see those for 1912–13 in Table 5 (above, p. 94). The ratios of women to men were 1:7.4 and 1:5.9 respectively.

23 This expression is derived from *kuuza bulongo*, to buy a building site: see Van de Weyer and Quets 1929: 52

5 Talking tough and bad: pidginization in Katanga

1 See Société des Pères Blancs 1932: 6

2 See Van Spaandonck 1965: no. 756, and above, Chapter 3, p. 89.

3 According to Van Spaandonck 1965: no. 759. On Thielemans, see above, Chapter 3, p. 89

4 For references, see above, Chapter 1, note 4.

5 See De Bauw 1920: 65; on Africans as suppliers of the mines, *ibid.*: 30; on counter-measures taken by industry and colonial administration, *ibid.*: 45–52.

6 There must have been a flurry of publication of guides for colonists expected to seek their fortune in Katanga after the rail connection to the south was established in 1910. Apart from Leplae's guide for future farmers, I found the following: Ministère des Colonies – Office Colonial 1911. A paragraph on language from this guide was quoted above, Chapter 4, note 3. In the same year the local Government also published, for general distribution, building regulations (Vice Gouverneur du Katanga 1911) and a bilingual legal guide (Katanga–Congo Belge n.d. [1911]). The latter was written by Nicolas Fourir, 'ex-greffier du Tribunal de Ière Instance d'Elisabethville', and deals especially with regulations for fire arms, labor recruitment, and employment.

7 They were discovered in the Van Iseghen collection at St Andries Abbey near Bruges. Both had escaped the attention of Swahili bibliographers. Printed copies of this sort of guide most likely 'disappeared' among their users before they found a place in scientific libraries. As is the case with other documents used in this study, there is often an inverse relationship between their linguistic and historical values.

8 On Edmond Leplae (1868–1941), see *Biographie coloniale belge*, Vol. IV, 1954: 515–18, and Claessens 1946. The very extensive bibliography of Leplae's writings in Claessens does not mention the *Guide*, nor is there any reference to linguistic interests. Leplae was recruited to colonial service (in 1910) from a career in agronomy and knew Katanga only from occasional travel. All in all, it is unlikely that he compiled the Swahili manual which is part of this *Guide*.

9 For the wordlists to be reproduced in this chapter the following abbreviations and conventions have been adopted: ECS = East Coast Swahili; KS = Katanga Swahili. Items from the two texts are rendered as they occur in the sources; KS and ECS terms appear in

italics. Incidentally, 'Katanga Swahili' here designates the 'improved pidgin' of later authors (Verbeken, Annicq); see below, Chapter 6.

10 More recently, on the basis of sizeable corpora of recorded texts, phonetic traits characteristic of Katanga/Shaba Swahili were described by Rossé (1977: 35–43) and Schicho (1982: 5–13). Both refer to Polomé and confirm his findings. Only Schicho somewhat expands Polomé's list with examples (sometimes recent) of influences from Kiluba, Tshiluba, and Bemba. For our purposes it proved practical to follow Polomé; some of the phonetic symbols he uses were simplified.

11 Does this have a bearing on the question whether or not Katanga Swahili 'descended' from Kingwana? The documentary value of our source is too slight to support any definitive conclusion. Nevertheless, it allows us to formulate several hypotheses: (a) If Kingwana is taken as the standard a direct connection with Katanga Swahili appears questionable unless (b) 'Kingwana' in 1912 differed significantly from the form described by Lecoste and Polomé, in which case it would be (c) more plausible to assume that both northern (Kingwana) and southern (Katanga Swahili) varieties of Congo Swahili differ from East Coast forms not so much in terms of a few, discrete phonetic traits but through a kind of 'return to variability'. This variability made them permeable to re-bantuization, either in the form of an emergence of general (proto-)bantu traits (as is hypothesized by Rossé 1977: 39) or as direct influence from bantu vernaculars.

12 As elsewhere is this study, the ECS entries were checked with Madan – Johnson 1939 (here the 1963 reprint). In some cases, Sacleux' *Dictionnaire* (1939) was consulted. Entries under KS were checked against Verbeken (edition of 1965), Annicq 1967, and my own repertoire.

13 Only five items could be traced neither to ECS nor to Kiluba (no. 18,19,21,24,43). No. 24 Kalamu, Lion, occurs in Tabwa (Van Acker 1907: 137, *nkalamu*) with the same meaning. No. 43 Zariba, Enceinte, more often *zeriba*, one encounters as a synonym for ECS *boma*, fortified enclosure, government post, in reports from the Sudan and northwestern Congo. Lingala could have been its 'carrier' into our source.

14 Openness is asserted in the title and introductory remark of this wordlist. Unlike the vocabulary of Dutrieux (see above, Chapter 1, p. 19 and note 17) and the *Petit vocabulaire* (see below), the *Guide* does not provide blank space for notes by its users. Those few gaps that occur – French terms without Swahili glosses – are probably mistakes that escaped the editor's attention and remained as traces of the author's inability to complete his own list. Instead of a Swahili term we find hyphens next to Voile, Antilope noire, Faisan, Vautour, Puceron, Rigole (but later a Swahili term, Kiferedji, is given on p. 10), Machette, Drap and Bougie (pp. 6, 7, 8, 10). One would think that at least the last three were common enough items. Failure to list Swahili words for them supports the assumption that the compiler worked from his own memory and that the gaps reflect his (temporary) inability to find a term. One oddity should be noted: the two unidentified terms for valley are listed as 'Dembo (vallée)' in the French and 'Ilongo' in the Swahili columns (p. 5) only to be followed on p. 6 by 'Vallée Bonde' (a current ECS/KS term).

15 References in the form 'Kil. [page no.]' are to Van Avermaet and Mbuya 1954. The entry under 'Source' was left blank in fifteen cases, although the gaps could eventually be reduced to six by questioning a speaker of Tshiluba and Lingala and by a cursory check of available dictionaries/grammars in the following languages that belong to the environment of Katanga Swahili: Hemba (Vandermeiren 1913), Sanga (Roland 1937), Kaonde (Broughall Woods 1924), Tabwa (Van Acker 1907), Lamba (Doke 1933), Bemba (White Fathers 1954), Tshiluba (Frère Gabriel 1921) and Kikongo/Kituba (Swartenbroeckx 1973). As will be seen from the following list, there is no reason to doubt that Kiluba (i.e. Luba–Katanga) was the dominant source for non-Swahili items in the *Petit vocabulaire*. (Note: all transcriptions were simplified.)

180

Petit vocabulaire	Possible source	English gloss
2 Moganga buka	KS *munganga* + Tabwa *mu-buku* (Van Acker, p. 22)	medical plant
22 Buluba	Kaonde *maluba* (pl.) (B. Woods, p. 200)	flowers
27 Tshofwe	Kaonde *chovwe* (B. Woods, p. 204) cf Tabwa *kyofwe* (Van Acker 130)	hippopotamus
35 Katwa	? Hemba *utwa* (*katwa* = 100) (Vandermeiren, p. 782)	numeral
36 Gondo	Tshiluba *ngondu* Kituba/Kikongo *ngonda* (Swartenbroeckx, p. 240)	moon, month
41 mampa	Tshiluba *dimpa* (plur. *mampa*) (F. Gabriel 327)	bread
43 Wembe	?Sanga *mbembe* (Roland, p. 112)	pigeon
49 Mosebo	Sanga *mosebo* (Roland, p. 130) or Tabwa *musebo* (Van Acker, p. 160)	road
50 Moio	Sanga *moyo* (Roland, p. 131) (but common in Tshiluba a.o.)	greeting
55 Kine	Sanga *kine* (Roland, p. 148) or Tabwa *kine* (Van Acker, p. 31)	truth

16 *Awa*, a Luba term for 'here', occurs as Apa in the wordlist of the *Petit vocabulaire*. This corresponds to KS *hapa*, with deletion of initial *h*. The latter is quite common in KS (see Schicho 1982: 6) and could perhaps be added to the list of distinctive phonetic traits except that *Petit vocabulaire* has it only in one other instance, Apana-yô, KS *(h) apana*, no (unless Oku, which in the wordlist appears for *Aku*, corresponds to KS *huku*, here).

181

17 Possibly it is derived from Kiluba *ka-balo*, reason, motive: see Van Avermaet and Mbuya 1954: 45.

18 Compare this to Chapter 1, p. 38, where the same procedure was followed (using the Swedesh list as adapted by Heine 1973: 46ff.). Several items from the *Guide* are put in brackets because their French glosses indicate that they were used in that text with a slightly different meaning. Term no. 20, *Kwisa*, whose origin I have been unable to identify, occurs not in the annex but in the text of the *Guide*, in the phrase Kwisa hapa, come here: see above, p. 115.

6 The end: illusions of colonial power

1 In the 1970s, *mumbunda na mampala* (under that name) had become a genre of popular painting. With scenes of fighting and air raids it was appreciated as a reminder of troubled times during the Katanga secession. But the scenes of war were additions, as it were, to the basic motive which had become a symbol of the city. On historical consciousness and popular painting in Shaba, see Szombati-Fabian and Fabian 1976.

2 This has been described, for instance, by Fetter 1976: Chapter 6.

3 A survey paper on 'symbolic studies' by the late Victor Turner (1975) is still valuable. I should also note that a concept of 'symbolic domination' was developed by, among others, Rabinow (1975).

4 On May 29, 1911, for instance, the Elisabethville paper *Journal du Katanga* published a circular notice from the Vice-Governor to territorial administrators according to which they were each sent a French wordlist and an ethnographic map of the Congo. They were asked to fill in the native terms. Special attention was to be paid to dialect borders showing up in 'pronunciation'. The note concludes: 'The Government attaches great importance to this work, which will allow us not only to pursue the scientific classification of Congolese languages but also, where necessary, the revision, according to these ethnographic data, of the territorial divisions of Katanga.'

5 The Salesians (like other mission orders of the time) placed a high value on manual work as a means of education. Undoubtedly this pedagogical practice nicely converged with the need for skilled workers and craftsmen in industry and commerce. On Salesian educational work in Katanga, see an article by Ntambwe Beya Ngindu which is partly based on research in local archives (1979).

6 As it turned out, this was not an ephemeral choice. Well into the 1950s, Sanga was the principal African language in their schools, even on the highest levels, as at the seminary near Kapolowe.

7 As a recent bibliography shows, Salesian publications in and about Swahili remained few (see Verbeek 1982: 112–21). The one major teaching aid they published – the *Kitabu cha kusoma*, a primer which first appeared in 1918 and had subsequent editions in 1921, and 1925, each time revised and extended – shows in form and content how closely education in Swahili for Africans was tied to the purpose of training workers.

8 What we shall have to say is restricted to Swahili and that is, of course, already a second-degree simplification. In 1920–30 Swahili was, as much as it is today, part of a multilingual repertoire of almost all its speakers. Phenomena such as code-switching and diglossia are frequent in such situations. Functional differentiation (including incipient class distinction) that was expressed by the use of different varieties of Swahili could also be served by choosing among different languages. Needless to say, there are no studies of the period we are concerned with now, but recent research on linguistic 'stratification' and on the determinants of code-switching in Lubumbashi show how complicated the situation must have been in those earlier times when Swahili had not quite attained the unifying function it has now; see Kabamba Mbikay 1979, also Schicho 1980: 19–27, and Rossé 1977: 224–44.

9 Thus in the prefatory note of Quinot (1926: 2).

10 All this applies only to expatriates who were, or thought they were, part of the colonial establishment. Numerous Italians, Greeks, Portuguese, marginal Belgians and immigrants from other countries lived, as petty traders, small entrepreneurs and craftsmen, outside the formal colonial hierarchy. In the absence of direct information about their linguistic behavior during that period (it is not even known how many of them learned and used French), we can again only extrapolate from later observations. These show that such intermediate groups interacted much more closely with the African population. Especially during childhood and adolescence, contacts were informal and intense. It is safe to say that members of these groups were the only expatriates ever to acquire perfect command of Katanga Swahili.

11 These sexual and generational distinctions overlap in part with social differences based on access to education, printed information, contacts with expatriates, and so forth. They continue to be operative today, as any researcher who learned his Swahili in one sociolect only is quick to find out. Women and children are notoriously difficult to understand, the latter often for their own parents.

12 Because informal writing in Swahili belonged to the uncontroled sector, it is not surprising that we lack first-hand documentation and must rely on retro-diction from observations made at a later time. In my own research on the Jamaa movement (1966–7) and on language use among workers (1972–4), I noticed a surprisingly high volume of writing in the form of letters, even diaries (sometimes as collections of dreams), and occasional autobiographical sketches. We have at least one major document of this sort in a popular history of Elisabethville: *Vocabulaire de ville de Elisabethville/Vocabulaire ya munji wa Elisabethville*, 'edited' by an organization of former domestics and written by a certain Yav André in 1965. This polycopied text was discovered by Bruce Fetter and has to my knowledge not been properly studied and analyzed (one of the difficulties being its peculiar literary form). It is more than likely that other documents of this sort, as well as texts of a more private nature, are still preserved. They should make a fascinating subject of study. Changes, or at least developmental tendencies, in the phonology, syntax, and lexicon of Katanga Swahili should be easy to detect in this private form of literacy, which was certainly inspired by models from administrative, religious, and newspaper writing but grew without pressure to conform to official standards.

13 See Jewsiewicki 1976 and Fetter 1976: Chapter 7. Greschat 1967 remains one of the best general references for the expansion of Kitawala into the Belgian Congo.

14 The standard reference for the theory of speech events and their components is Dell Hymes 1964, later revised and reprinted in 1972. In my own work on and with Shaba Swahili I have found these ideas useful (e.g. in application to religious communication in the Jamaa, Fabian 1974) but in need of critique when it comes to the notion of 'rules' (see Fabian 1979).

15 These fears were voiced by Schebesta in an early contribution to the Congolese 'language question' (1930: 408–9). His tirade against 'Kingwana' has an ironical twist in view of the fact that most of his famous work on the Bambuti pygmies was carried out in that language. See also Heremans 1978: II 428, on criticism of the White Fathers.

16 See Heremans 1978: II 407–8, 409–10. This author also found that Swahili was used by the White Fathers for missionizing only along the eastern and western shores of Lake Tanganyika. Up country, and especially in relatively homogeneous areas such as Rwanda, vernacular languages were employed.

17 The inter-War period was also the time of linguistic stock-taking and of concentrated efforts at improvement and standardization in British East Africa. Contemporaneous attempts to solve the growing manpower problems of the colonies through long-term educational planning (see my remarks above, Chapter 3) may explain otherwise surprising chronological coincidences in the field of Swahili-description. To begin with the Germans, who no longer had a direct political hold on these territories, it appears that the former colonial establishment, administrative as well as missionary, continued to participate in the debates about language choice and standardization. B. Struck's argument for Swahili as the common language of East

Africa appeared in 1921 (and was one of the best-founded surveys of this sort). In the same year two Benedictine missionaries, A. Reichart and M. Küsters, published a Swahili manual which was an extraordinary text, combining high linguistic standards with ethnographic and sociolinguistic attention to actual language use that was far ahead of its time. On German policies toward Swahili in historical perspective, see Wright 1965 and Mehnert 1973. Under British rule, efforts to standardize and thereby control Swahili were not left to more or less academic disputes or occasional administrative intervention, as they were in the Belgian Congo. An Education Conference held at Dar es Salaam in 1925 made a beginning by settling the choice of Swahili. By 1930 an institutional basis was created for coordinated efforts at standardization in the form of the Interterritorial Language Committee; see Whiteley 1969: Chapter 5, on its activities. Controversies, however, continued between advocates of an indigenist bent who envisaged an improved and re-bantuized popular Swahili as a point of departure, and others who took a more elitist, philological approach; see the debate between Roehl 1930 and Broomfield 1930, 1931 in the journal *Africa*, and, more recently, the ranting and raving critique of standardization by Khalid (a pseudonym) 1977. Because authoritative scholars with great achievements in the fields of translation and linguistic description were so prominent in the East African debates it is perhaps not surprising that later commentators, including Whiteley, all but ignored an entire history of amateurish attempts to codify 'practical' varieties of up-country Swahili (the scholarly literature contains nothing but deprecatory asides before Heine 1973 and Vitale 1980 paid serious attention to pidgin Swahili in Kenya; see also Angogo 1980). If we disregard the nineteenth century, as early as 1909 (possibly 1903: see Hendrix 1982: no. 2249) the Mombasa-based newspaper *East African Standard* sponsored a vocabulary and useful phrases. Basset 1937 (first edition in 1915?), Burt 1923 (first edition in 1917 or even 1910: see Van Spaandonck 1965: no. 52), and G. M. Jardine 1927 wrote introductions to a simplified Swahili. Ratcliffe and Elphinstone published their more ambitious *Modern Swahili* in 1932 but also a pocket-size *English–Swahili Phrase Book* (in the same year and again sponsored by the *East African Standard*). And then there was Le Breton's *Up-Country Swahili: Simplified Swahili for the Farmer, Merchant, Business Man and their Wives* (for 'The Soldier, Settler, Miner, Merchant, and their Wives' in a later edition) *and for all who deal with the up-country African*. It first appeared in 1936 and reached a total of 93,000 copies, with its sixteenth edition of 1968. Chronologically and in other respects this text parallels pidgin manuals in Katanga we are about to examine now. A thorough comparison of Le Breton and Verbeken should make an interesting study. One slightly later text that is often overlooked should also be mentioned here: *Kiswahili: A Kiswahili Instruction Book for the East African Command* (East African Army Education Office n.d.; first edition 1942).

18 Its designation as the 'fourth edition' poses a problem. No earlier editions could be found, nor are they cited in the bibliographies. One can only assume that this was the first *printed* edition and that it was preceded by manuscript or polycopied versions. It is therefore likely that this was the first company-sponsored language aid to appear after the UMHK had taken the decision for Swahili in 1918. No information could be gotten about Van de Weyer. Jérôme Quets is mentioned as 'ingenieur des mines' in the UMHK monograph, where it is said that he came to Katanga in 1914 (UMHK 1956: 113). Much later he was a leading figure in an organization of alumni of the university of Louvain, and of its journal *Lovania*.

19 As far as orthography is concerned, *ou* is no longer used for *u*, *tch* has become *tsh*, and *j* is used instead of *dj*, among other changes and idiosyncrasies. The lexicon has some very peculiar forms, mostly due to the author's uncertainty about, or disregard for, pronunciation or morphology. Some examples are: 'allemand: daki' (7; colon added here and in the following) which looks like a hypercorrected form for *datshi*, a somewhat obsolete expression in KS for German (from *deutsch*). There is 'froid: marili' (21) in KS *baridi*; 'dessus: yulu' (16), on the other hand, is a typical KS form for ECS *juu*. Morphological uncertainty shows in forms such as 'aller (s'en): ku kwenda' (7), KS *kwenda*; 'attendre: kun 'gohela' (8), KS *kuongolea*; or when

'garcon: mutoto mwanamume' (22) is given next to 'homme: muntu wana mume' (23), KS *mutoto/muntu mwanaume*. Occasionally there are expressions with a distinctly KS flavor, such as 'bien portant: iko muzima' (10). The phrase section consists almost exclusively of imperatives and imperative requests. Compared to earlier texts (see above, Chapter 5) there are now traces of at least a 2nd person singular form: for example: 'as-tu rĕu la ration de viande: una isha ku kamata posho na niama' (47). The use of *unaisha* to mark an action concluded is typical of KS (it is roughly equivalent to the -*me*- tense in ECS) but in popular usage 'to receive' would be *kupata*, instead of 'ku kamata', 'to take', and the connective would not be 'na' but *ya*. More or less correct forms such as 'mi nataka' for 'I want' are found next to pidgin expressions that must have made a slightly demented impression on African listeners: 'je pars pour l'Europe: meye ata kwenda bulaie' (44) and 'nous ne voulons pas que les travailleurs arrivent en retard: sheye hapana taka bantu anafika niuma' (46)

20 Here are some examples. Loans: 'bureau: ofisi (de office)' (53, colon added here and in the following) from English; 'magasin: Sitoro (de store)' (54) from English; 'bottine, galoche: nsapatu (K. et B.)' (60) from Portuguese via Kitchen-Kaffir and Bemba; 'poussière: chitofu (K.) (de stof)' (63) from Afrikaans via Kitchen Kaffir. Paraphrases: 'infirmerie de l'usine: kwa muntu wa munganga (litt. chez l'homme du docteur)' (54); limer: kukata na tupa (Sw.) (litt. couper à la lime)' (66); 'menuserie: chapu cha mbau (Sw.)' (69).

21 See above, note 7. As far as I know there was no other Swahili guide published by missionaries in Katanga until the Benedictine Father (and later archbishop of Elisabethville) F. Cornelis published his *Le Kiswahili pour débutants* in 1958.

22 On Verbeken, see *Biographie belge d'Outre-Mer* (the former *Biographie coloniale belge*), Vol. VI, 1967: 1050–3. I was able to consult the 'Fonds Verbeken' at the Royal Museum of Central Africa at Tervuren. Only two brief autographs were found that have a direct bearing on our topic. One is a short list (ca. 70 items) of 'termes spéciaux' in Swahili. These are technical terms used in railroad operation and maintenance in the mines. The other is an account on sales and revenues for his *Petit cours*.

23 On the complicated maneuvers carried out by various factions to coopt and control the rising black elite of Elisabethville, see Fetter 1976: Chapter 8.

24 Verbeken shared this conviction with E. De Jonghe, from whom he quotes this sentence in his article on 'Les langues véhiculaires au Congo belge', in *L'Essor du Congo*, May 1936, nos. 2989, 2990. That article, incidentally, shows that Verbeken read widely in the literature on Swahili. He may have taken from Roehl's 1930 paper his rather peculiar etymology of Kingwana as being Kilungwana, derived from 'walungu' = 'warungu' = 'wazungu', hence 'language of the foreigners' (this was proposed by Roehl 1930: 198).

25 See Fetter1976: 164–5, and Jewsiewicki 1976: 48, note 2.

26 See, for references to Verbeken's writings, the bibliography in *Biographie belge d'Outre-Mer* (cf. above, note 22). The Kishila vocabulary is mentioned in a letter from A. van Iseghem of April 11, 1913. Van Iseghem was then district commissioner of Haut Luapula and acknowledges receipt of Verbeken's work. Verbeken's personal file, including periodic evaluations by superiors, contains several references to his linguistic interests. In 1923 it is mentioned that he speaks 'Kituba' very well, and sufficient Swahili and Kanioka (he was then serving in the region of Kabinda). 'Kituba' here undoubtedly means vehicular Tshiluba.

27 See on this Jewsiewicki 1976: 62–5, but notice that he concludes from the fact that elementary teaching was done in vernacular languages (outside of the city) that there was no 'language common to all' (p. 65). True, immigrants to the cities did not all *arrive* with a common language; yet they quickly found one in Swahili and, on a deeper level, in the many expressions of a new urban culture which made communication possible even when verbal means were (still) limited. Earlier in his article Jewsiewicki found a fitting formulation when he observed that, in religious movements such as the Kitawala, 'the solidarity of beliefs, reinforced by

---

solidarity in the face of repression, made less rigid the ethnic frontiers between people *to whom colonization offers a language of interethnic communications*' (1976: 56; my emphasis).

28 Here are short specimens of three varieties of Swahili used in *Ngonga* (not including Verbeken's instalment course). Notice that all of them bear traces of (editorial) lubaization, which shows up, for instance, in a more frequent occurrence of intervocalic *l* and *y/j* or *d/l* substitution than would be typical for the popular language. The varieties are:

1. 'Refined' translations of Verbeken's French column:

La coutume	*Setuli (Desturi)*
Beaucoup d'européens pré-	Wazungu wingi wanasema:
tendent que les indigènes	Watu weusi hawataweza
ne seront jamais capables	kabisa kuhakikisha
de raisonner comme eux, même	sawasawa siye, hata wata-
quand ils seront éduqués,	koposilimuka, kwa sababu
parce que la pensée des in-	uzani wao hauhakikishi
digènes ne suit pas la même	namuna sawa siye.
logique que celle des européens.	

2. Excerpts and adaptations from *Elimu ya intshi*, a geography text published by the White Fathers at Albertville (actually *Elimu ya Inchi*, 2 vols. (Baudouinville, 1920): see Mioni 1967: 505)

Géographie	*Elimu ya intshi*
1-LE MONDE EST ROND	1-DUNIA NA WATU
Notre monde est rond comme un	Dunia hii yetu ni muvilin-
citron. Cette boule, Dieu l'a	go kama ndimu. Huo muvilingo,
placée dans le ciel comme les	Mungu aliuweka mbinguni
étoiles, la lune et le soleil;	kama vile nyota na mwezi na
elle n'est soutenue ni par une	yuwa. Usisekemea wala nguzo
colonne ni par un soutien quelconque.	wala sekemeo lolote.

3. Tales and fables provided in Katanga Swahili by other contributors:

HALISI	A STORY
MUNGU NI MUKUU	GOD IS GREAT
Siku moya Sulutani mukubwa ali-	One day a big chief sat in
kuwa akikala katika boma lake,	his fortified court. He
akasikia viyana wawili wali-	heard two youngsters argu-
kombana. Kiyana mumoya alisema:	ing among each other. One
"Mungu ni Mukuu kuliko wote."	of the young people said:
Lakini mwenzake akamuyibu:	"God is greater than anyone
"Sulutani wetu ni Mukuu; aki-	else." But his friend (i.e.
taka kuua hakuna mutu awezaye	fellow-youngster) replied:
kukuokola!"	"Our chief is great; if he
	wants to kill there is no
	one who could save you!"
	(My translation.)

All examples from *Ngonga*, No. 9, July 28, 1934.

29 See *Ngonga*, No. 28, December 8, 1934, and especially the last issue, No. 46, April 13, 1935.

30 At the time of writing I have been unable to find a copy of the first edition of Verbeken's *Petit cours*; the earliest edition I saw was the second of 1944. For a while I worked on the assumption that the first edition and the UMHK manual of 1938 were identical. For a number of reasons this now appears unlikely, though it cannot definitely be ruled out.

31 It would now be appropriate to describe in some detail this point of arrival of a long process of descriptive appropriation (although this has been done already by a contemporary critic: see Mélignon). But precisely because we are at the end of a line of development, and because we

know by now fairly well the general shape and purpose of Verbeken's Swahili, we can avoid a tedious description of a tedious manual. How strong its hold on the market was may be taken from the fact that the *Petit cours* had no serious competition until the 1960s. Spinette published a Kingwana–French vocabulary for use in the Ituri and Stanleyville/Kisangani regions in 1960 (still sponsored by the Belgian Colonial Ministry). In the same year the first introduction on an acceptable scholarly level by a Belgian who was not a missionary appeared with Natalis' two-part *La Langue swahilie*, followed by a pocket dictionary in 1961. This work has no regional orientation, unlike the grammar–dictionary by Annicq (1967), which continues Verbeken's codification of a pidgin variety supposedly spoken by expatriates at Lubumbashi. By that time Zairean scholars had begun to formulate their own visions of Swahili: see, for example, Kajiga 1967; but see Heylen 1977, which is still based on the grammar by Fr Delaunay.

32 Thus the title as it appears on the folder holding the carbon copy of Mélignon's typed text. On the first page of the résumé it says 'Réhabilitation de la langue Swahili'.

33 With this Mélignon anticipated statements that appeared in print (in *L'Essor du Congo*) at the end of World War II and immediately after, and were collected in a volume edited by A. Rubbens, *Dettes de guerre* (1945). Placide Tempels' *Bantu Philosophy* belongs in this context: see on this Fabian 1970 (revised 1975).

34 The hypothesis was summarized, with references to the principal authors, by Heine (1973: 23–5).

35 This was an allusion to fears for the existence of the colony. As we know now, there were talks between Great Britain and Germany in 1937–8 which embraced the possibility of a take-over of the Congo basin by the latter: see Cornevin 1970: 181.

36 This was confirmed in the interview with Fr Boniface Poulens: see above Chapter 4, note 8.

37 In the 'Fonds Verbeken' at the Royal Museum at Tervuren there is a typed text with corrections and annotations in Verbeken's handwriting. It is titled 'Pourquoi et comment apprendre le Kiswahili?' and was destined for oral delivery. This may explain, and excuse, the author's failure to give acknowledgements to Mélignon for numerous formulations that obviously inspired his memorandum.

Bibliography

(The list contains mainly published sources and secondary works. References to archival material, government circulars, newspapers and journals are given in the notes. The principal bibliographic sources were: Catalogue of the C. M. Doke Collection, Diemer, Fodor, Hair (1966), Hendrix, Mioni, Société des Pères Blancs (1932), Starr, Streit and Dindinger, Struck (1909), Van Spaandonck, Verbeek, Walraet, Whiteley and Gutkind.)

Abel, A. 1960. *Les Musulmans noirs du Maniema*. Brussels: Centre pour l'Étude des Problèmes du Monde Musulman Contemporain.

Abemba, J. I. 1971. *Pouvoir politique traditionnel et Islam au Congo Central*. Brussels: Cahiers du CEDAF.

À l'assaut des pays nègres. Journal des missionnaires d'Alger dans l'Afrique equatoriale. 1884. Paris: Oeuvre des Écoles d'Orient.

Angogo, Rachel. 1980. 'An Inventory of KiSwahili-related pidgins and creoles'. *Ba Shiru* 10: 22–8.

Annicq, Camille. 1967. *Le Swahili véhiculaire*. Lubumbashi: Imbelco.

Barth, Heinrich. 1862 (repr. 1971). *Collection of Vocabularies of Central-African Languages*. London: Cass Library of African Studies.

Bassett, Udy. 1937 [3rd edition]. *Everyday Swahili Phrases and Vocabulary*. Nairobi: Caxton.

Becker, Herbert Theodor. 1943. *Das Schulwesen in Afrika*. Berlin: W. de Gruyter.

Becker, Jérôme. 1887. *La Vie en Afrique, ou Trois Ans dans l'Afrique centrale*, 2 vols. Paris–Brussels: J. Lébègue.

Beidelman, Thomas O. 1981. 'Contradictions between the Sacred and the Secular Life: The Church Missionary Society in Ukaguru, Tanzania, East Africa, 1876—1914.' *Comparative Studies in Society and History* 23: 73–95.

_____ 1982. *Colonial Evangelism: A Socio-Historical Study of an East African Mission at the Grassroots*. Bloomington: Indiana University Press.

Bennett, N. R. 1969. Introduction to A. W. Dodgshun, *From Zanzibar to Ujiji*. Boston, Mass.: Boston University African Studies Center.

_____ 1971. *Mirambo of Tanzania, 1840?–1884*. London: Oxford University Press.

Bentley, (Mrs) H. Margo. 1911. *Guide de conversation français–congolais*. Brussels: Ministère des Colonies.

Bickerton, Derek. 1976. 'Pidgin and Creole Studies.' *Annual Review of Anthropology* 5: 169–93.

Biographie coloniale belge–Belgische Koloniale Biographie. 1948– . Brussels: Institut Royal Colonial Belge.

Bontinck, François. 1966. *Aux origines de l'État Indépendant du Congo*. Louvain: Nauwelaerts.

_____ with K. Janssen (ed. and transl.). 1974. *L'Autobiographie de Hamed ben Mohammed el-Murjebi Tippo Tip (ca. 1840–1905)*. Brussels: Academie Royale des Sciences d'Outre-Mer.

Bontinck, François. 1974. *L'autobiographie de Hamed ben Mohammed el-Murjebi Tippo Tip (ca. 1840–1905) traduite et annotée. Avec la collaboration de Koen Janssen*. Brussels: ARSOM.

Boyd, Edgar. 1978. 'The White Fathers in Katanga–Ally or Adversary of Belgian Imperial

188

Interests, 1884–1910?'. Paper presented at the 21st Annual Meeting of the African Studies Association, Baltimore, Md.

Braekman, E. M. 1961. *Histoire du protestantisme au Congo.* Brussels: Éditions de la Librairie des Éclaireurs Unionistes.

Broomfield, G. W. 1930. 'The Development of the Swahili Language'. *Africa* 3: 516–22.

——— 1931. 'The Re-Bantuization of the Swahili Language'. *Africa* 4: 77–85.

Brutel, Emile. 1911. *Vocabulaire français–kiswahili et kiswahili–français, précédé d'une grammaire.* Brussels: C. Marci.

——— 1914. *Vocabulaire français–kiswahili et kiswahili–français.* Algiers: Maison Carrée.

Buell, Raymond Leslie. 1928. *The Native Problem in Africa,* 2 vols. New York: Macmillan.

Burssens, Amaat. 1954. *Introduction à l'étude des langues bantoues du Congo Belge.* Antwerp: De Sikkel.

Burt, A. (Mrs. F. Burt). 1923. [1st edition 1917]. *Swahili Grammar and Vocabulary.* London: Society for Promoting Christian Knowledge.

Buttaye, R. n.d. [1909]. *Dictionnaire kikongo–français, français–kikongo.* Roulers: J. De Meester.

Calloc'h, J. 1911. *Vocabulaire français–sango et sango–français: Langue commerciale de l'Oubangi-Chari, précédé d'un abrégé grammatical.* Paris: P. Geuthner.

Calvet, Louis-Jean. 1974. *Linguistique et colonialisme: Petit traité de glottophagie.* Paris: Payot.

——— 1981. *Les Langues véhiculaires.* Paris: Presses Universitaires de France.

Cameron, Verney Lovett. 1885. *Across Africa,* 2 vols. London: Dalby, Isbister & Co.

Campbell, Dugald. 1922. *In the Heart of Bantuland.* London: Seely, Service & Co.

Caprile, Jean-Pierre (ed.). 1982. *Contacts de langues et contacts de cultures. 4. L'Expansion des langues africaines peul, sango, kikongo, ciluba, swahili,* Paris: Laboratoire de Langues et Civilisations à Tradition Orale/Association d'Études Interculturelles Africanes.

Catalogue of the C. M. Doke Collection on African Languages in the Library of the University of Rhodesia. 1972. Boston, Mass.: G. K. Hall.

Certeau, Michel de. 1984 [2nd edition]. *L'Écriture de l'histoire.* Paris: Gallimard.

Ceulemans, P. 1959. *La Question arabe et le Congo (1883–1892).* Brussels: Académie Royale des Sciences Coloniales. Classe des Sciences Morales et Politiques. Mémoires. Collection in 8°, N. S. Tome XXII, fasc. 1.

Claessens, J. 1946. 'Edmond Leplae'. *IRCB Bulletin* 17. 1: 109–65.

Club Africain d'Anvers–Cercle d'Études Coloniales. n.d. [1913]. *Enseignement colonial: Programme des cours de vulgarisation. (10ᵉ Année) Session 1913–1914.* Antwerp: J.-E. Buschmann.

Colle, Pierre. n.d. [before 1912]. *Abrégé de grammaire swahilie.* Brussels: Ministère des Colonies.

——— n.d. [before 1912]. *Guide de conversation en langue swahilie.* Brussels: R. Weverbergh.

——— n.d. *Guide de conversation en langue swahilie. Précédé d'un abrégé de grammaire swahilie. À l'usage des émigrants se rendant au Katanga et au Haut-Congo Belge* [bilingual French-Flemish]. Brussels: ['Publié par les soins du Ministère des Colonies'].

——— 1913. *Les Baluba,* 2 vols. Brussels: A. Dewit.

——— and Thielemans (Père). 1928. *Guide de conversation en langue swahili, précédé d'un abrégé de grammaire swahili, à l'usage des émigrants se rendant au Katanga, au Haut-Kivu, Urundi-Ruanda.* Brussels.

Congo Belge. 1918. *Rapport d'Ensemble Annuel 1916.* London: Imprimerie Belge.

Congo Belge–Service de l'Enseignement. 1948. *Organisation de l'Enseignement Libre Subsidié pour indigènes avec le concours des Sociétés de Missions Chétiennes.* Brussels.

Cooper, Robert L. (ed.). 1982. *Language Spread: Studies in Diffusion and Social Change.* Bloomington: Indiana University Press.

Cornet, René J. 1950. *Terre katangaise. Cinquantième anniversaire du Comité Spécial du Katanga.* Brussels: Comité Spécial du Katanga.

Cornevin, Robert. 1970. *Histoire du Congo Léopoldville–Kinshasa.* Paris: Berger-Levrault.

Courboin, Albert. 1908. *Bangala, langue commerciale du Haut-Congo: Eléments et manuel de conversation avec lexique.* Antwerp: O. Forst.

Daull, R. P. 1879. *Grammaire kisouahili*. Colmar: M. Hoffmann.

Davis, J. Merle. 1967 [1st edition 1933]. *Modern Industry and the African: An Enquiry into the Effect of the Copper Mines of Central Africa upon Native Society and the Work of the Christian Missions*. London: Frank Cass.

De Bauw, Anatole. 1920. *Le Katanga: Notes sur le pays, ses ressources et l'avenir de la colonisation belge*. Brussels: F. Larcier.

De Boeck, A. 1904. *Grammaire et vocabulaire de lingala, langue du Haut-Congo*. Brussels: Polleunis & Ceuterick.

　　1927 [1st edition 1920]. *Cours théorique et pratique de lingala, avec vocabulaire et phrases usuelles*. Turnhout: H. Proost.

De Clercq, Auguste. 1911. *Grammaire pratique de la langue luba*. Brussels: Polleunis & Ceuterick.

　　1934. 'Les Langues communes au Congo Belge'. *Congo* 14.2: 161–7.

De Clercq, Louis. n.d. [1921]. *Grammaire du Kiyombe*. Brussels: Goemaere.

De Jonghe, E. 1933. 'Les Langues communes au Congo Belge'. *Congo* 13.2: 509–23.

'De la légalité des villages chrétiens'. *Congo* 3: 501–34.

Delaunay, Henri. 1885. *Dictionnaire français–kiswahili*. Paris.

　　1884. *Grammaire kiswahili*. Tours: Mame.

De Leeuw, Georges. 1911. *Le Commerce au Katanga: Influences belges et étrangères*. Brussels–Leipzig: Misch & Thron.

Diemer, E. 1961. 'Essai de bibliographie des travaux des Pères Blancs en Afrique'. *Neue Zeitschrift für Missionswissenschaft* 17: 127–33.

Dodgshun, A. W. 1969. *From Zanzibar to Ujiji: The Journal of Arthur W. Dodgshun, 1877–1879*, ed. N. R. Bennett, Boston, Mass.: Boston University African Studies Center.

Doke, Clement C. 1933. *English–Lamba Vocabulary*. Johannesburg: The University of Witwatersrand Press.

Dolan, Norbert. 1912. *Éléments pour un manuel Zande. Avec phrases, conversations et vocabulaire*. Averbode: Imprimerie de l'Abbaye.

Doob, Leonard W. 1961. *Communication in Africa: A Search for Boundaries*. New Haven, Conn.: Yale University Press.

[Dutrieux, Pierre]. Association Internationale Africaine. 1880. *Vocabulaire français–kisouahili*. Brussels: Verhavert.

Etat Indépendant du Congo. 1894. *Vocabulaire français–kisouahili*. Brussels: Van Campenhout.

East African Army Education Corps. n.d. [1st edition 1942]. *Kiswahili: A Kiswahili Instruction Book for the East Africa Command*. Entebbe: Government Printer.

East African Standard. 1909. '*Swahili.' A Vocabulary of Useful Phrases, etc., etc. Compiled to meet a Long Felt Want for the Traveller in East Africa*. Mombasa: The Standard.

École Coloniale de Liège. n.d. *Règlements et programmes*. Liège: A. Dubuisson.

École Coloniale Supérieure d'Anvers. n. d. [1920] [Bilingual brochure]. Brussels: E. Mertens. n.d. [ca. 1921–3]. [Brochure]. Antwerp: Neptune.

Elisabethville 1911–1961. 1961. Brussels: L. Cuypers.

Etat Indépendant du Congo–Département de l'Intérieur. 1904. *Recueil administratif*. Brussels: F. Van Buggenhoudt.

Etherington, Norman. 1983. 'Missionaries and the Intellectual History of Africa: A Historical Survey'. *Itinerario* 7: 116–43.

Fabian, Johannes. 1970. *Jamaa: A Charismatic Movement in Katanga*. Evanston, Ill.: Northwestern University Press.

　　1970. *Philosophie bantoue: Placide Tempels et son oeuvre vus dans une perspective historique*. Brussels: CRISP. (Revised and reprinted in A. J. Smet (ed.). *Autour de la 'Philosophie Africaine'*. Kinshasa: Presses Universitaires du Zaire. 1975. pp. 383–409).

　　1973. '*Kazi*: Conceptualizations of Labor in a Charismatic Movement among Swahili-Speaking Workers'. *Cahiers d'études africaines* 13: 293–325.

1974. 'Genres in an Emerging Tradition: An Approach to Religious Communication'. In A. W. Eister (ed.), *Changing Perspectives in the Scientific Study of Religion*. New York: Wiley Interscience, pp. 249–72.

1979. 'Rule and Process: Thoughts on Ethnography as Communication'. *Philosophy of the Social Sciences* 9: 1–26.

1981. 'Six Theses Regarding the Anthropology of African Religious Movements'. *Religion* 11: 109–26.

1983. 'Missions and the Colonization of African Languages: Developments in the Former Belgian Congo'. *Canadian Journal of African Studies* 17: 165–87.

1983. *Time and the Other: How Anthropology Makes its Object*. New York: Columbia University Press.

1985. *Language on the Road: Notes on Swahili in Two Nineteenth Century Travelogues*. Hamburg: H. Buske.

Fetter, Bruce. 1968. 'Elisabethville and Lubumbashi: The Segmentary Growth of a Colonial City 1910–1945'. Unpublished Ph. D. thesis, Department of History, University of Wisconsin.

1973. *L'Union Minière du Haut Katanga, 1920–1940: La Naissance d'une sous-culture totalitaire*. Brussels: Cahiers du CEDAF.

1974. 'African Associations in Elisabethville, 1910–1935: Their Origins and Development'. *Études d'histoire africaine* 4: 206–10.

1976. *The Creation of Elisabethville 1910–1940*. Stanford, Calif.: Hoover Institution Press.

[Flament, F. *et al.*]. 1952. *La Force publique de sa naissance à 1914*. Brussels: Institut Royal Colonial Belge. Section des Sciences Morales et Politiques. Mémoires. Collection in 8°. Tome XXVII.

Fodor, István. 1975. *Pallas und andere afrikanische Vokabularien vor dem 19. Jahrhundert*. Hamburg: H. Buske.

Foucault, Michel. 1973. *The Order of Things: An Archeology of the Human Sciences*. New York: Vintage Books.

Frères Maristes. n.d. [1936]. *Swahili–français–français–swahili (Grammaire, exercices, conversation, lectures, vocabulaires)*. Stanleyville: Imprimerie des Frères Maristes.

Gabriel, Frère [Henri Vermeersch]. 1921. *Dictionnaire français–kiluba*. Brussels: A. Dewit.

1921 [3rd edition]. *Étude du Tshiluba*. Brussels: Ministère des Colonies.

Galton, Francis. 1891 [1st edition 1853]. *Narrative of an Explorer in Tropical South Africa. Being an Account of a Visit to Damaraland in 1851*. London: Ward, Lock & Co.

Gilliard, Leo. 1928. *Grammaire pratique lontomba*. Brussels–Elisabethville: Editions de l'Essorial.

Gilman, Charles. 1970. 'Indicateurs de la variation stylistique dans le Swahili de Kisangani'. *Révue congolaise des sciences humaines* 1: 57–62.

1976. 'Lexical reinterpretation in Zairean Swahili'. *Swahili* 46: 13–16.

Giraud, Gaston. *Vocabulaire des dialectes sango, bakongo et a' zande*. Paris: A. Challamel.

Goffiné, Leonhard. 1913. *Kitabu cha Wakristu. Postilla catholica seu epistolarum et evangeliorum dominicarum ac festorum explanationes homileticae breviores quas ad usum christianorum Africae orientalis et in linguam suahelicam vertit etc*. Averbode: Ex Typographia Abbatiae.

Greschat, Hans-Jürgen. 1967. *Kitawala. Ursprung, Ausbreitung und Religion der Watch-Tower-Bewegung in Zentral-Afrika*. Marburg: N. G. Elwert.

Grévisse, F. 1951. *Le Centre extra-coutumier d'Elisabethville. Quelques aspects de la politique indigène du Haut-Katanga industriel*. Brussels: Institut Royal Colonial Belge. Section des Sciences Morales et Politiques. Mémoires. Collection in 8°. Tome XXI.

Guebels, L. 1949. *Aperçu rétrospectif des travaux de la Commission Permanente pour la Protection des Indigènes d'après les rapports des Sessions*. Elisabethville: Editions CEPSI.

Guillerme, Père. 1920. *Grammaire et dictionnaire français–chibemba*. Malines.

Hair, P. E. H. 1963. Introduction to S. W. Koelle, *Polyglotta Africana*.

1966. 'Collections of Vocabularies of Western Africa before the Polyglotta: A Key'. *Journal of African Languages* 5: 208–17.

191

Language and colonial power

Halewyck, Michel. 1910. *La Charte Coloniale. Commentaire de la loi du 18 octobre 1908 sur le gouvernement du Congo belge*. Brussels: M. Weissenbruch.

Hamiss-Kitumboy, L. W. 1973. 'Lugha ya Kiswahili katika Zaire'. *Kiswahili* 43: 64–7.

Harries, Lyndon. 1956. 'Le Swahili au Kongo belge'. *Congo Overzee* 22: 395–400.

Harris, Zellig, and Fred Lukoff. 1942. 'The phonemes of Kingwana–Swahili', *Journal of the American Oriental Society* 62: 333–8.

Hartog, François. 1980. *Le Miroir d'Hérodote*. Paris: Gallimard.

Hautefelt, J. B. n.d. [ca. 1912]. *Livre de lecture français–swahili pour indigènes du Congo Belge (traduction en Swahili par le R. P. Van den Eynde)*. Dison: Imprimerie Disonaise.

Heine, Bernd. 1973. *Pidgin-Sprachen im Bantu-Bereich*. Berlin: D. Reimer.

1977. 'Vertical and Horizontal Communication in Africa'. *Africa-Spectrum* 12: 231–8.

Hendrix, Melvin K. 1982. *An International Bibliography of African Lexicons*. Metuchen, NJ–London: Scarecrow Press.

Heremans, Roger. 1966. *Les Établissements de l'Association Internationale Africaine au Lac Tanganika et les Pères Blancs. Mpala et Karéma, 1877–1885*. Tervuren: Musée Royale de l'Afrique Centrale. Annales-Série in 8°. Sciences Historiques, nr. 3.

1978. 'Mission et Écoles: L'éducation dans les missions des Pères Blancs en Afrique centrale avant 1914. Objectifs et réalisations'. Doctoral dissertation, Department of Modern History, University of Louvain.

Heylen, Walter. n.d. [1977]. *Initiation pratique au Swahili*. Bukavu: Centre d'Études de Langues Africaines.

Hodgkin, Thomas. 1957. *Nationalism in Colonial Africa*. New York: New York University Press.

Hulstaert, G. 1939. 'La Langue véhiculaire dans l'enseignement.' *Aequatoria* 2: 85–9.

Hurel, Père. 1911. *Manuel de la langue kinyarwanda*. Berlin.

1921. *Grammaire kinyarwanda*. Algiers: Maison Carrée.

1926. *Dictionnaire runyarwanda–français et français–runyarwanda*. Algiers: Maison Carrée.

Hymes, Dell. 1964. 'Introduction: Towards Ethnographies of Communication'. In J. J. Gumperz and Dell Hymes (eds.), *The Ethnography of Communication*. Menasha, Wis.: American Anthropologist. pp. 1–34.

(ed.). 1971. *Pidginization and Creolization of Languages*. Cambridge: Cambridge University Press.

1972. 'Models of Interaction of Language and Social Life.' In J. J. Gumperz and Dell Hymes (eds.), *Directions in Sociolinguistics*. New York: Holt, Rinehart and Winston. pp. 35–71.

Inspection Générale de l'Enseignement. 1931. *Instructions relatives aux programmes à suivre et aux méthodes à employer dans les écoles de la Colonie*. Léo-Kalina: Imprimerie du Gouvernement.

Jadot, J.-M. 1950. 'Un Tournaisien, médecin de l'A.I.A.: P.-J. Dutrieux'. *Bulletin des Séances* (Institut Royal Colonial Belge) 21: 350–70.

Janzen, John M., and Wyatt MacGaffey. 1974. *An Anthology of Kongo Religion: Primary Texts from Lower Zaire*. Lawrence: University of Kansas.

Jardine, G. Murray. 1927. *Abridged Swahili Grammar: Phrases, Stories and Vocabulary*. London: Sheldon Press.

Jenniges, E. 1909. *Dictionnaire français–kiluba exposant le vocabulaire de la langue kiluba telle qu'elle se parle au Katanga*. Bruxelles: Spineux & Cie.

Jewsiewicki, Bogumil. 1976. 'La Contestation sociale et la naissance du prolétariat au Zaire au cours de la première moitié du XXᵉ siècle'. *Canadian Journal of African Studies* 10: 47–71.

1979. 'Zaire enters the World System: Its Colonial Incorporation as the Belgian Congo'. In G. Gran (ed.), *The Political Economy of Underdevelopment*. New York: Praeger. pp. 29–53.

Johnston, Harry H. 1919. *A Comparative Study of the Bantu and the Semi-Bantu Languages*, 2 vols. Oxford: Clarendon Press.

Jones, Thomas Jesse. n.d. [ca. 1924]. *Education in East Africa: A Study of East, Central and South Africa by the Second African Education Commission under the Auspices of the Phelps-Stokes*

192

Fund, in Cooperation with the International Education Board. London: Edinburgh House Press.

Kabamba Mbikay. 1979. 'Stratigraphie des langues et communications à Lubumbashi'. *Problèmes Sociaux Zairois* 124–5: 47–74.

Katanga-Congo Belge. n.d. [1911]. *Notes sur les lois à l'usage des Résidents et Voyageurs. Handy Note Book on the Laws in Use for Residents and Travellers.* Bulawayo: Argus Co.

Katzenellenbogen, S. E. 1973. *Railways and the Copper Mines of Katanga.* Oxford: Clarendon Press.

Kajiga, G. 1967. *Initiation à la culture ntu. Grammaire Swahili.* Goma: 'B.P. 50'.

Khalid, Abdallah. 1977. *The Liberation of Swahili from European Appropriation.* Nairobi: East African Literature Bureau.

Koelle. S. W. 1853 [reprinted 1963]. *Polyglotta Africana, or A Comparative Vocabulary of Nearly Three Hundred Words and Phrases in More than One Hundred Distinct African Languages.* London: Church Missionary House.

Krapf, Johann Ludwig. 1850. *Vocabulary of Six East African Languages: Kisuaheli, Kinika, Kikamba, Kipokomo, Kihiau, Kigalla.* Tübingen: L. Friederichsen.

Kuypers, Père. 1920. *Grammaire ruhaya.* Boxtel: [White Fathers].

Labeye (Lieutenant-Colonel). 1928. *Cours de langue indigène.* Brussels: R. Louis.

La Conférence de Géographie de 1876: Recueil d'études. 1976. Brussels: Académie Royale des Sciences d'Outre-Mer.

Lagergren, David. 1970. *Mission and State in the Congo: A Study of the Relations between Protestant Missions and the Congo Independent State Authorities with Special Reference to the Equator District, 1885–1903.* Uppsala: Gleerup.

Lanteri-Sem, Monique. 1981. 'Discours et prâtiques missionnaires aux origines de la colonisation du Zaire (1885–1908)'. Doctoral dissertation, University of Nice.

Last, J. T. 1885. *Polyglotta Africana Orientalis.* London: Society for the Promotion of Christian Knowledge.

Le Breton, F. H. n.d. [1st edition 1936]. *Up-Country Swahili: Simplified Swahili for the Farmer, Merchant, Business Man, and their Wives and for all who deal with the Up-Country Native.* Richmond: Simpson & Co.

Lecoste, Baudouin. 1954. 'Le Ngwana, variété congolaise du Swahili'. *Kongo-Overzee* 20: 391–408.

Lemaire, Charles. 1897 [2nd edition]. *Vocabulaire pratique: français, anglais, zanzibarite (swahili), fiote, kibangi–irébou, mongo, bangala.* Brussels: Ch. Bulens.

Les Jésuites belges et les missions. Bruges: Houdmont Frères.

Lieberson, Stanley. 1982. 'Forces Affecting Language Spread: Some Basic Propositions'. In R.L. Cooper (ed.), *Language Spread.* Bloomington: Indiana University Press. pp. 37–62.

Liesenborghs, O. 1938. 'Wat is Kingwana?: *Kongo-Overzee* 4: 233–49.

Luwel, Marcel. 1976. 'Verney Lovett Cameron ou l'échec d'un concurrent de Stanley'. In *La Conférence de Géographie de 1876. Recueil d'études.* Brussels: Académic Royale des Sciences d'Outre-Mer. pp. 57–169.

Madan, A. C., and. F. Johnson. 1939. *A Standard Swahili–English Dictionary.* London: Oxford University Press.

Markowitz, Marvin D. 1973. *Cross and Sword: The Political Role of the Christian Missions in the Belgian Congo, 1908–1960.* Stanford, Calif.: Hoover Institution Press.

Maus, Albert. 1938, 1939. 'Le Nouveau programme de l'enseignement libre'. *Congo* 1938, 2: 490–525; 1939, 1: 1–20.

Mazrui, Ali A. 1975. *The Political Sociology of the English Language: An African Perspective.* The Hague: Mouton.

and Pio Zirimu. 1978. 'Church, State, and Marketplace in the Spread of Kiswahili: Comparative Educational Implications'. In B. Spolsky and R. L. Cooper (eds.), *Case Studies in Bilingual Education.* Rowley, Mass.: Newbury House. pp. 427–53.

Mehnert, W. 1973. 'The Language Question in the Colonial Policy of German Imperialism'. In T.

Büttner and G. Brehme (eds.) *African Studies–Afrika Studien.* Berlin: Akademie-Verlag. pp. 383–97.

Mélignon, A. 1939. 'Réhabilitation du Swahili au Katanga'. Unpublished typescript. Jadotville.

Ménard, François. 1908. *Grammaire kirundi.* Algiers: Maison Carrée.

— 1909. *Dictionnaire français–kirundi et kirundi–français.* Roulers: J. de Meester.

Millman, W. 1917. *Petit vocabulaire de français–anglais–swahili.?* Yakusu: Baptist Missionary Society.

Ministère des Colonies. n.d. [ca. 1912–14]. *Petit vocabulaire des mots Ki-Swahili les plus usités dans le Katanga.* Brussels: Imprimerie Industrielle et Financière.

[E. Leplae]. 1912. *Guide pour les émigrants agricoles belges au Katanga. Annexe: Quelques mots de la langue Swahili parlée au Katanga.* Brussels: Imprimerie Industrielle et Financière.

— 1914. *Annuaire officiel pour 1914.* Brussels: A. Lesigne.

— 1925. *Projet d'organisation de l'Enseignement libre au Congo belge avec le concours des Sociétés des Missions nationales.* Brussels: M. Weissenbruch.

Ministère des Colonies de Belgique, 1ᵉ Direction. 1918. *Recueil à l'usage des fonctionnaires et des agents du Service Territorial.* London.

Ministère des Colonies – Office Colonial. 1911 [4th edition]. *Renseignements à l'usage des colons et des commerçants désireux de s'établir au Katanga.* Brussels: Hayez.

Mioni, A. 1967. 'La Bibliographie de la langue swahili'. *Cahiers d'études africaines* 7: 485–532.

Missions Catholiques du Congo. 1907. *Aperçu sur certaines questions dans la réunion tenue à Léopoldville en Février 1907.* Kisantu: Imprimerie De Bergeyck S. Ignace.

Missions Catholiques du Congo Belge. 1910. *Instructions aux Missionaires.* Antwerp: De Vlijt.

— 1920. *Instructions aux Missionnaires.* Wetteren: J. De Meester.

— 1930. *Recueil d'instructions aux Missionnaires.* Louvain: J. Kuyl-Otto.

Moltedo, G. 1905. *Petit vocabulaire des langues arabe et ki-swahili.* Brussels: Mounom.

Monchamp, Georges. 1904. *L'Oeuvre linguistique des Pères Blancs d'Afrique.* Brussels: Hayez.

Mottoulle, L. 1946. *Politique sociale de l'Union Minière du Haut-Katanga pour sa main-d'oeuvre indigène et ses résultats au cours de vingt années d'application.* Brussels: Institut Royal Colonial Belge. Section des Sciences Morales et Politiques. Mémoires. Collection in 8°. Tome XIV, fasc. 3.

Muhlowe, E. 1969. *La Communauté musulmane de Kasongo dans l'évolution politique récente (1958–1965).* Mémoire de licence, University of Louvain.

Munongo, A. Mwenda. 1967. *Pages d'histoire Yeke.* Lubumbashi: CEPSI.

Mwalimu Yoani [J. B. Hautefelt]. 1912. *Kitabu cha kusoma Kingwana.* Brussels: J. Vanderhoeven.

Natalis, Ernest. 1960. *La langue Swahilie,* 2 vols. Liège: Editions FULREAC.

— 1961. *Dictionnaire de poche français–kiswahili: Kanusi ya mfukoni Kiswahili–Kifaransa.* Liège: Editions FULREAC.

Nida, Eugene A. 1949. 'Some Language Problems in the Congo'. *Congo Mission News* 145: 14–16.

Norris, Edwin. 1841. *Outline of a Vocabulary of a Few of the Principal Languages of Western and Central Africa; Compiled for the Use of the Niger Expedition.* London: J. W. Parker.

Ntambwe Beya Ngindu. 1979. 'L'Enseignement salésien et son impact au Shaba (1911–1949)'. *Problèmes sociaux zairois* 124–5: 147–56.

Ntamunoza Mambo-Mbili. 1980. 'Vocabulaire et idéologie dans la chronique des missionnaires d'Afrique (Pères blancs) 1892–1900: Essai sur la fonction socio-culturelle d'un langage missionaire', 2 vols. Doctoral dissertation, Faculté des Lettres, National University of Zaire, Lubumbashi.

Olsen, F. V. 1950. 'L'Historique des troupes du Katanga pendant la période 1910 jusqu'à l'offensive en A.O.A pendant la première guerre mondiale'. In Comité Spécial du Katanga (ed.) *Comptes rendus du Congrès Scientifique Elisabethville 1950.* Brussels: CSK.

Pallas, Simon Peter. 1787–9. *Linguarum totius orbis vocabularia comparativa etc.,* 2 vols. [Text in Russian.] Moscow: C. Schnoor.

Pères Blancs. 1902. *Grammaire en Kiswahili à l'usage des nègres du Haut Congo*. Algiers: Maison Carrée.

1907. *Vocabulaire français – kitabwa et kitabwa – français*. Algiers: Maison Carrée.

1909. *Manuel kitabwa*. Algiers: Maison Carrée.

1920. [1st version 1903]. *Elimu ya Inchi*, 2 vols. Baudouinville: Vicariat Apostolique du Haut-Congo.

1921. *Vocabulaire kiswahili – latin*. Algiers: Maison Carrée.

1925. *Grammaire latine – kiswahili*. Algiers: Maison Carrée.

1925. *Vocabulaire latin – kiswahili*. Algiers: Maison Carrée.

1929. *Sarufi ya Kiswahili*. Albertville: Procure des Pères Blancs.

1939. *Exercises de grammaire en kiswahili*. Algiers: Maison Carrée.

Pères Jésuites, 1915. *Petit manuel pratique à l'usage des missionnaires*. [In Swahili.] Kisantu: Pères Jésuites.

Perrings, Charles. 1979. *Black Mineworkers in Central Africa*. London: Heinemann.

Philippson, Gérard. 1981. 'Le Swahili et l'expansion des langues africaines'. In J. -P. Caprile (ed.) *Contacts des langues et contacts de cultures*. Paris: LACITO. pp. 87–104.

Pirotte, J. 1973. *Périodiques missionnaires belges d'expression française (1889–1940), reflets de cinquante années d'évolution d'une mentalité*. Louvain: Recueil de Travaux d'Histoire et de Philologie. 6ᵉ série, no. 2.

Polomé, Edgar C. 1967. *Swahili Language Handbook*. N.p.: Center for Applied Linguistics.

1968. 'The Choice of Official Languages in the Democratic Republic of the Congo'. In J. Fishman, C. Ferguson and J. Das Gupta (eds.) *Language Problems in Developing Nations*. New York: Wiley. pp. 295–311.

1968. 'Lubumbashi Swahili'. *Journal of African Languages* 7: 14–25.

1972. 'Sociolinguistic Problems in Tanzania and Zaire'. *The Conch* 4: 64–83.

Quinot, H. 1925. *Vocabulaire français – kiswahili – lingala. Élaboré spécialement à l'usage des agents au Congo des Sociétés Congolaises*. Brussels: Schicks.

1926. *Petite grammaire de la langue kiswahilie (Swahilie) du Congo Belge (Katanga et Province Orientale)*. Brussels: R. Weverbergh.

1926. *Vocabulaire français – kiswahili-tshiluba (Kiluba) du Congo belge*. Brussels.

Rabinow, Paul. 1975. *Symbolic Domination*. Chicago, Ill.: University of Chicago Press.

Raddatz, Hugo. 1892. *Die Suahili-Sprache (enthaltend Grammatik, Gespräche, Dialekte aus dem Innern und Wörterverzeichnisse mit einem Anhang: Sudan-Arabisch und einer Einführung in die Bantusprachen)*. Leipzig: C. A. Koch.

Raison-Jourde, Françoise. 1977. 'L'Échange inégal de la langue: La pénétration des techniques linguistiques dans une civilisation de l'oral'. *Annales* 32: 639–69.

Ratcliffe, B. J., and H. B. Elphinstone. 1932. *Modern Swahili*. London: Sheldon.

n.d. [1932]. *A New English – Swahili Phrase Book*. Nairobi: East African Standard.

Reichart, A., and M. Küsters. 1926. *Elementary Kiswaheli Grammar or Introduction into the East African Negro Language and Life*. Heidelberg: J. Groos.

Renault, François. 1971. *Lavigerie, l'esclavage africain et l'Europe*, 2 vols. Paris: E. De Boccard.

Rigby, Peter. 1981. 'Pastors and Pastoralists: Differential Penetration of Christianity among East African Cattle Herders'. *Comparative Studies in Society and History* 23: 96–129.

Roehl, K. 1930. 'The Linguistic Situation in East Africa'. *Africa* 3: 191–202.

Roelens, Victor. 1938. *Instructions aux Missionnaires Pères Blanc du Haut-Congo*. Baudouinville: Vicariat Apostolique du Haut-Congo.

1948–9. *Notre Vieux Congo 1891–1917. Souvenirs du premier evêque du Congo belge*, 2 vols. Namur: Grands Lacs-Collection Lavigerie.

Roeykens, Auguste. 1965. *La Politique religieuse de l'État Indépendant du Congo. Documents* I. Brussels: Académie Royale des Sciences d'Outre-Mer. Classe des Sciences Morales et Politiques. Mémoires. Collection in 8°, N. S. Tome XXXII, fasc. 1.

Roland, H. 1937. *Grammaire de la langue kisanga (Haut-Katanga)*. St André-les-Bruges: Missions Bénédictines.

Rossé, René. 1977. 'Le Swahili populaire de Lubumbashi'. Doctoral dissertation, University of Nice.

Rossie, Jean-Pierre. 1976. *Bibliographie commentée de la communauté musulmane au Zaire des origines à 1975*. Brussels: Cahiers du CEDAF.

Rotberg, Robert I. 1967. 'Introduction to the Second Edition'. In J. Merle Davis, *Modern Industry and the African*. London: F. Cass & Co. pp. vii–xxix.

Royaume de Belgique – Ministère des Colonies. 1930 [5th edition]. *Recueil à l'usage des fonctionnaires et des agents du Service Territorial au Congo Belge*. Brussels: M. Weissenbruch.

Rubbens, A. (ed.). 1945. *Dettes de guerre*. Elisabethville: Imbelco.

Sacleux, Charles. 1939. *Dictionnaire swahili–français*. Paris: Institut d'Ethnologie.

Salesian Missions. 1918. *Kitabu cha kusoma. Livre de lecture*. Capetown: Salesian Press.

[J. Sak and F. Verboven]. 1921. *Kitabu cha kusoma kwa wanafunzi ya Madarasa wa 'Don Bosco'*. Lubumbashi: Mapadiri Salesiani.

Samain, A. n.d. [1923]. *La Langue kisonge: Grammaire, vocabulaire, proverbes*. Brussels: Goemaere.

Samarin, William S. 1982a. 'Colonization and Pidginization on the Ubangi River'. *Journal of African Languages and Linguistics* 4: 142.

1982b. 'Goals, Roles, and Language Skills in Colonizing Central Equatorial Africa'. *Anthropological Linguistics* 24: 410–22.

Schebesta, Paul. 1931. 'Meine Forschungsreise in Belgisch-Kongo, 1929–1930'. *Africa* 4: 401–17.

Schicho, Walter, with M. Ndala. 1980. *Kiswahili von Lubumbashi*. Vienna: Veröffentlichungen der Institute für Afrikanistik der Ägyptologie der Universität Wien, 10.

with M. Ndala. 1981. *Le Groupe Mufwankolo*. Vienna: Veröffentlichungen der Institute für Afrikanistik und Ägyptologie der Universität Wien, 14.

1982. *Syntax des Swahili von Lubumbashi*. Vienna: Veröffentlichungen der Institute für Afrikanistik and Ägyptologie der Universität Wien, 16.

Schieffelin, Edward L. 1981. 'Evangelical Rhetoric and the Transformation of Traditional Culture in Papua New Guinea'. *Comparative Studies in Society and History* 23: 150–6.

Schmidt, Wilhelm. 1930. 'The Use of the Vernacular in Education in Africa'. *Africa* 3: 117–46.

Seidel, A., and I. Struyf. 1910. *La Langue congolaise: Grammaire, vocabulaire systématique, phrases graduées et lectures*. Paris: J. Groos.

Shapiro, Judith. 1981. 'Ideologies of Catholic Missionary Practice in a Postcolonial Era'. *Comparative Studies in Society and History* 23: 130–49.

Shihabuddin Chiraghdin, and Mathias Mnyampala. 1977. *Historia ya Kiswahili*. Nairobi – Dar es Salaam: Oxford University Press.

Slade Reardon, Ruth. 1968. 'Catholics and Protestants in the Congo.' In C. G. Baeta (ed.), *Christianity in Tropical Africa*. London: Oxford University Press. pp. 83–98.

Smith, Edwin E. 1926. *The Christian Mission in Africa: A Study based on the Proceedings of the International Conference at Le Zoute, Belgium, September 14th to 21st, 1926*. London: The International Missionary Council.

Société des Missionnaires d'Afrique (Pères Blancs). 1914. *Directoire des Constitutions*. Algiers: Maison Carrée.

Société des Pères Blancs. 1932. *Publications en langues africaines*. Algiers: Maison Carrée.

Société d'Études Coloniales. 1885. *École Coloniale: Programme des cours et règlement d'ordre*. Brussels: Imprimerie des Travaux Publics.

1895, 1896, 1897. *Manuel du Voyageur et du Résident au Congo*, 3 parts. Brussels: Imprimerie des Travaux Publics (1895), A. Lesigne (1896), P. Weissenbruch (1897).

Sohier, A. 1938. *Droit de procédure du Congo belge: le régime pénitentiaire congolois*. Corpus juris Belgici. Brussels.

Soors, M. 1927. *Le Suaheli usuel: Guide de conversation à l'usage des fonctionnaires et agents territoriaux au Congo Belge.* Brussels: L'Essor Colonial et Maritime.

— 1933. *Termes swahili employés en justice. Ufundisho wa sultani na hakimu wao na wanyampara wao kama uliotungwa ku inchi ya Bakusu.* Stanleyville: Imprimerie du Gouvernement.

Spinette, J. 1960. *Vocabulaire kingwana – français (kiswahili). Environ 1300 mots et expressions rassemblés en Ituri et à Stanleyville.* Brussels: Direction de l'Agriculture, des Forêts et de l'Élevage.

Stanley, Henry Morton. 1878. *Through the Dark Continent*, 2 vols. London: Sampson Low, Marston, Searle & Rivington.

Stapleton, Walter Henry. 1903. *Comparative Handbook of Congo Languages.* Yakusu: Baptist Missionary Society.

Starr, Frederick. 1908. *A Bibliography of Congo Languages.* Chicago, Ill.: University of Chicago Press.

Steere, Edward. 1870. *A Handbook of the Swahili Language, As Spoken at Zanzibar.* London: Society for the Promotion of Christian Knowledge.

— 1870. *Swahili Tales, As Told by Natives of Zanzibar.* London: Bell and Daldy.

— 1878. *Swahili Exercises.* Zanzibar: UMCA.

Stengers, Jean. 1963. *Belgique et Congo: L'élaboration de la Charte Coloniale.* Brussels: Renaissance du Livre.

Stipe, Claude E. 1980. 'Anthropologists versus Missionaries: The Influence of Presuppositions'. *Current Anthropology* 21: 165–79.

Streit, Robert, and Johannes Dindinger. 1952–4. *Bibliotheca Missionum. Afrikanische Missionsliteratur*, Vols. 17, 18, 19, 20. Freiburg: Herder.

Struck, Bernhard. 1909. *Suaheli-Bibliographie. Mit einer Einführung in die moderne Suaheli-Literatur.* Leipzig: R. Haupt.

— 1921. 'Die Einheitssprache Deutsch – Ostafrikas.' *Koloniale Rundschau* 4: 164–96.

Swartenbroeckx, Pierre. 1973. *Dictionnaire kikongo et kituba – français.* Bandundu: Centre d'Études Ethnologiques.

Szombati-Fabian, I., and J. Fabian, 1976. 'Art, History and Society: Popular Painting in Shaba, Zaire'. *Studies in the Anthropology of Visual Communication* 3: 1–21.

Tempels, Placide. 1945. *La Philosophie bantoue.* Elisabethville: Imbelco.

Thibaut, Emile. 1911. *Les Jésuites et les fermes-chapelles.* Brussels: Goemaere.

Torrend, J. 1891. *A Comparative Grammar of the South-African Bantu Languages.* London: Kegan Paul, Trench, Trübner & Co.

Tournay-Detillieux, J. 1909. *Loi sur le gouvernement du Congo Belge: Résumé complet des discussions.* Brussels: A. et G. Bulens.

Troubetzkoy, Nicolas. 1982 [first publ. 1926]. 'Une oeuvre littéraire: "Le Voyage au delà des trois mers" d'Athanase Nikitine'. In Athanase Nikitine, *Le Voyage au delà des trois mers.* Paris: Maspéro. pp. 79–114.

Tuckey, J. K. 1818 [reprinted 1967]. *Narrative of an Expedition to Explore the River Zaire Usually Called the Congo, in South Africa, in 1816.* London: J. Murray [Frank Cass].

Turner, Victor. 1975. 'Symbolic Studies'. *Biennial Review of Anthropology* 4.

Union Coloniale Belge. 1912. *Cours de préparation coloniale: Session 1912–13.* Brussels: Imprimerie de 'L'Expansion Belge.'

— 1914. *Cours de préparation coloniale.* Brussels: Imprimerie de 'L'Expansion Belge.'

— 1924. *Cours de préparation coloniale.* Brussels: R. Louis.

— 1927. *Cours de préparation coloniale.* Brussels: R. Louis.

Union Minière du Haut-Katanga. 1938. *Langage kiswahili: Vocabulaires et éléments de conversation à l'usage des agents de la société.* Brussels: Imprimerie Industrielle et Financière.

— 1956. *Union Minière du Haut-Katanga 1906–1956.* Brussels: L. Cuypers.

— n.d. *Monographie 1943.* Elisabethville: Imbelco.

Université Coloniale de Belgique. n.d. [1927]. *Faculté des Sciences Politiques et Administratives.*

Section commerciale annexée. Année académique 1927–1928. Antwerp.

1928. *Faculté des Sciences Politiques et Administratives.* Antwerp: E. Stockmans & Co.

n.d. [after 1928]. *Faculté des Sciences Politiques et Administratives. Section commerciale coloniale annexée.* Antwerp: Imprimerie Anvers-Bourse.

Valdman, Albert (ed.). 1977. *Pidgin and Creole Linguistics.* Bloomington: Indiana University Press.

1981. 'Pidgins et créoles'. In J. Perrot (ed.) *Les Langues dans le monde ancien et moderne.* Paris: CNRS 2ᵉ partie.

Van Acker, Auguste. 1907. *Dictionnaire kitabwa – français et français – kitabwa.* Brussels: Publication de L'État Indépendant du Congo.

Van Avermaet, E., and B. Mbuya. 1954. *Dictionnaire kiluba – français.* Tervuren: Musée Royal de l'Afrique Centrale.

Van Bulck, G. 1948. *Les Recherches linguistiques au Congo Belge.* Brussels: Institut Royal Colonial Belge. Section des Sciences Morales et Politiques. Mémoires. Collection en 8°. Tome XVI.

Van der Burgt, J. M. M. 1903. *Dictionnaire français – kirundi.* Bois-le-Duc: Sociéte 'L'Illustration Catholique.'

Vandermeieren, J. 1912. *Grammaire de la langue kiluba – hemba telle qu'elle est parlée par les Baluba de l'est-Katanga.* Brussels: Ministère des Colonies.

1913. *Vocabulaire kiluba hemba – français, français – kiluba hemba.* Brussels: Ministère des Colonies.

Van de Weyer, P., and J. Quets. 1929. *Vocabulaire français – kiswahili (et bemba) et éléments de conversation.* Brussels: Imprimerie Industrielle et Financière.

Vanheusden, R. 1928. *Grammaire et exercises pratiques chibemba français.* Kafubu: Imprimerie de l'École Professionnelle Salésienne.

Van Overbergh, C. 1913. *Les Nègres d'Afrique.* Brussels: A. Dewit.

Vansina, Jan. 1966. *Kingdoms of the Savanna.* Madison: University of Wisconsin Press.

1976. 'L'Afrique centrale vers 1875'. In *La Conférence de Géographie de 1876.* Brussels: Académie Royale des Sciences d'Outre-Mer. pp. 1–31.

Van Spaandonck, Marcel. 1965. *Practical and Systematical Swahili Bibliography. Linguistics 1850–1963.* Leiden: E. J. Brill.

Verbeek, Léon. 1982. *Les Salésiens de l'Afrique Centrale. Bibliographie 1911–1980.* Rome: Libreria Ateneo Salesiano.

Verbeken, Auguste. 1928. *Abrégé de grammaire Tshiluba.* Brussels – Elisabethville: Éditions de l'Essorial.

1934–5. 'Pour apprendre le Kingwana'. Weekly column in *Ngonga* (Elisabethville).

1936. 'Les Langues véhiculaires au Congo Belge'. *Essor du Congo,* May 1.

1936–7. 'Petit cours de Swahili'. Column in *L'Essor du Congo* (Elisabethville).

1938. *Petit cours de Kiswahili pratique, suivi d'un vocabulaire français – kiswahili et kiswahili – français.* Elisabethville: Imbelco.

1956. *Msiri: Roi du Garenganze.* Brussels: L. Cuypers.

Vertongen, Lucien. 1912. *La Cléricalisation du Congo.* Brussels: H. Kumps-Robyn.

Vicariat de Buta. 1909. *Kitabu tca kusoma Kingwana: Livre de lecture en Langue Swahili qui est la plus répandue parmi les langues bantou au Congo Belge. A l'usage des Ecoles-Chapelles.* Averbode. Imprimerie de l'Abbaye.

Vice Gouverneur du Katanga. 1911. *Règlement sur les constructions dans les circonscriptions urbaines.* Brussels: S. A. Belge d'Imprimerie.

Vitale, Anthony J. 1980. 'KiSetla: Linguistic and Sociolinguistic Aspects of a Pidgin Swahili in Kenya.' *Anthropological Linguistics* 22: 47–65.

Vocabulaire de Ville de Elisabethville ... Edité par les agents anciennes domestiques aux communes de Elisabethville. Hiyi vocabulaire ya munji wa Elisabethville ... yenye kufanziwa kwa watu hawo wazamani wa chama ya yitwa waboyi (domestiques) wenye kupatikana mu makaponi tatu ya Elisabethville. 1965. [compiled by Yav André]. Polycopied text. Lubumbashi.

Vocabulaire français – fiote pour le chemin de caravanes de Matadi à Léopoldville. n.d. [1886]. Brussels: Van Campenhout.

Walraet, M. 1954, 1960. *Bibliographie du Katanga.* Brussels: Institut Royal Colonial Belge. Mémoires Collection in 8°. Tom. xxxii, N. S. Tom. xxiii.

White Fathers. 1954. *The White Fathers' Bemba – English Dictionary: Revised Edition.* London: Longmans, Green & Co.

Whitehead, John, and L. Whitehead. 1928. *Manuel de Kingwana, le dialecte occidental de Swahili etc.* Waiyika: La Mission.

Whiteley, Wilfred. 1969. *Swahili: The Rise of a National Language.* London: Methuen.

and A. E. Gutkind. 1954. *A Linguistic Bibliography of East Africa.* Kampala: The East African Swahili Committee and The East African Institute of Social Research.

Woods, R. E. Broughall. 1924. *A Short Introductory Dictionary of the Kaonde Language with English – Kaonde Appendix.* London: The Religious Tract Society.

Wright, Marcia. 1965. 'Swahili Language Policy, 1890–1940'. *Swahili* 35: 40–8.

Wtterwulghe, George-François. 1904 [1st edition 1903]. *Vocabulaire à l'usage des fonctionnaires se rendant dans les territoires du district de l'Uele et de l'enclave Redjaf-Lado.* n.p.: ['Publication de l'Etat Indépendant du Congo'].

Yanga, Tshimpaka. 1980. 'A Sociolinguistic Identification of Lingala (Republic of Zaire)'. Ph.D. dissertation, Department of Anthropology, University of Texas at Austin.

Yates, Barbara Y. 1978. 'Shifting Goals of Industrial Education in the Congo, 1878–1908'. *African Studies Review* 21: 33–48.

1980. 'The Origins of Language Policy in Zaire'. *Journal of Modern African Studies* 18: 257–79.

Index

Abel, A., 169
Abemba, J. I., 169
administration, administrators, 42, 47, 51,
  73, 81, 95, 98, 102, 137, 141, 144, 148,
  152, 159, 165, 174, 177; responding to
  survey on education, 51, 53–8, 66, 170–1
administrative divisions, *see* Congo, Belgian
agriculture, 74, 98–9; and settlers, 99,
  114–15, 123
Angogo, R., 184
Annicq, C., 125, 130, 187
appropriation, of language, 8, 12, 13, 34, 76,
  83, 93, 111, 135–6, 148, 156, 186
Arabic, 22, 23, 25, 33, 46, 147, 160, 163
Arabs, *see* Swahili, people
Arnot, F. S., 7, 163
assimilationists vs. indigenists, 78, 81, 152,
  184
Association Internationale Africaine, AIA,
  19, 24ff, 167, 168, 174
Atlantic coast, 7, 35, 72

Barth, H., 18, 165
Basset, U., 184
Becker, H. T., 76, 173–4
Becker, J., 24–33, 91, 117, 161, 167, 168
Beidelman, T. O., 172
Belgianization, 63, 103–4, 105
Bemba, 6, 44, 59, 82, 86, 118, 133, 138, 150,
  151, 153, 159, 180, 185
Bennett, N. R., 168
Bickerton, D., 110, 176
Bloomfield, L., 160
Boma, 21, 22, 49, 50, 52, 58, 62, 66, 166,
  167, 170, 171
Bontinck, F., 164, 168
borders, colonial, 11, 62–5, 77, 168
Bourse du Travail du Katanga, BTK, 63,
  64, 104, 137, 171, 177, 178
Boyd, E., 164
Braekman, E. M., 172–3

British colonial policy, and Swahili, 16, 57,
  157, 184; *see also* Swahili, Standard;
  Whiteley
Broomfield, G. W., 184
Brutel, E., 112–13, 114, 117, 119, 124, 133,
  156
Buell, R. L., 81, 176, 177, 178
Bunkeya, 6, 100, 177
Burssens, A., 91, 175–6
Burton, W. F., 59, 61, 62, 171
business and industry, 66, 73, 81, 137, 148;
  responding to survey on education, 51,
  53–8, 170–1, 172
Buttaye, R., 113–14, 165

Callewaert, Ch., 166
Calvet, L.-J., 163, 175, 176
Cameron, H. L., 164, 167, 168
Campbell, D., 176, 177
Catherine the Great, 1–2
Certeau, M. de, 168
Ceulemans, P., 169
Charter, Colonial, 44–9, 65, 66, 74, 113,
  170, 174
Chimoyo, 178
Claessens, J., 179
Clarke, J. A., 59
classification, taxonomy, of languages, 2, 17,
  26, 34, 76, 81–2, 91, 109–10, 159, 175
Colle, P., 89, 113, 114, 117, 119, 124, 133,
  147, 156, 173, 174
colonization: aims of, 72–4, 137, 158; of
  language, 32, 42, 175; *see also* Charter,
  Colonial; borders, colonial; ideology,
  colonial; power, colonial
Comité Spécial du Katanga, CSK, 63–5, 66,
  67, 98, 101, 102, 114, 171, 176
communication: and command, 21, 23, 30,
  40, 67, 84, 107, 109–10; control of, 3, 14,
  34, 35, 74, 138, 148; verbal vs. non-verbal
  means of, 3, 23, 37, 136, 141, 185

201

Printed in the United States
126633LV00003B/62/A